Life Sciences

Life Sciences

Curriculum Resources and Activities for School Librarians and Teachers

Amy Bain

Janet Richer

Janet Weckman

2001
Teacher Ideas Press
A Division of
Libraries Unlimited, Inc.
Englewood, Colorado

TEACHER IDEAS PRESS
A Division of
Libraries Unlimited, Inc.
P.O. Box 6633
Englewood, CO 80155-6633
1-800-237-6124
www.lu.com/tip

ISBN 1-56308-679-4

Contents

Section 2—Habitats

Section 3—The Human Body

Introduction

The recent explosion of children's literature has drastically changed the way many educators now teach. Teachers are electing to leave many of the "basal textbooks" behind and incorporate children's literature into the classroom. Teachers are finding that these books, bursting with photographs and colorful illustrations, capture readers' interest and keep the students involved with the topic longer than traditional textbooks. The books on the market offer something for everyone, matching interests and reading abilities of the students to various books. By using children's books, students can go beyond the basic concepts that a textbook presents and delve into the topic.

In addition to nonfiction, many creative fiction books are available that are artistically illustrated and cleverly written. Teachers have discovered that these books are fun to read and, often, they can be tied into a science or social studies topic. Students may find that, while studying insects, they're also reading fiction stories such as "The Very Hungry Caterpillar," who undergoes metamorphosis, or "Two Bad Ants," who are *supposed* to be collecting food for the queen and the colony. The subjects of reading and science begin to overlap, giving students more time to do both. Tie in writing activities, art projects, and hands-on activities involving insects, and the concept of "unit studies" comes alive. A unit study incorporates skills and information from several subjects and connects them in a meaningful, stimulating way.

Life Sciences: Curriculum Resources and Activities for School Librarians and Teachers was created to provide educators with the resources they need to prepare interesting and informative science unit studies quickly and easily. Each chapter provides resources for creating a thematic unit on one specific topic. Using *Curriculum Resources* to plan a unit, teachers can easily pick and choose books and activities to match students' interests and academic abilities. Teaching multilevel classes will no longer be intimidating, and planning time will be dramatically decreased. Teachers who make use of all of the units included in *Curriculum Resources* will cover all the material contained in a standard textbook series, and much more.

Included in this book are the resources needed to prepare stimulating science units for grades K–8. Each topic includes:

1. Key Concepts (Objectives)

   A teacher must have specific goals in mind to plan appropriate activities and lessons. Each major part of *Curriculum Resources* contains a "Key Concepts" section that outlines learning objectives by age level. These "Key Concepts" were derived from studying scope and sequence statements for several school districts, examining textbooks and other printed material, and reviewing standardized tests.

   Through the use of these "Key Concepts," the teacher maintains the flexibility of determining what will be taught and how in-depth the lessons will be. These concepts serve as a guide for lesson planning.

2. Comprehensive Teaching Resources

   Books in the "Comprehensive Teaching Resources" section are in-depth resources that cover more than one unit topic. One of these books can serve as a reference guide for your unit and be used to investigate information related to the topic but not specifically covered in that topic.

3. Teaching Resources (Nonfiction Children's Literature)

In the individual subject chapters, books summarized in this subsection are written for children using text they can understand and incorporate illustrations that capture children's interest. These books can be used in place of textbooks to teach the science topic in a more stimulating manner.

Each book is designated "P" for Primary (K–2), "I" for Intermediate (3–5), or "U" for Upper (6–8) grades. These designations indicate what age level each book's text is geared toward. Each teacher can then decide how best to use a specific book in overall lesson planning. Not all books will be needed to teach the basic concepts of a topic, but the variety of books listed will give teachers the opportunity to choose books that complement their own teaching style.

4. Reading Selections (Fiction Children's Literature)

Each subject chapter includes summaries of a variety of fiction books. These books build on the science topic through engaging stories and enjoyable illustrations. Select a variety of fiction books at various reading levels for independent reading and for shared reading times as well. Not only will these fiction books reinforce reading skills, they can also be used to reinforce the science goals and the vocabulary associated with them.

5. Science Activities

A key segment of any unit study is hands-on experimenting by the student. It is important to supplement teaching resources with projects and experiments from the "Science Activities" subsection of each subject chapter. Ideas are presented for projects that actively involve the students and expand on the science topic. Choose activities that employ a variety of skills—such as research, prediction, and comparison—and incorporate other subjects such as mathematics and English.

Rather than providing page after page of worksheets, enrichment and enhancing activities challenge students to think more creatively and in-depth about the topic. The large variety of activities offered allows the teacher to choose those that most closely match the interests and needs of the students.

Most of the activities listed require the use of everyday household items. This keeps preparation time simple and costs low. Also, activities can be easily modified to different ability levels. Incorporating a few of these activities into the teaching of a subject will increase the interest level of the student and make the lesson more fun for teacher and student alike.

6. Creative Writing and Art Activities

Immediately following the science activities are subsections that expand the science topic into other subject areas. Activities are provided in the areas of reading, writing, and art. Some activities correspond to a fiction book listed in the "Reading Selections" subsection of the chapter and relate the activity to the story. Other activities stand alone and can be assigned with no prior reading required. Again, these activities can be easily modified to various ability levels and encourage creative expression and reasoning skills.

7. Additional Resources

The "Additional Resources" section at the end of each major part lists experiment books, addresses of agencies and related organizations, names of magazines, and Web sites that will provide teachers with more information on the unit topic. The experiment books are available from the library and provide ideas for additional experiments. With all of these resources at their fingertips, teachers should never run out of ideas.

Curriculum Resources places a variety of resources at your fingertips to plan lessons for an entire unit. If you are a person who likes to be very structured, you can write an outline for each unit, with daily lessons. If you are a flexible, go-with-the-flow type of person, you can simply pick and choose from the resources and activities as your day develops. With the variety of books and activities included, you can quickly select an activity that will engage your class for 5 minutes or 45 minutes, based on your needs.

Using *Curriculum Resources*, the process of selecting activities and resources and planning your unit can be accomplished in less than an hour. The result can be three weeks or more of lessons. After planning several units, this process will become second nature and take even less time. With unit studies, lesson planning becomes easier and teaching becomes more fun. Watch the enthusiasm for science in your classroom grow, and revive the joy of learning.

Experiments and the Scientific Method

An important part of science education is teaching children how to think "scientifically" and develop problem-solving skills. This can be done effectively through hands-on demonstrations, activities, and experiments. The "Experiment Books" subsection in the "Additional Resources" section in each major part lists books that are filled with experiments relating to the topic. In addition to these books, some books (noted with a "+") in the "Teaching Resources" subsection in each chapter also contain experiments.

Science education would be incomplete without studying different methods researchers use to make discoveries and develop new theories. Students should learn how to apply the scientific method by doing experiments themselves. Understanding this process will strengthen problem-solving skills.

Scientific research can involve a variety of techniques. Some of the methods scientists use are:

1. *Observing nature*: Learning about the life cycle of a butterfly or how average temperatures determine when crops should be planted are examples of how observing nature provides information that can be used in other areas of study.

2. *Classifying data*: By comparing and contrasting characteristics of different objects or animals, relationships can be determined.

3. *Using logic*: When a specific principle is demonstrated repeatedly, it may logically become a scientific principle of law. For example, objects with less density than water will float. Obviously, not every object in existence was tested before this principle was formed.

4. *Conducting experiments*: This is the major process for developing and proving theories.

5. *Forming a hypothesis*: Scientists may try to explain information received by creating a theory. For example, astronomers found that Uranus was not always in the position they calculated it should be. They then hypothesized the existence of another planet, and later discovered Neptune.

6. *Expressing findings mathematically*: Scientists often explain observations through the use of mathematics. For example, scientists may observe a gravitational relationship between two planets and derive a mathematical equation expressing that relationship. This equation can then be used to predict the gravitational relationship between other planets.

7. *Pure accident*: There is always the unique case of "stumbling onto a discovery." The discovery of penicillin is an excellent example.

When performing a science experiment or project, students should strive to follow a logical, scientific method, such as the following example:

1. *Identify the problem*: What does the student want to find out or expect to learn?

2. *Develop a hypothesis*: What does the student predict will happen?

3. *Describe the procedure and materials*: What steps will be taken to try to solve the problem? What materials will be used?

4. *Record observations/data*: What happened? What results were obtained? When appropriate, data should be recorded in graph form to make it easier to determine patterns and relationships.

5. *Generate conclusions*: What can be learned from the observations made? What conclusions can be made from the data collected?

By following this scientific method, students should learn problem-solving skills and be able to identify a problem and determine possible methods to solve it. The more frequently the students perform experiments, the more familiar they will become with the scientific method. For this reason, educators should strive to include as many hands-on activities as possible in their lesson plans.

Problem-solving skills can be used in many activities included in the subject chapters. Strengthening life-long skills such as problem solving will benefit any student.

ANIMALS

- Key Concepts

- Comprehensive Teaching Resources

- Chapter 1: Insects and Spiders

- Chapter 2: Other Invertebrates

- Chapter 3: Reptiles and Amphibians

- Chapter 4: Fish

- Chapter 5: Birds

- Chapter 6: Mammals

- Chapter 7: Dinosaurs

- Additional Resources

Key Concepts

■ Primary Concepts

Students will be able to:

1. Identify and describe the characteristics of insects (Chapter 1).

    They have no bones.

    They have three body parts.

    They have six legs.

    They hatch from eggs.

2. Recognize that some animals develop through different stages of growth (e.g., the butterfly, the tadpole) (Chapters 1, 3).

3. Identify different ways in which animals move (Chapters 1–6).

4. Classify animals according to the habitats in which they live and recognize that animals need water, food, and air found in these habitats (Chapters 1–6).

5. Classify animals according to their coverings (Chapters 1–6).

6. Match the adult animal to the appropriate baby animal (Chapters 1–6). Describe similarities and differences between adults and their young.

7. Identify and describe the characteristics of reptiles (Chapter 3).

    They are cold blooded.

    Most lay eggs and have four legs.

    They have bony skeletons.

8. Identify and describe the characteristics of amphibians (Chapter 3).

    They can live on land and in the water.

    They have bony skeletons.

    They lay eggs.

    Most go through metamorphosis.

9. Identify and describe the characteristics of fish (Chapter 4).

    They live in water.

    They use gills to take in oxygen from water.

    They have bony skeletons.

10. Identify and describe the characteristics of birds (Chapter 5).

> They have feathers and a beak.
>
> They hatch from eggs.
>
> They have bony skeletons.
>
> Most can fly.

11. Identify and describe the characteristics of mammals (Chapter 6).

> They are warm blooded.
>
> They nurse on milk from their mothers.
>
> They have bony skeletons.
>
> They have skin covered with hair.
>
> Most are born alive from within their mother. (Most do not lay eggs.)

12. Describe ways in which scientists learn about dinosaurs. Compare dinosaur skeletons (Chapter 7).

13. Explain the characteristics of meat-eating and plant-eating dinosaurs (Chapter 7).

14. Explain the characteristics of flying, land, and water dinosaurs (Chapter 7).

15. Discuss the appearance of the Earth when the dinosaurs lived on it (Chapter 7).

16. Describe changes on the Earth and their effects on the life of the dinosaurs (Chapter 7).

17. Identify animals that lived after the dinosaurs and explain the ways in which they adapted to their environment (Chapter 7).

18. Discuss why dinosaurs could not survive today (Chapter 7).

■ Intermediate Concepts

Students will be able to:

1. Identify the major parts of the body of an insect (Chapter 1).

2. List and name animals that live in groups and why (Chapters 1–6). Identify the appropriate vocabulary for each group (e.g., colonies, packs, herds, schools).

3. Explain the basic structure of invertebrates and how they function (Chapters 1, 2). Identify the main invertebrate groups and provide examples of each:

> arthropods   sponges
> mollusks   coelenterates
> protozoa   echinoderms
> worms

4. Classify animals as vertebrates or invertebrates (Chapters 1–6).

5. Identify the characteristics of each animal group and how these groups work together (Chapters 1–6).

6. Identify the main characteristics of cold-blooded animals (Chapters 3, 4).

7. Describe how scientists classify animals and name the main characteristics of each group (Chapters 3–6) (amphibians, fish, reptiles, mammals, birds).

8. Contrast and compare different bones and feathers from various animals (Chapters 3–6).

9. Explain the basic structure of vertebrates and how they function (Chapters 3–6). Identify the main vertebrate groups and give examples of each (reptiles, birds, amphibians, mammals, fish).

■ Upper Concepts

Students will be able to:

1. Compare protective coloration, protective resemblance, and mimicry and give examples of each (Chapters 1–6).

2. Identify the major anatomy and physiology of these animal phyla (Chapters 1–6): *Porifera*, *Arthropoda*, *Coelenterates*, *Echinodermata*, *Platyhelminthes*, *Mollusca*, *Nematoda*, *Chordata*, *Annelida*.

3. Place animals within their correct phyla by using their characteristics (Chapters 1–6).

4. Identify similar characteristics in each phylum (Chapters 1–6).

5. Understand the increasing complexity from one phylum to another (Chapters 1–6).

6. Label the parts of an animal cell and contrast it to a plant cell (Chapters 1–6).

7. Describe the relationship between body temperature and heart rate during hibernation (Chapters 3, 6).

Comprehensive Teaching Resources

The following table lists books that cover a wide range of topics about animals. One of these books could serve as your main teaching guide while studying this unit. Each book is listed with a short summary, and the chapters in this book that it applies to are noted. Books containing more difficult subject matter are listed in the second table.

BOOK AND SUMMARY	AUTHOR	CHAPTERS					
		1	2	3	4	5	6
Two Lives (Steck-Vaughn, 1992) Describes how amphibians, insects, and fish have two lives (emphasizing the larval stage and metamorphosis).	Joyce Pope	X	X	X		X	
The New Book of Popular Science—Vol. IV & V (Grolier, 1998) Details the animal world, including insects, fish, birds, amphibians, reptiles, and mammals.	Grolier	X	X	X	X	X	

Several series have been published on the subject of animals. Some of these are listed in the following table. The books are listed by degree of difficulty, easiest to most difficult.

SERIES	BOOK TITLE	AUTHOR
Books for Young Explorers (National Geographic Society)*	*How Animals Care for Their Babies*, 1996 *How Animals Talk*, 1987 *Ways Animals Sleep*, 1983	Roger Hirschland Susan McGrath Jane R. McCauley
Animal Ways (Newington Press)	*Animals At Home*, 1991 *Animals At Night*, 1991 *Animals At Rest*, 1991 *Animals At Work*, 1991 *Animals Talking*, 1991	Jane Burton
Wild World (Newington Press)	*Animal Builders*, 1991 *Animal Communications*, 1991 *Animal Families*, 1991 *Animal Helpers*, 1991 *Animal Hunters*, 1991 *Animal Movement*, 1991 *Animal Senses*, 1991 *Animal Travelers*, 1991	Jim Flegg

*Series contains wonderful, detailed photographs and easy text.

Each chapter in this section lists reference books that focus on the specific area of the animal kingdom being addressed. These books can be used to complement and expand upon the basic information provided in the comprehensive resource books listed in the previous tables.

The reference books in each chapter have been classified by age level to help you select those that best fit the needs and interests of your student(s).

Chapter 1
Insects and Spiders

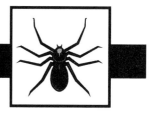

■ Teaching Resources

Books containing experiment(s) relating to the subject matter are marked with a plus sign (+) before and after the title.

P   +*Butterflies and Moths*,+ by Dean Morris (Raintree, 1987)
Discusses the life cycles and behavior patterns of various species of butterflies and moths.

P   *Dragonfly*, by Emery Bernhard (Holiday House, 1993)
An introduction to the physical characteristics, life cycle, natural environment, and relationship of humans to the dragonfly.

P   *Fireflies,* by Sylvia A. Johnson (Lerner, 1986)
Describes the physical characteristics, habits, and habitat of fireflies.

P   *It's a Good Thing There Are Insects,* by Allan Fowler (Childrens Press, 1990)
Identifies the characteristics of insects and describes some of their useful activities and products.

P   *Life of the Butterfly,* by Heiderose Fischer-Nagel and Andreas Fischer-Nagel (Carolrhoda Books, 1988)
Describes the physical characteristics, habits, and behavior of butterflies and includes photographs of different species.

P   +*Monarch Butterfly*,+ by Gail Gibbons (Holiday House, 1991)
Describes the life cycle, body parts, and behavior of the monarch butterfly.

P   *Spiders,* by Gail Gibbons (Holiday House, 1994)
Examines the physical characteristics, behavior, and habitats of different kinds of spiders.

P   +*Where Butterflies Grow*,+ by Joanne Ryder (Lodestar Books, 1989)
Describes what it must feel like to change from a caterpillar into a butterfly.

P/I *Amazing Butterflies and Moths,* by John Still (Alfred A. Knopf, 1991)
The life cycles and characteristics of various kinds of caterpillars, moths, and butterflies are depicted in photographs.

P/I *Amazing Spiders,* by Claudia Schnieper (Carolrhoda Books, 1989)
The appearance, behavior, and life cycles of spiders are described.

P/I *Backyard Hunter: The Praying Mantis,* by Bianca Lavies (Econo-Clad, 1999)
Describes the physical characteristics, behavior, and life cycle of the praying mantis.

P/I *Bugs,* by Nancy Winslow Parker & Joan Richards Wright (Econo-Clad, 1999)
Brief description of the physical characteristics, habits, and natural environment of many common insects. Includes jokes and general information.

P/I *Butterflies and Moths,* by Bobbie Kalman and Tammy Everts (Crabtree, 1994)
A look at the physical characteristics and behavior of butterflies and moths.

P/I *The Honey Makers,* by Gail Gibbons (William Morrow, 1997)
Covers the physical structure of honeybees and how they live in colonies, as well as how they produce honey and are managed by beekeepers. Wonderful illustrations.

P/I *The Housefly,* by Heiderose Fischer-Nagel and Andreas Fischer-Nagel (Carolrhoda Books, 1990)
Describes, in text and illustrations, the physical characteristics, habits and natural environment of the housefly and its relationship to humans.

P/I *An Insect's Body,* by Joanna Cole (William Morrow, 1987)
Examines the common house cricket and shows why its body is ideally suited for survival.

P/I *Life of the Honeybee,* by Heiderose Fischer-Nagel and Andreas Fischer-Nagel (Carolrhoda Books, 1986)
Text and photographs present aspects of the honeybee's life.

P/I *Spiders Are Not Insects,* by Allan Fowler (Childrens Press, 1996)
Introduces the spider, an eight-legged creature that is not an insect.

P/I *Web Weavers and Other Spiders,* by Bobbie Kalman (Crabtree, 1996)
An overview of spiders, including physical characteristics, web building, mating behavior, and defensive techniques.

I *Ant Cities,* by Arthur Dorros (Thomas Y. Crowell, 1987)
Describes how ants live and work together to build and maintain their cities.

I +*Butterflies,*+ by Beth Wagner Brust (Creative Education, 1991)
Discusses butterflies, their metamorphosis, and their migration. Colorful photographs.

I *Chirping Insects,* by Sylvia A. Johnson (Lerner, 1986)
Describes how chirping insects such as crickets, katydids, and grasshoppers produce their songs and use them to send messages.

I *Creepy, Crawly Baby Bugs,* by Sandra Markle (Walker, 1996)
A close look at baby insects, those animals often called "bugs."

I *The Fascinating World of Bees,* by Angels Julivert (Barron's Juveniles, 1991)
Describes the appearance, life cycle, activities, and social habits of bees, and provides information on beekeeping.

I *The Fascinating World of Spiders,* by Maria Angels Julivert (Forest House, 1992)
An introduction to the physical characteristics, habitats, and natural environment of various kinds of spiders.

I   *Insect Metamorphosis, from Egg to Adult,* by Ron Goor and Nancy Goor (Atheneum, 1990)
Explains how insects grow, describing the various stages of incomplete and complete metamorphosis.

I   *Killer Bees,* by Kathleen Davis and Dave Mayes (Dillon, 1993)
Describes the origin, characteristics, behavior, and dangerous aspects of this hybrid honeybee.

I   *Killer Bees,* by Bianca Lavies (Dutton Children's Books, 1994)
An introduction to killer bees through text and photographs.

I   *Magic School Bus Inside a Beehive,* by Joanna Cole (Scholastic, 1998)
Ms. Frizzle takes her class to a beehive in her magical bus.

I   *+Milkweed Butterflies: Monarch, Models, and Mimics,+* by Hilda Simon (Vanguard Press, 1969)
Explores the world and life cycle of milkweed butterflies.

I   *Spiders,* by Kevin Holmes (Bridgestone Books, 1998)
An introduction to spiders covering their physical characteristics, habits, prey, and relationship to humans.

I/U   *+Meet the Arthropods,+* by Ellen Doris (Thames & Hudson, 1996)
The characteristics of arthropods are discussed along with ideas for projects, field trips, and suggestions that can be explored.

■ Reading Selections

Books marked with an asterisk (*) before and after the title are related to activities in the activity sections of this chapter.

Anansi the Spider: A Tale from Ashanti, by Gerald McDermott (Econo-Clad, 1999)
> Anansi must decide which of his sons to reward for saving his life, and becomes responsible for placing the moon in the sky.

The Ant and the Elephant, by Bill Peet (Houghton Mifflin, 1972)
> Of all the animals Elephant helps, only the tiny ant returns the favor.

Ant Plays Bear, by Betsy Byars (Viking, 1997)
> Ant and his brother learn to be friends while playing a game, discussing growing up, and hearing a scary noise.

Antics: An Alphabetical Anthology, by Cathi Hepworth (G. P. Putnam's Sons, 1992)
> Alphabetical entries from A to Z all have "ant" in them.

Berlioz the Bear, by Jan Brett (Paper Star, 1996)
> Berlioz the Bear and his fellow musicians have a surprising day when Berlioz's bass begins to buzz.

Buggy Riddles, by Katy Hall and Lisa Eisenberg (Econo-Clad, 1999)
> An illustrated collection of insect riddles.

The Caterpillar and the Polliwog, by Jack Kent (Econo-Clad, 1999)
> A polliwog longs to become a beautiful butterfly and tries to imitate the caterpillar.

Caterpillar, Caterpillar, by Vivian French (Candlewick Press, 1993)
> A girl learns about caterpillars and butterflies as she watches her grandfather "grow" them on the nettles in his garden.

Charlie the Caterpillar, by Dom DeLuise (Simon & Schuster, 1990)
> Charlie is rejected when he is an ugly caterpillar but is able to befriend another caterpillar when he becomes a beautiful butterfly.

Charlotte's Web, by E. B. White (Harper Trophy, 1999)
> As friends, Wilbur the pig and Charlotte the spider share several experiences. (Chapter Book)

The Cricket in Times Square, by G. Selden (Yearling Books, 1970)
> The adventures of a country cricket who arrives in New York and is befriended by a mouse and a cat. (Chapter Book)

Going Buggy!, by Peter Roop and Connie Roop (Lerner, 1986)
> A collection of jokes and riddles about bugs.

*The Grouchy Ladybug,** by Eric Carle (HarperCollins Juveniles, 1996)
> A grouchy ladybug is looking for a fight, challenging everyone she meets, regardless of size or strength.

The Hardy Boys: The Sting of the Scorpion, by Franklin W. Dixon (Price Stern Sloan, 1979)
> Frank and Joe try to solve a mystery after witnessing the explosion of an aircraft. (Chapter Book)

How to Hide a Butterfly and Other Insects, by Ruth Heller (Econo-Clad, 1999)
> Rhyming text describes how various insects camouflage themselves.

I Know an Old Lady, by Nadine Bernard Westcott (Oxford University Press, 1988)
> Depicts a popular folk song with pictures.

I Wish I Were a Butterfly, by James Howe (Econo-Clad, 1999)
> A wise butterfly helps a cricket discover his own uniqueness and that he is special in his own way.

Insects Are My Life, by Megan McDonald (Orchard, 1995)
> No one at home or at school understands Amanda's fascination with insects until Maggie comes along.

The Lady and the Spider, by Faith McNulty (Harper Trophy, 1987)
> A lady saves a spider living in a head of lettuce when she finds it and puts it back in the garden.

*The Lamb and the Butterfly,** by Arnold Sundgaard (Scholastic, 1996)
> An independent butterfly and a secluded lamb compare lifestyles.

Maggie and the Pirate, by Ezra Jack Keats (Scholastic, 1992)
> Maggie goes off in search of "the pirate" after he kidnaps her prized pet cricket.

The Napping House, by Audrey Wood (Red Wagon Books, 1996)
> The entire household gathers for a nap, but when a flea joins the group, the restful situation is disrupted.

Old Black Fly, by Jim Aylesworth (Henry Holt, 1998)
> Rhyming text and illustrations follow a mischievous fly through the alphabet. The fly has a hard time when he lands where he shouldn't.

Quick as a Cricket, by Audrey Wood (Child's Play, 1998)
> Creates metaphors, using common animal traits, to describe a boy's characteristics. Beautiful illustrations.

Sam's Sandwich, by David Pelham (Dutton Children's Books, 1991)
> When Sam's sister asks for a sandwich with "everything" on it, Sam decides to slip in some little surprises.

Spiderweb for Two: A Melendy Maze, by Elizabeth Enright (Econo-Clad, 1999)
> Randy and Oliver find a surprise message in their mailbox that must be decoded and that leads to another message. The messages turn their dreary winter into an adventure. (Chapter Book)

There's an Ant in Anthony, by Bernard Most (Mulberry Books, 1992)
> Anthony discovers "ant" in his name and then looks for "ant" in other words.

Two Bad Ants, by Chris Van Allsburg (Houghton Mifflin, 1988)
> When two bad ants decide to leave their colony, they experience a dangerous adventure that convinces them to return home.

The Very Busy Spider, by Eric Carle (Econo-Clad, 1999)
> The farm animals try to divert a busy little spider from spinning a web, but she persists and produces a beautiful web.

The Very Hungry Caterpillar, by Eric Carle (Philomel, 1994)
> A hungry caterpillar eats a large amount of food until, once full, it forms a cocoon and becomes a butterfly.

The Very Quiet Cricket, by Eric Carle (Putnam, 1997)
> A very quiet cricket, who wants to rub his wings together and make a sound, finally gets his wish.

Where Butterflies Grow, by Joanne Ryder (Lodestar Books, 1989)
> Describes what it must feel like to turn into a butterfly from a caterpillar.

Why Mosquitoes Buzz in People's Ears, by Verna Aardema (Dial Press, 1992)
> Retells a folk tale from West Africa about a series of animals trying to discover who killed an owlet, causing Mother Owl great sadness. Because of this, she wouldn't wake the sun.

The following books are out of print, but may be available at the local library.

Ants Can't Dance, by Ellen Jackson (Macmillan, 1991)
> No one believes that Jonathan has an ant that dances, a peanut that talks, and a stone that whistles.

Flit, Flutter, Fly, by Lee Bennett Hopkins (Doubleday, 1992)
> A collection of poems about bugs and other creatures that crawl or fly. Composed by a variety of authors.

Grasshopper to the Rescue, by Bonnie Carey (Wm. Morrow, 1979)
> The grasshopper must meet the demands of several animals to save his friend, the ant.

Lady Bugatti, by Joyce Manner (Lothrop, Lee, & Shepard, 1991)
> Lady Bugatti and her insect guests dine together and visit the theatre.

Remember the Butterflies, by Anna Grossnickle Hines (Dutton Children's Books, 1991)
> When Grandpa can't revive a dead butterfly, they stop and celebrate the butterfly's life. When Granpa dies, Holly and Glen remember the special times with him.

Spiders in the Fruit Cellar, by Barbara Joosse (Random House, 1983)
> Even though Elizabeth is old enough to go to the fruit cellar, she finds that she is afraid of the spiders lurking there.

Tarantulas on the Brain, by Marilyn Singer (Harper & Row, 1982)
> Lizzie, a scientific fifth-grader, and her friend create a plan to get a tarantula for a pet. (Chapter Book)

■ Science Activities

Ants

With the students' help, make an ant farm using the following instructions:
- Fill a jar three-quarters full with loose soil. Dampen the soil slightly.
- Place a small, moist sponge in the jar. Add water to the sponge daily.
- Put 12 to 14 ants and a small amount of honey or sugar in the jar. Cover the top of the jar with a small mesh screen.
- Tape a piece of black paper around the sides of the jar. Remove this paper daily and observe the ants. Record observations as a class.

Ants and Food

- Experiment to see which foods attract ants. Place several foods outdoors on pieces of paper. Check every 10 minutes for ant activity. Take pictures each time you check, then construct a poster showing your results.
- Depending on the age of your students, you can work individually or in groups. Have older students choose the foods, guess which one(s) will attract the most ants, and explain why.
- Results can be graphed (by older students) or be used to practice addition and subtraction (how many more/fewer than before).

Observing Ants

Take the students outside to observe an ant colony. Watch the ants and try to discover how the ants' needs (such as food, water, shelter, and communication) are met.

Cootie

Play the game "Cootie" with the students and compare the created bug with an ant. Ask the students to name the parts of an ant's body.

Butterflies

- Study both sides of a butterfly. (Students can catch butterflies with a small net out in their backyards or in a nearby park.) Explain symmetry to the students and discuss it in reference to the butterfly.

- Have the students research the migration habits of monarch butterflies. Trace their migration pattern on a map.
- Chart and discuss similarities and differences between butterflies and moths.

Plant a Butterfly Garden

Butterflies love pink. As a class, write a proposal to your principal to suggest the creation of a flower garden. When you plant your flower garden in the spring, choose lots of pink bushes, perennials, and annuals. Watch the butterflies flock! (This garden will also attract hummingbirds.) There is also a "butterfly bush" that can be purchased from your local nursery. The blooms on this bush also attract butterflies.

Honeycombs

Research how bees make honeycombs. Purchase some honeycomb and examine it with a magnifying glass. As a group, record your observations. Ask the students: What do the "combs" look like? What shape are they? Are they all the same size, or do they vary in size? How are different flavors possible in honey? What causes honey to be light or dark?

Comparing Insects

Compare different insects. If possible, collect specimens of the insects you are studying. Try to determine characteristics they all have in common and what characteristics differ among varieties. Make a chart categorizing the specimens and listing their similarities and differences. Ask the students if they can think of six or seven major groups or orders that insects can be divided into. (These are listed below.)

1. Bees, wasps, ants = Hymenoptera
2. Caterpillars, butterflies, moths = Lepidoptera
3. Beetles = Coleoptera
4. Aphids = Hemiptera
5. Flies, mosquitoes = Diptera
6. Grasshoppers, crickets = Orthoptera
7. Spiders = *not insects*!

Younger students can combine this exercise with an author study on Eric Carle. Books that could be studied include *The Very Hungry Caterpillar, The Grouchy Ladybug, The Very Quiet Cricket*, and *The Very Busy Spider*.

Moths

Have the students try to collect moths by placing a sheet of white paper outside on a tree or on the side of their houses. The moths will be attracted to the white in the evening when it is dark outside. Students can catch the moths with a small insect net. Have them look in a field guide to identify the different moths.

Bugs and Crops

- Farmers use insecticides to prevent insects from eating their crops. Research what particular types of insects do the most harm to crops. See if the students can find cases where areas have been "plagued" by insects. Discuss what types of insects they were.

- Older students can do some research on the effects of the insecticides used by farmers on the consumers of their crops. Ask them to find out if there are particular insecticides that farmers are not permitted to use and how the farmers feel about this restriction.

Bees

Research the different types of bees. Ask the students: How many different types can you find? Do killer bees really exist? Do they really kill people if they sting them? Where are killer bees located?

Ladybugs and Spiders

- Compare ladybugs and spiders. Ask the students: How are they similar? How do they differ? Why are ladybugs considered insects but spiders are not? What characteristics define an insect?
- Research the different types of spiders. Ask the students to explain how they are similar and how they are different.

Make a Pooter

A pooter is a device that aids in collecting tiny insects without hurting them. You simply suck them into the jar. You'll need a jar that has a rubber stopper that fits tightly. You will also need 2 feet of flexible plastic tubing with an inside diameter of 1/4 inch. These items can be purchased from a hardware store or from a winemaking supplies store.

- Using a power drill with a 1/4-inch drill bit, drill two holes in the rubber stopper.
- Cut the plastic tubing in half using scissors. Push each piece of tubing through one of the holes in the stopper.
- Use a small rubberband to attach a 1-inch square piece of gauze over one end of one piece of the tubing. Be sure that end is inside the jar.
- Place the stopper in the opening of the jar.
- Take the students outside to search for a small insect. (One that is small enough to fit through the tubing.) Quietly move the end of the tube without the gauze up to the bug. Place the other tube (the one with the gauze) in your mouth and suck on it. (The insect will be sucked into the pooter. The gauze keeps the bug from being sucked into your mouth.)
- Study the insect with a magnifying glass. Be sure to release the bug where you found it after you have finished your studies.

You Dirt Bug!

- Have the students gather some fresh soil and put it in a pail. There are many different types of invertebrates living in the soil found under the dead leaves that have fallen from the trees in their yards.
- They should put a couple of handfuls of the soil into a strainer and sift it onto a piece of white paper.
- Have them use a magnifying glass to look for any animals that may have fallen onto the paper.
- Ask the students to draw pictures of any animals they can see on the paper and place them in a notebook.
- Have them use a reference book to find out what animals they have found.

Lift a Web

Discuss with the class that different spiders spin different types of webs. You can "lift" a web by spraying hair spray on one that is vacant and carefully lifting it onto a piece of black construction paper. Have the students look at the intricate design created by such a tiny creature! Research spiders and decide which type created this masterpiece.

Metamorphosis

Students enjoy bringing insects to school to share with the class. By following these instructions, caterpillar specimens have a better chance to survive and undergo metamorphosis.

- Collect some moss and twigs and place them in the bottom of a large jar along with some potting compost.
- Collect a few caterpillars from a plant outside. (Be sure to keep the leaves that the caterpillars are sitting on because this is what they eat—they won't eat just any plant.)
- Place the caterpillars in the jar. Make a lid by putting a piece of paper over the top of the jar and tying a string around it to kccp it in place. Poke a few holes in the paper lid using the point of a pencil.
- Feed your caterpillars each day with fresh leaves from the same kind of plant on which you found them. Record what you see daily in a log.
- When the pupae become butterflies or moths, let them go.

How Does It Do That?

You will need a sheet of clear plastic for this activity.

- Collect some small animals (earthworms, snails, beetles, or wood lice). Keep them in a dark, cool box while you and the students are observing them.
- Carefully place them on the clear plastic, one at a time.
- Have one person hold the plastic flat while another person is underneath it looking up at how each animal moves. From this angle, you can see the animals' movements more clearly. Record your findings in a class notebook.

Invertebrate Traps

The following is an exciting class (or family) activity if the school yard can accommodate it.

- Dig some holes in the ground just big enough for a plastic cup to fit into.
- Place two cups (one inside the other) into each hole. When pushed down all the way, the rim of the top cup should be level with the top of the hole.
- Place a piece of thin wood over the top cup to keep the rain out. Use some small stones to prop the cover up so there is a gap of about 3/4 inch (2 centimeters) between the cover and the top of the cup. Glass won't make a good cover because it will make the trap too hot when the sun is shining.
- Check your traps regularly. Take out the inner cup and take a closer look at what you have caught. Be sure to let the animals go when you are finished observing them. Then replace the cup in the hole.
- Ask the students to guess whether they would catch different kinds of animals in long grass areas as opposed to short grass.
- Do the same kinds of animals fall into your traps during the day and at night?

- Ask the students to guess what would happen if you put some small pieces of fruit or meat or some sugar water into your traps. Do they think you would catch more or fewer animals?
- Be sure to fill in whatever holes you dig when you finish this experiment.

Curds and Whey

Read the nursery rhyme, "Little Miss Muffett." Make butter by whipping heavy whipping cream until it separates into the curds and whey. Explain that curds are the fat that separates to form the butter, and whey is the liquid that is left over. Have the children taste a little of each.

■ Creative Writing Activities

Following are instructions to give the students for various writing activities.
- Design a restaurant menu for caterpillars and butterflies. What type of plants would caterpillars prefer? What plants and parts of plants do butterflies like? What type of artwork would you use on your menu to make it appealing to your customers?
- Make up riddles describing your favorite insects. (For inspiration, read *Buggy Riddles* by Hall and Eisenberg or *Going Buggy* by Roop and Roop).
- Pretend you are a 17-year locust and are coming out of the ground. It is now the year 2010. What is the world you see around you like? How has it changed from 17 years ago? Write down your thoughts.
- Pretend you have been changed into a spider. What kind of skills do you need to survive? Where do you make your home? What do you eat and how do you obtain your food? Who are your enemies?
- You are a research scientist for the government. You have been given a grant to study insects and determine if we can adapt any of their habits and skills to our lifestyle. Which insects would you decide to study? What characteristics of these insects are you interested in studying? Why?
- Write down as many words as you can that contain "ant." (Use the dictionary for help, if needed.) Afterwards, read *There's an Ant in Anthony* by Most. Did Anthony find any words you missed?
- Write a letter to a parent telling him or her why you are happy being you. Include all the qualities and skills you possess that make you special. (*I Wish I Were a Butterfly* by Howe)
- Pick one of your favorite possessions (a toy, a rock/fossil, a seashell, etc.) and write a letter to a friend to convince him or her that it has an unusual ability: It can talk, dance, sing, glow, and so forth. (*Ants Can't Dance* by Jackson)
- Create a newspaper for the insect world. Think up an appropriate title for it and also appropriate titles for the different columns you include. You could cover events such as "Miss Muffett scared away," "Old lady swallows a fly," or "Ants invade local picnic."
- Write a story about a grouchy ladybug and a friendly ladybug. How many different adjectives can you use to describe the two bugs? (*The Grouchy Ladybug* by Carle)
- Pretend that you are inside a cocoon waiting to emerge. Write a story about what you are thinking and feeling while you wait. What do you turn into inside the cocoon (a moth, a butterfly, or something completely different)?
- It is the day of the Insect Olympics! The air is charged with excitement! Design the Olympic program listing the events to take place, the competitors in each event, and the judges (suggestions: ant weight-lifting competition, grasshopper long jump/high jump competition). Design an Olympic logo/symbol for the games, write an Olympic anthem, or design a poster depicting

the games. Have students write summaries of each event describing the action that took place and naming the winners. (Older students can write short, concise news articles; younger students can simply write a paragraph telling what happened.)

- Imagine that all the garden insects gathered together to celebrate their own Thanksgiving Day. Write an account of their celebration. What "food" would they serve? Who would attend? What would they be thankful for?

- A magician will turn you into any insect that you choose for a day. Decide what insect you want to be. Keep an hourly journal describing your activities and your feelings while you are transformed.

- Have the children talk about themselves as they add their feelings to this poem: "It's fun to see what I can be. To imagine a world that suits just me!" I can be:

  quiet as a _____

  noisy as a _____

  shy as a _____

  bold as a _____

  calm as a _____

  fast as a _____

  peaceful as a _____

  lazy as a _____

  busy as a _____

Have the children complete the phrases above (and make up more of their own). Let the children pick one of the phrases and write a story about an incident in their lives (real or imaginary) that exemplifies the trait.

■ Art Activities

Following are instructions to give the students for various art activities.

- Make fingerprint bugs. Press your finger down on a stamp pad, then press the finger onto a piece of paper to make a fingerprint. (Connect several fingerprints to make the body of a caterpillar.) Draw or paint legs, wings, antennae, and so forth onto the fingerprint body to create your own special bugs. You can also use scraps of material, pipe cleaners, or other household items to create your bugs.

- Make a waxed paper butterfly using the following instructions:

  Lay a piece of waxed paper out on a kitchen table or counter. Using several different colors of crayon, shave pieces off the crayons and let these shavings drop onto the waxed paper. Small pencil sharpeners can shave crayons easily. Very young students may need adult supervision, or their crayons can be shaved ahead of time by an adult. Cover the shavings with another piece of waxed paper.

  Place a light cloth over the sheets of waxed paper and iron with a dry, hot iron. The shavings will melt, causing the two sheets of waxed paper to stick together.

  Cut butterfly wings out of the colored waxed paper. Add antennae to complete your butterfly.

- Dip a round sponge into a bowl containing tempera paint. Dab the sponge onto a piece of scrap paper to remove the excess, then dab it onto your art paper to make paintings of caterpillars and butterflies. (Use different-shaped sponges to create any type of bug you wish. You can also draw a scene around your sponge-painted insects.)

- Glue colored yarn to a paper plate in any pattern you wish to make a spider's web. Add a spider to your web by making it out of black construction paper. Use pipe cleaners for the legs.
- Look through nature magazines to find as many pictures of insects and spiders as you can. Cut out and paste the pictures to a piece of colored cardboard to make a buggy collage.
- Make a caterpillar out of an egg carton. Cut the egg carton lengthwise, making two long sections with six "humps" each. Paint the caterpillar's body, add pipe cleaner antennae, and draw on eyes. Use a paper bag stuffed with cotton as a cocoon. Later, remove the "caterpillar" from the bag and add wings for a butterfly.
- Obtain a recording of "Flight of the Bumblebees" by Rimsky-Korsakov from your local library. Make up a dance to do to the music.
- For an afternoon snack, consider serving spiders: Use a chocolate sandwich cookie for the spider's body. Insert short pieces of black (or red) string licorice into the filling on two sides for the legs. Or make a cracker "sandwich" using two round crackers with peanut butter in the center. Insert chow mein noodles into the peanut butter to make the spider's legs.
- Read *I Know an Old Lady Who Swallowed a Fly* by Westcott. Make a mural of the story using a hand-drawn lady, insects, and animals or using pictures cut out of a magazine.
- Make a spider by painting (or coloring) a paper plate black and adding legs made out of construction paper or crepe paper folded accordion-style.
- Read *The Grouchy Ladybug* by Carle. Make a puppet resembling each of the animal characters in the book. The puppets can be made out of paper lunch bags decorated with crayons, paint, material, and sequins or out of old socks on which you glue or sew yarn, buttons, sequins, and so forth. Act out the story for your family or friends.
- Fold a piece of paper in half. Cut out a shape resembling a butterfly wing. Open up the paper and paint one wing. Fold the paper back together again and press the painted wing to the unpainted wing. Open the paper back up and let your butterfly dry.
- Make the life cycle of a butterfly out of pasta. Divide a paper plate into four equal sections. Label the sections Egg, Cocoon, Caterpillar, and Butterfly. Glue rice in the "Egg" section, glue rotini in the "Caterpillar" section, glue shell pasta in the "Cocoon" section, and glue bowtie pasta in the "Butterfly" section.
- Make a large "old woman," as depicted in the story, *I Know an Old Lady Who Swallowed a Fly* by Westcott, out of cardboard. Leave a "window" in the middle of the old woman's stomach. Cut out an opening for her mouth. Draw pictures of the insects and other animals that the old woman swallowed in the story. Attach each picture to a piece of wire or string. Retell the story, putting each creature into the old woman's mouth at the proper time and feeding it down into her stomach.

Chapter 2
Other Invertebrates

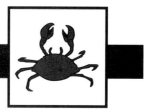

■ Teaching Resources

Books containing experiment(s) relating to the subject matter are marked with a plus sign (+) before and after the title.

P   *It Could Still Be a Worm,* by Allan Fowler (Childrens Press, 1996)
A simple introduction to many kinds of worms, including the earthworm, roundworm, and flatworm.

P   *An Octopus Is Amazing,* by Patricia Lauber (Econo-Clad, 1999)
Gives an introduction to one of the most intelligent inhabitants of the sea, the many-tentacled octopus.

P   *Octopuses,* by Jenny Markert (The Child's Word, 1992)
Colorful photographs and large text introduce the physical and behavioral characteristics of octopuses.

P   *Sponges Are Skeletons,* by Barbara Juster Esbensen (HarperCollins, 1993)
Gives information about sponges' lives in the ocean, how they are harvested, and how they are used by human beings.

I   *Crabs,* by Kathleen Pohl (Raintree, 1990)
Discusses the life cycle and behavior patterns of freshwater crabs.

I   *Discovering Crabs and Lobsters,* by Jill Bailey (Bookwright, 1987)
Examines the physical characteristics, feeding, reproduction, and defenses of crabs and lobsters.

I/U *Simple Animals,* by John Stidworthy (Facts on File, 1990)
Introduces the invertebrate animals, which include protozoa, sponges, crabs, and octopuses.

■ Reading Selections

Books marked with an asterisk before and after the title (*) are related to activities in the activity sections of this chapter.

The Adventures of Lowly Worm, by Richard Scarry (Someday Isle, 1995)
     Lowly Worm has so much fun in Busytown that he is saddened when his bike accident keeps him at home. With all of the get well cards and a visit from his friends, he realizes he'll be up in no time.

Chadwick the Crab, by Priscilla Cummings (Tidewater, 1988)
     Chadwick the crab searches for adventure, but soon finds himself in trouble and must rely on the birds and marine animals to rescue him.

Charlie's Great Escape, by Jane Luck Wilson (Ozark, 1996)

Billy's fishing pails are filled with hundreds of worms, but two special friends are determined to escape to return to their family.

Clams All Year, by Maryann Cocca-Leffler (Yearling Books, 1998)

All summer long the children go clam digging at their grandparents' beach house, with no luck. After a big storm, they discover enough clams to last all year.

4 Pups and a Worm, by Eric Seltzer (Random Library, 1996)

When a problem arises, four pups and a worm are there to solve it.

Here's Juggins, by Sally Smith Bryant (North Country Press, 1997)

When Juggins's father, a lobster fisherman on the coast of Maine, is accused of stealing from other fishermen, Juggins tries to clear his name. (Chapter Book)

Herman the Helper, by Robert Kraus (Econo-Clad, 1999)

Herman, the octopus, is always willing to help—old or young, friend or foe.

Hooray for Snail!, by John Stadler (Econo-Clad, 1999)

Slow Snail hits the ball so hard during a baseball game that it flies to the moon and back. Will Snail have time to slide in for a home run?

How to Eat Fried Worms, by Thomas Rockwell (Franklin Watts, 2000)

Two boys try to convince others that worms can be delicious. (Chapter Book)

How to Hide an Octopus and Other Sea Creatures, by Ruth Heller (Platt & Munk, 1992)

Rhyming text describes how different sea animals change color to blend in with their surroundings.

I'm Going to Pet a Worm Today: And Other Poems, by Constance Levy (McElderry Books, 1991)

Contains 39 poems about everyday things from petting worms to eating peas.

Inch by Inch, by Leo Lionni (Mulberry Books, 1995)

An inchworm outsmarts a hungry robin by displaying his measuring skills.

Is This a House for Hermit Crab?, by Megan McDonald (Orchard, 1990)

A crab outgrows his shell and looks for a new home.

The Jellyfish Season, by Mary Downing Hahn (Avon Books, 1996)

Personal problems make living conditions tense when, for economic reasons, two families must move in together on the eastern shore of Maryland. (Chapter Book)

The Lobster and Ivy Higgins, by Nancy Buss (Boyds Mills Press, 1992)

Ivy Higgins is determined to save the 27-pound lobster at her father's fish market, when her father announces he will raffle him off to bring in needed business. (Chapter Book)

Lobster's Secret, by Kathleen M. Hollenbeck (Soundprints, 1996)

Lobster searches for dinner while watching for predators, an even more dangerous feat after he molts.

Moving Day, by Robert Kalan (Greenwillow Books, 1996)

A hermit crab looks for a new home.

My Brother Louis Measures Worms, by Barbara Robinson (Harper Trophy, 1990)

Mary Elizabeth relates the humorous misadventures of her brother Louis and the other wacky members of her family. (Chapter Book)

National Worm Day, by James Stevenson (Greenwillow Books, 1990)
>A worm, a snail, a rhinoceros, and their animal friends enjoy several adventures together.

Octavia Warms Up, by Barbara Beak (Child's Play, 1995)
>Octavia Octopus learns to knit to make leg-warmers to keep her legs from getting stiff when she dances. Instructions for making a yarn octopus are included.

An Octopus Followed Me Home, by Dan Yaccarino (Viking, 1997)
>When a girl brings home an octopus and wants to keep him as a pet, her daddy reminds her of the crocodile, seals, and other inappropriate animals she has already brought into the house that created chaos.

Octopus Hug, by Laurence Pringle (Price Stern Sloan, 1996)
>While Mom is out for the evening, Dad and the kids have fun inventing new games and learning how to give an octopus hug.

Oliver's High Five, by Beverly Swerdlow Brown (Health Press, 1998)
>Oliver the Octopus faces many rejections based on his appearance. Even with only five legs, Oliver demonstrates his abilities.

Oyster Moon, by Margaret Meacham and Marcy Dunn Ramsey (Tidewater, 1996)
>A 14-year-old girl rescues her twin brother from the clutches of the cruel captain of an oyster dredge during the height of the Oyster Wars. (Chapter Book)

Simpson Snail Sings, by John Himmelman (Puffin Books, 1997)
>Simpson Snail has several fun days as he and his friends attend a costume party, have a sleepover, and learn to sing.

Snail and Buffalo, by Jim Latimer (Orchard, 1995)
>Snail, who is tiny, fearful, and slow, and Buffalo, who is large, brave, and fast, find they can each do things the other cannot.

Snail Started It, by Katja Reider, Angela Von Roehl, and Rosemary Lanning (North South Books, 1997)
>Snail starts a chain of insults when he calls Pig fat, but eventually it catches up with him and he learns that each animal is right just the way he or she is.

The Snail's Spell, by Joanne Ryder and Lynne Cherry (Viking, 1988)
>The reader imagines how it must feel to be a snail.

Something New to Do, by Michael Pellowski, Ski Michaels, and Jan Palmer (Troll, 1989)
>A young octopus, who is constantly searching for things to do, has some scary experiences.

The Story Snail, by Anne F. Rockwell (Aladdin, 1997)
>John can do nothing right until a snail gives him 100 fabulous stories to tell.

The Tickle Octopus, by Audrey Wood (Harcourt Brace, 1994)
>The lives of Bup and his family are changed forever when an extraordinary creature teaches them to laugh and play.

Walking the Edge, by Alice Mead (Whitman, 1995)
>Frustrated by his life of near-poverty and the unreliability of his divorced, drunken father, 13-year-old Scott throws himself into a science project raising clams to restock the bay of his Maine village. (Chapter Book)

Waterman's Child, by Barbara Mitchell (Lothrop, Lee & Shepard, 1997)
>Annie reflects on the life of her great-grandmother, who married a waterman and moved to Chesapeake Bay. There they made a living from oyster and crab fishing.

Why the Crab Has No Head, by Barbara Knutson (Lerner, 1988)
>An African legend in which the creator is concerned with Crab's pride and makes him "headless" to instill humility.

The Winter Worm Business, by Patricia Reilly Giff (Econo-Clad, 1999)
>Leroy and Tracy are in business selling worms, but the arrival of Leroy's bossy cousin Mitchell (who looks like Leroy) causes havoc. (Chapter Book)

The Worm Club, by Laurie Lawlor (Minstrel Books, 1994)
>Arthur is headed for trouble when the class bully befriends him. Will this ruin his chances to be on the school safety patrol? (Chapter Book)

■ Science Activities

Catch Me If You Can!

Ask students to speculate how sea animals are harvested or caught. In small groups, have students research the different methods for catching shrimp, lobsters, and clams. Ask them to find what type of equipment they would need for each of these methods. Have each student write a classified ad to hire someone to work in this area. Students should consider what types of skills and knowledge the potential hire should possess.

One Shell or Two?

Have students bring in several different types of shells to compare. Look at the difference in structure and together deduce that there are two basic structures: univalved (like a hermit crab's shell) and bivalved (like a clam or oyster). Ask the students what would be the function of a bivalved shell that can open and close? What would be the function of a univalved shell? What other differences can be observed?

Lobster Anyone?

For a real "hands-on" experience, purchase a live lobster from your local seafood market. (Make sure the pincers are banded!) Have the students observe the lobster and make careful notes on: the number of legs, the number of antennae, the structure of the tail, appendages under the tail, the length of the body and the tail, and so forth. (Crayfish can also be used for this activity. In most areas crayfish cannot be purchased in live form, but they can be purchased as precooked, frozen specimens. If these specimens are used, you can also dissect them and note the absence of bones.) **Teacher's note:** To prepare a one-pound lobster for dinner, boil in salted water 8 to 10 minutes.

Seafood Facts

Make a classroom seafood menu. On chart paper, make an outline of an open book, representing an open menu. Inside list several entrees such as lobster, shrimp, crab, mussels, and clams. Under each entree have students record facts that they discover about that animal. For example, they could discover how spiny lobsters differ from the lobsters we usually eat, how lobsters molt, where blue lobsters are found, or the approximate age of a one-pound lobster. Be sure to list any "fun facts" the students discover on your menu and do research on some of them.

World Invertebrates

As a class, highlight on a map of the world where different types of seafood are found. Ask the students what area is known for serving fresh lobster, king crab, shrimp, crayfish, and crab cakes? Why wouldn't these creatures swim from place to place and live all around the world?

Arthropod Investigation

Create a data sheet that compares the four main types of arthropods (i.e., animals with "jointed bodies"). Create five vertical columns on a piece of paper, labeling the columns "Characteristics," "Insects," "Crustaceans," "Arachnids," and "Millipedes/Centipedes." Under "Characteristics," list several features that help scientists classify animals into groups, such as number of legs, number of antennae, number of body segments, number of legs per body segment, number of claws, number of wings, and position of eyes. If possible, have specimens available for students to compare along with lots of books and photos. When finished, give examples of different animals and classify them in the appropriate groups (bee, tick, lobster, crab, spider, scorpion, housefly, butterfly, millipede, crayfish, etc.).

Sponges and Coral

Often, we forget that coral and sponges are invertebrates, too. As a class, look at the structure of coral, sponges, and sea anemones. (It is preferable to examine actual specimens.) Ask the students how these animals get their food? Why are they considered animals and not plants? Research different types of coral and where they are found. Students can make ocean scenes to show the different types of coral. (See "Art Activities" in this chapter.)

A Surprise Inside

Some shells open and close ("bivalved shells"). Often, if a grain of sand or other foreign matter is caught inside, a pearl forms. Have the students investigate pearls and answer these questions: How are pearls made and harvested? What is mother of pearl? Where is it found? What are cultured pearls? What are freshwater pearls? Why are pearls different colors? Who are the Japanese pearl divers? Why are pearls expensive and considered a treasure? Cut out two large identical shell shapes and tape or staple them together at the top. Record the answers to the questions inside the bottom shell.

Inch by Inch

Ask the students: How did the inchworm get its name? Is it really 1 inch long? As a class, share information on the inchworm to find the answers to these questions. (see *It Could Still Be a Worm* by Fowler) As a math activity, have a "measuring" treasure hunt. Make a list of specific measurements (3 inches, 5 inches, 10 inches, etc.). Give the list to your student(s).Each student must search the house/school for objects that are exactly that length. You can also read *Inch by Inch* by Lionni with the class.

A Worm Farm

Did you know that there are as many as 2 million earthworms per acre in some areas of the United States? Watch how worms eat dirt in your own "wormery" (see following instructions). You'll need a quart-sized glass jar.

- Place a layer of sand (about 1-1/2 -inches deep) in the bottom of the jar. Place a layer of soil, about the same depth, on top of the sand. Keep alternating the layers of soil and sand until the jar is nearly full. Be sure to end with a layer of soil. Smooth out each layer as you go.

- Dig up, or purchase, three or four earthworms and place them on the top layer of soil. Then place a layer of rotted leaves or compost over the earthworms. Spray this top layer lightly with water. (You will need to spray this top layer, lightly, throughout this experiment, whenever the soil looks or feels dry.)

- Take a piece of black construction paper and cut it to the same height as the glass jar. Wrap the construction paper around the jar and tape it to itself to make a tube that can be slipped down over the jar and be removed when you want to observe the earthworms. (You may want to decorate your black tube to make your "wormery" more festive looking.) Place the tube over the jar and set the "wormery" in a safe place.

- After a few days, remove the tube and observe what the worms have done to the layers of sand and soil. Record this information in a log every few days by making sketches of the worms' tunnels and writing a short description next to your drawings.

■ Creative Writing Activities

Following are instructions to give the students for various writing activities.

- Write a story about a sad jellyfish who, although beautiful to look at, has no friends because other fish are afraid of being stung by her. Does the jellyfish resolve her problem? How?

- Write your own story of "The Crabby Crab." How did he get the name "crab" in the first place? Do you know any people who are considered crabby? What do you suppose would cheer them up?

- Pretend you have eight arms, like the octopus. Make a list of the advantages of the situation. Then, compile a list of disadvantages. After you are finished, review your list and decide if you would like to have eight arms, or if you are happy with the two arms you have. (*Something New to Do* by Pellowski, Michaels, and Palmer)

- Choose one of the invertebrate animals and give it a physical handicap (e.g., a lobster with just one claw; a squid that can't squirt ink). Write a story showing how your character overcomes this disability. (*Oliver's High Five* by Brown)

- Write a story in which an activity occurs "at a snail's pace." Describe the characters' reactions and how they deal with the situation.

- Write a descriptive narrative from the perspective of a fish that is swimming in the Caribbean Sea. Describe the underwater sites he sees and any adventures he encounters.

- You are an oyster fisherman and have discovered a huge pearl in one of the oysters. What do you do about it?

- One of your friends tends to "clam up" whenever she meets new people. Write her a friendly letter with suggestions on how to be more outgoing.

- Your pet hermit crab needs a bigger home, but you have no larger shells to offer him. What item can you provide that he can use temporarily while you search for a larger shell? Write a humorous story about how your hermit crab adjusts to his temporary home.

■ Art Activities

Following are instructions to give students for various art activities.

- Make a 3-dimensional picture with worms. Each student will need one piece of white paper, one-half piece of green paper, and some brown yarn.

  1. Using a hole puncher, have students punch several holes in the green paper.

  2. Students then cut the brown yarn into 3-inch segments to serve as worms. Insert the yarn through the holes in the green paper so that the yarn extends 1 to 2 inches beyond the holes. Tape the yarn into place on the back of the green paper. (Each hole should have a "worm" coming out of it.)

  3. Glue or paste the green paper onto the white paper so that the worms are on the outside. Students can draw a scene "above ground" or simply add the sun and clouds to their artwork.

- Using modeling clay (preferably one that hardens), create a 3-dimensional scene of the ocean floor. Look at photos of different types of coral. Have students create different types of corals with different colors of clay (or paint the clay when it is hard). Add starfish that can be cut out of sandpaper. Add different shells. Cover the scene with blue plastic wrap.

- Design a keepsake picture frame. Cut out a cardboard rectangle the desired size of your frame. Decorate the frame with colored sand and small shells.

- Create a watercolor scene of the ocean floor. With crayons, draw pictures of several different invertebrate animals, such as starfish, coral, sea anemones, or clams. When you are finished, paint over the entire scene with blue watercolor paint.

- Sew together the outer edges of two old gloves from the base of the index finger to the hand hole and from the base of the pinkie finger to the hand hole (leaving the ends where you insert your hands open and pushing the two "thumbs" to the inside). Fill the gloves with fiberfill so that you have an octopus with eight legs. Sew the hand-hole edge closed. Add eyes and any other features that you want to make your own personalized octopus.

- Look at the different types of shells (either in an encyclopedia or library book, or by collecting specimens). Try to make similar shells using modeling clay or bread dough. You can even use marbles or beads as pearls in an oyster shell that you construct. Decorate your shell using paint, glitter, or any material of your choice.

- Using a bag of small, pearl-colored beads, make a picture of your favorite invertebrate. Arrange the beads on a piece of colored construction paper (dark colors such as red, purple, orange, or black will provide the best contrast) to form your animal, then glue them in place.

Chapter 3
Reptiles and Amphibians

■ Teaching Resources

Books containing experiment(s) relating to the subject matter are marked with a plus sign (+) before and after the title.

P   *Eyewitness Juniors Amazing Crocodiles and Reptiles,* by Mary Ling (Alfred A. Knopf, 1991)
Text and photographs depict the habits, diet, and characteristics of crocodiles, alligators, turtles, snakes, and lizards.

P   *Never Kiss an Alligator!,* by Colleen Stanley Bare (Puffin, 1994)
An easy-to-read book discussing the characteristics and habits of alligators.

P   *Snakes Are Hunters,* by Patricia Lauber (Harper Trophy, 1989)
Describes the characteristics of a variety of snakes and how they hunt and eat their prey.

P   *The Yucky Reptile Alphabet Book,* by Jerry Pallotta (Charlesbridge Pub, 1990)
Introduces the letters of the alphabet by describing a reptile for each letter.

P/I *Alligators and Crocodiles,* by Michael George (Child's World, 1991)
Describes the characteristics, habitat, behavior, and life cycle of these reptiles.

P/I *Frogs, Frogs, Everywhere,* by D. M. Souza (Carolrhoda Books, 1994)
An introduction to the physical characteristics, life cycle, and behavioral characteristics of frogs.

P/I *The Fascinating World of Frogs and Toads,* by Angels Julivert (Carolrhoda Books, 1993)
Describes the physical characteristics, behavior, and habitats of various kinds of frogs and toads.

P/I *A Frog's Body,* by Joanna Cole (Wm. Morrow, 1980)
A frog's anatomy is explained through photographs and text.

P/I *Frogs, Toads, Lizards, and Salamanders,* by Nancy Winslow Parker (Greenwillow Books, 1990)
Describes the physical characteristics, natural environment, and habits of frogs, toads, lizards, and salamanders.

P/I *Rattlesnakes,* by Mary Ann McDonald (Child's World, 1996)
An introduction to the physical characteristics, behavior, and life cycle of rattlesnakes. (Also, *Boas,* 1996; *Cobras,* 1996; *Garter Snakes,* 1996; and *Pythons,* 1996.)

P/I *Reptiles,* by Carson Creagh (Time Life Books, 1996)
Describes the physical characteristics and behavior of reptiles.

P/I *Reptiles and Amphibians,* by Andres Llamas Ruiz (Sterling Publishing, 1996)
Colorful illustrations and brief text cover the birth and growth of reptiles and amphibians.

P/I *Shy Salamanders,* by D. M. Souza (Carolrhoda Books, 1994)
A look at the life cycle, habits, and characteristics of salamanders.

P/I *Snake,* by Caroline Arnold (Morrow Junior Books, 1991)
Discusses, in detailed pictures and text, the physical characteristics, behavior, and life cycle of a variety of snakes, especially the boas and pythons.

P/I *Snakes,* by Seymour Simon (Harper Trophy, 1994)
Describes, in text and photographs, the physical characteristics, habits, and environment of snakes.

I *Chameleons,* by Claudia Schnieper (Carolrhoda Books, 1988)
Text and excellent photographs detail the physical characteristics, behavior, and life cycle of the chameleon.

I *Chameleons,* by Kathy Darling (Lee & Shepard Books, 1997)
Text and photographs vividly describe chameleons.

I *Chickens Aren't the Only Ones,* by Ruth Heller (Paper Star, 1991)
An introduction to animals that lay eggs including: reptiles, amphibians, fishes, insects, birds, and a few mammals.

I *Roaring Reptiles,* by D. M. Souza (Carolrhoda Books, 1992)
Describes the characteristics, habitat, and life cycle of crocodiles, alligators, caimans, and gavials.

I *Salamanders,* by Cherie Winner (Carolrhoda Books, 1993)
Describes the physical characteristics, habitat, and life cycle of salamanders.

I *Snakes and Other Reptiles,* by Mary Elting (Simon & Schuster, 1987)
Describes the characteristics, habits, and habitat of an often-misunderstood group of animals that includes: snakes, crocodiles, turtles, and lizards.

I/U *Alligators,* by Frank Staub (Lerner Publishing, 1995)
Text and photographs examine alligators.

U *Alligators and Crocodiles,* by Lesley Dow (Child's World, 1990)
Discusses the biological features of alligators and crocodiles, their habitat, lifestyle, and history.

U *A Water Snake's Year,* by Doris Gove (Atheneum, 1991)
Details a year in the life of a female water snake.

■ Reading Selections

Books marked with an asterisk (*) before and after the title are related to activities in the activity sections of this chapter.

Alligator Arrived with Apples, by Crescent Dragonwagon (Aladdin, 1992)
> From Alligator's apples to Zebra's zucchini, a multitude of alphabetical animals and foods celebrate Thanksgiving with a grand feast.

Alligator in the Basement, by Bob Keeshan (Fairview Press, 1996)
> A boy discovers the power of imagination when he visits his grandfather and meets the alligator that lives in the washing machine.

Alligators and Others All Year Long!, by Crescent Dragonwagon (Macmillan, 1993)
> A collection of animals celebrate the months of the year in poetry.

Apples, Alligators and Also Alphabets, by Odette Johnson and Bruce Johnson (Oxford University Press, 1990)
> An alphabet book of different animals.

Baby Rattlesnake, by Te Ata (Children's Book Press, 1989)
> Willful Baby Rattlesnake throws tantrums to get his rattle before he's ready, but misuses it and learns a lesson.

To Bathe a Boa, by C. Imbior Kudrna (Carolrhoda Books, 1986)
> A youngster finds it's not easy to bathe an uncooperative boa.

Bill and Pete Go Down the Nile, by Tomie de Paola (Paper Star, 1996)
> Pete and his crocodile friend, Bill, encounter a jewel thief at the museum in Cairo.

Box Turtle at Long Pond, by William George (Greenwillow, 1989)
> A box turtle spends a day at Long Pond searching for food, basking in the sun, and escaping from a raccoon.

A Boy, a Dog, a Frog, and a Friend, by Mercer Mayer (Dial Books, 1993)
> When something unusual bites on the fishing line, a quiet fishing adventure changes.

The Day Jimmy's Boa Ate the Wash, by Trinka Noble (E. P. Dutton, 1992)
> A field trip becomes chaotic when Jimmy brings along his boa. (Video by Great Plains National Television Library)

The Enormous Crocodile, by Roald Dahl (Alfred A. Knopf, 2000)
> An enormous crocodile tries several attempts to secure lunch, only to be foiled by neighbors.

Franklin Fibs, by Paulette Bourgeois (Kids Kan Press, 1997)
> Franklin, the turtle, has to live with the results of a fib he tells his friends. (Other "Franklin" books are available.)

Frog and Toad All Year, by Arnold Lobel (Econo-Clad, 1999)
> As the seasons change, two friends share different experiences. (Other "Frog and Toad" books are available.)

Frog and Toad Are Friends, by Arnold Lobel (HarperCollins Juvenile, 1979)
> Two friends enjoy several activities together. (Other "Frog and Toad" books are available.)

Frog in Winter, by Max Velthuijs (Tambourine Books, 1993)
> Frog's physiology does not permit him to enjoy winter, but his friends help him to make the best of the cold weather.

A Frog Inside My Hat, by Fay Robinson (Bridgewater Books, 1993)
> A collection of short, whimsical poems.

Frog on His Own, by Mercer Mayer (Econo-Clad, 1999)
> Frog ventures away from his friends for an adventure on his own. (Video by Phoenix Learning Group, 1992)

The Frog Prince Continued, by Jon Scieszka (Puffin Books, 1994)
> The Frog Prince finds life with the Princess unfulfilling and seeks out a witch to turn him back into a frog. However, finding the right witch can be difficult, giving the Frog Prince time to re-think his decision.

Frog Where Are You?, by Mercer Mayer (Econo-Clad, 1999)
> A wordless book depicting a boy who searches the woods for his frog and experiences several mishaps along the way.

Frogs Jump, by Alan Brooks (Scholastic, 1999)
> Illustrations (by Steven Kellogg) provide humorous interpretations of the actions of animals, from one frog to twelve whales.

Funny, Funny Lyle, by Bernard Waber (Houghton Mifflin, 1987)
> Many changes are ahead as Lyle's mother moves in, and Mrs. Primm announces she is expecting a baby.

Gator Pie, by Louise Mathews (Sundance, 1995)
> Two alligators face a dilemma when they try to share a pie, dividing it into halves, thirds, fourths, eighths, and eventually, hundredths.

Gila Monsters Meet You at the Airport, by Marjorie Weinman Sharmat (Econo-Clad, 1999)
> A New York City boy's ideas of life in the West make him worried about his family's plans to move there.

Harvey's Horrible Snake Disaster, by Eth Clifford (Houghton Mifflin, 1984)
> Nora visits her cousin Harvey and trouble with snakes is the result. (Chapter Book)

How to Hide a Crocodile, by Ruth Heller (Price Stern Sloan, 1994)
> Different reptiles are shown individually and again hiding in their environment. For beginning readers.

Hurry up, Franklin, by Paulette Bourgeois (Kids Kan Press, 1997)
> Franklin the turtle learns to be happy with what he is and find the good in it. (Other "Franklin" books are available.)

Jimmy's Boa and the Big Splash Birthday Bash, by Trinka Hakes (E. P. Dutton, 1989)
> Jimmy's birthday party at Sea Land turns out to be a big splash when everyone ends up in the big tank.

Jimmy's Boa Bounces Back, by Trinka Hakes Noble (E. P. Dutton, 1992)
> Jimmy's boa adds chaos to a posh garden club meeting.

The Lizard and the Sun, by Alma Flor Ada (Doubleday Books for Young Readers, 1997)
> A traditional Mexican folk tale in which a faithful lizard finds the sun, which brings light and warmth back to the world.

Lizard in the Sun, by Joanne Ryder (Morrow Junior Books, 1994)
> A child discovers what it is like to be an anole, a tiny lizard, lying in the sun and changing colors.

Lizard's Song, by George Shannon (Mulberry Books, 1992)
> A lizard repeatedly teaches his song to Bear, who, when distracted, forgets the words.

Lovable Lyle, by Bernard Waber (Houghton Mifflin, 1977)
> A little girl's mother forbids her to play with Lyle, until she evidences how kind and brave he is.

Lyle at the Office, by Bernard Waber (Houghton Mifflin, 1994)
> When Lyle visits Mr. Primm's advertising office, he is almost recruited as the cereal spokesperson.

Lyle, Lyle, Crocodile, by Bernard Waber (Houghton Mifflin, 1987)
> A grumpy neighbor sends Lyle to the zoo, but Lyle's bravery wins Mr. Grump's acceptance and permission to return home.

The Mixed up Chameleon, by Eric Carle (HarperCollins Juvenile Books, 1998)
> A chameleon wishes to be like the other animals it sees, but soon realizes it's better to be yourself.

The Monkey and the Crocodile, by Paul Galdone (Econo-Clad, 1999)
> A hungry crocodile tries his best to catch a monkey for dinner but must use his wits to do it.

The Mysterious Tadpole, by Steven Kellogg (Dial Books, 1993)
> Louis's pet tadpole does not seem to be growing into an ordinary frog.

One Frog Too Many, by Mercer Mayer (Dial Books, 1992)
> A pet frog becomes jealous when a little boy receives a second frog.

Rockin' Reptiles, by Stephanie Calmenson and Joanna Cole (William Morrow, 1997)
> When a new girl on the block has only one extra ticket to a concert, two best friends must try to decide which of them will go.

Tammy Turtle, by Suzanne Tate (Nags Head Art, 1991)
> The life story of a turtle who is often assisted by "helpful humans."

There's an Alligator under My Bed, by Mercer Mayer (Dial Books, 1987)
> Bedtime is challenging for a boy with an alligator under his bed, until he lures it out of his room and into the garage.

The Turtle and the Monkey, by Paul Galdone (Clarion Books, 1990)
> A turtle offers to share a banana tree with a greedy monkey but must outsmart the monkey to get her share.

Turtle Day, by Douglas Florian (Thomas Y. Crowell, 1989)
> The events of Turtle's day are described, including how he hides in his shell when frightened by a snake.

The Voyage of the Frog, by Gary Paulsen (Yearling Books, 1990)
> David goes out on his boat, *The Frog,* and must deal with a fierce storm as well as his feelings about his uncle's death. (Chapter Book)

The Wide-Mouthed Frog, by Rex Schneider (Stemmer House, 1991)
> A wide-mouthed frog is curious about the diets of the swamp animals until he meets an alligator who eats only wide-mouthed frogs.

■ Science Activities

Frogs

Frog or Toad?

As a class, list the differences between a frog and a toad. Discuss how they are similar and how they differ. Ask the students: Which would you prefer as a pet? Why?

Frog versus Human

The systems and organs of the frog are often compared with those of humans. Study the digestive system of the frog. How is it similar to our digestive system? How is it different? For an interactive Web site on frog dissection, try: http://curry.edschool.virginia.edu/go/frog.

Poisonous Frogs

Have the students research different types of frogs. Some frogs are brightly colored and some are more "naturally" colored. Ask the students to hypothesize why this is so. Discuss whether most poisonous frogs are brightly colored or a more natural shade.

Posters

Make two "Information Posters," one each for reptiles and amphibians. As the class discovers related information, list the facts about the appearance, habits, and habitat of animals on each poster. Once the facts are listed, illustrate the posters with pictures of the different members of the subject group. (Pictures can be cut out of magazines or drawn by the students.)

Crocodile versus Alligator

Make a chart with three columns. In the first column, have the students list characteristics unique to alligators. In the third column, list characteristics unique to crocodiles. In the center column, list characteristics common to both the alligator and the crocodile.

Snake Characteristics

- Have the students look at the colorings and markings of poisonous and non-poisonous snakes. Ask the students to determine some of the common characteristics of poisonous snakes (e.g., arrow shape of head) and non-poisonous snakes. (Snakes with stripes running from head to tail are usually harmless. Snakes with "bands" of color may or may not be harmless.)

- In small groups, have students research the snakes that inhabit North America. They should determine which snakes are poisonous and which are non-poisonous. Discuss whether the markings on North American snakes conform to the "rule" listed in the previous item in this list.

Lizards

Have the students research several types of lizards. Compare their markings and coloring. Ask the students: Where do the most colorful lizards live? What relationship does the coloring of a lizard have to its environment?

■ Creative Writing Activities

Following are instructions to give students for various writing activities.

- Snakes or serpents are often portrayed as the "bad" guys in movies and books. Discuss why you think snakes have this "bad guy" image. Write a story about a snake that is good and does something nice.
- Write a silly paragraph about a snake, using as many words beginning with the letter "s" as you can. (You can repeat this exercise substituting any of the other reptiles in place of the snake.)
- An alliteration is a phrase of two or more words that have the same initial sound (e.g., the alligator ate Annie). Make up a list of alliterations using the names of your favorite reptiles.
- Mercer Mayer wrote many stories about reptiles and amphibians. Do an author study on Mercer Mayer. Where did Mayer live while growing up? Did Mayer live near a pond?
- Read *Frog and Toad All Year* by Lobel. Write a story about Frog and Toad and what they would do during your favorite season.
- Read *What a Catastrophe!* by Campbell. Write your own ending for the story.
- Some children think that there is a "creature" living under their beds. Write a story telling about the animal that lives under your bed. What kind of animal is it? Have you found a way to live in harmony with it? (*There's An Alligator under My Bed* by Mayer)
- Read *The Enormous Crocodile* by Dahl. Write a letter to Enormous Crocodile explaining to him why he should not eat children.
- You are fishing at your favorite fishing hole. All of a sudden, something tugs at your fishing line! You think you've caught a whopper, but, when you pull it in, you can't believe what you see! Finish this story. (*A Boy, a Dog, a Frog, and a Friend* by Mayer)
- Imagine, like the turtle, that you carry your home around with you all the time, on your back. Write an essay describing your house and any contents it may have. Explain whether or not you like this arrangement.
- Write a letter to your parents giving the reasons why you believe they should allow you to have a snake as a pet.
- Pretend that, like the chameleon, your skin changed color so that you blended in with your surroundings and were hard to see. List some of the advantages you might find in this situation. Then list some of the disadvantages. Write a silly story about a child whose skin keeps turning the color of his surroundings (the couch, bed quilt, draperies, etc.).
- Write a story about several different animals that are joined together but don't get along (e.g., an animal with a lion's head, a lamb's body, and a monkey's tail). Your creature is confused because it reacts like each of the animals at different times. Explain how this mishap occurred. Write about the difficulties that your creature has dealing with its environment and what it must do to adjust. Is there a way out of its predicament? Be sure to include the importance of compromise and cooperation in your story. (*The Mixed up Chameleon* by Carle)

■ Art Activities

Following are instructions to give students for various art activities.

- Make a frog puppet using a lunch bag. Draw a face on the bottom of the paper bag. Glue on arms and legs made out of green paper that has been folded accordion style.
- Paint a picture of an alligator on a piece of sandpaper. (This will give your alligator a rough, bumpy feel.) Cut out the alligator and glue it onto a picture of a swamp that you painted on regular paper.

- Make a turtle swimming in a pond out of chalk dust using the following instructions:

  Make chalk dust by grating the chalk or mashing it with a hammer. The chalk dust must be very fine so that it will float on the water and not sink.

  Fill a tub (or a 9-by-13-inch pan) with water and sprinkle different colors of chalk dust on top of the water. Add blue first, which will become the water. Then, in the center, add green for the turtle and the colors you want for coloring on the turtle's shell.

  Gently lay a piece of paper on top of the water. The chalk will adhere to the paper. Remove the paper after a few seconds and let it dry.

  If you wish to make more than one picture, the water need not be changed between pictures; however, more chalk must be used for each additional picture.

- Make snakes out of old ties (the wilder the better) using the following instructions:

  Sew (or glue) closed the wide end of the tie.

  Add eyes made of felt, pom-poms, or sequins, and make a tongue and fangs out of felt. Glue these onto the wide end of the tie.

  Fill the tie with fiberfill (you may need a long stick or rod to push the fiber inside).

  Sew closed the narrow end of the tie. (*The Day Jimmy's Boa Ate the Wash* by Noble)

- Draw a picture of yourself, giving yourself any animal features you would like to have (elephant trunk for a nose, bird feathers, duck feet, a turtle shell, etc.). (*The Mixed up Chameleon* by Carle)

- Make a papier-mâché snake by taping crumpled newspaper around a bent coat hanger. (Bend the coat hanger to whatever snake shape you desire.) Apply the papier-mâché by dipping newspaper strips in a paste mixture (made by mixing 1/2 cup flour, 1 tablespoon of salt, and 1 cup warm water) and wrapping them around the newspaper and hanger. Continue dipping the newspaper strips and adding them to the hanger until you have four layers. Let your snake dry and paint it.

- Find a rock about the size of your fist in your yard or neighborhood. Wash and dry the rock and then paint it to look like a turtle shell. Draw legs, a head, and a tail on construction paper. Cut them out and glue them to your "shell."

- Paint a picture of a swamp, including as many different reptiles as you can. (You could also make the swamp a 3-dimensional scene. Make trees out of construction paper rolled like a tube for the trunk with leaves glued on and use blue construction paper glued on to cardboard for the water. Then draw and cut out the reptiles and place them in your swamp.)

Chapter 4
Fish

■ Teaching Resources

Books containing experiment(s) relating to the subject matter are marked with a plus sign (+) before and after the title.

P *Hungry, Hungry Sharks,* by Joanna Cole (Econo-Clad, 1999)
An introduction to the kinds of sharks and their behavior.

P *Sharks,* Gail Gibbons (Holiday, 1992)
Describes shark behavior and different kinds of sharks.

P *Sharks: Shark Magic for Kids,* by Patricia Corrigan (Gareth Stevens, 1996)
Contains information about sharks with many illustrations.

P/I *Amazing Fish,* by Mary Ling (Knopf, 1991)
Introduces memorable members of the fish world, explains what makes them unique, and describes important characteristics of the entire group.

P/I *Sharks,* by Seymour Simon (HarperCollins, 1995)
A look at sharks with photographs of several of the different species.

P/I *Tiger Shark,* by Anne Welsbacher (Capstone Press, 1995)
An introduction to the tiger shark with interesting stories and reports.

P/I *Whale Sharks,* by Anne Welsbacher (Capstone Press, 1998)
An introduction to the wonders and mysteries of the largest shark, the whale shark. Large print and vivid photos.

I *Chickens Aren't the Only Ones,* by Ruth Heller (Paper Star, 1991)
An introduction to animals that lay eggs including: fish, birds, reptiles, amphibians, and a few mammals.

I *Fish,* by Edward Ricciut (Blackbirch Press, 1994)
Examines the physical structure, metabolism, and life cycles of fish and discusses how they fit into the food chain.

I *Sharks,* by Kevin Holmes (Bridgestone Books, 1999)
An introduction to sharks covering their physical characteristics, habits, prey, and relationship to humans.

I/U *Sharks!,* by Catherine Gourley (Millbrook Press, 1996)
A collection of facts and stories, both historical and traditional, about sharks, their behavior, and their interaction with people.

■ Reading Selections

Books marked with an asterisk (*) before and after the title are related to activities in the activity sections of this chapter.

The Big Fish: An Alaskan Fairy Tale, by Marcia A. Wakeland (Misty Mountain, 1993)
Lena learns from a king salmon that she can do anything if she believes in herself.

The Carp in the Bathtub, by Barbara Cohen (Econo-Clad, 1999)
Two children try to rescue the fish their mother plans to cook for dinner.

Fish Eyes, by Lois Ehlert (Harcourt Brace Jovanovich, 1990)
A colorful counting book based on neon fish.

Fish Face, by Patricia Reilly Giff (Yearling Books, 1984)
One in a series of books centered around the Kids of the Polk Street School. (Chapter Book)

Fish Is Fish, by Leo Lionni (Alfred A. Knopf, 1987)
When a tadpole grows up and leaves the pond, a little fish decides that he doesn't need to remain in the pond either.

The Fish of Gold, by the Grimm Brothers, adapted by M. Eulalia Valeri (Silver Burdett, 1985)
A poor fisherman catches a golden fish that grants wishes until his wife's preposterous wishes cause a reversal of their fortune.

Fishy Riddles, by Katy Hall and Lisa Eisenberg (Econo-Clad, 1999)
A simple collection of riddles about fish.

The Great, White, Man-Eating Shark, by Margaret Mahy (Puffin Books, 1996)
Norvin pretends to be a shark and scares away swimmers to have the cave to himself. But he's soon joined by an amorous female shark.

Louis the Fish, by Arthur Yorinks (Farrar, Straus & Giroux, 1986)
An unhappy butcher finally achieves happiness.

The Magic Fish, by Freya Littledale (Scholastic, 1989)
A fisherman is granted a wish from a magic fish and enjoys wealth and riches until his wife's greed ruins the magic.

The Major, the Poacher, and the Wonderful One-Trout River, by Dayton O. Hyde (Boyds Mills Press, 1998)
The Major, who wants to raise a record-breaking trout, has to deal with a 14-year-old poacher. (Chapter Book)

Nate the Great and the Fishy Prize, by Marjorie Sharmat (Econo-Clad, 1999)
Nate agrees to search for the missing prize, forfeiting his time to prepare his dog for the pet contest.

Nessa's Fish, by Nancy Luenn (Aladdin, 1997)
Nessa protects her grandmother and the fish caught for the Eskimo village from a fox, a pack of wolves, and a bear.

Shark in the Sea, by Joanne Ryder (Morrow Junior Books, 1997)
> A hungry great white shark swims about watching, smelling, listening, and waiting for someone to become his next meal.

A Swim Through the Sea, by Kristin Joy Pratt (Dawn Publications, 1994)
> Travel through the alphabet and meet the many sea creatures that inhabit the seas.

The Two-Thousand-Pound Goldfish, by Betsy Byars (Harper Trophy, 2000)
> Warren escapes into movie fantasies while he awaits the return of his mother, who is hiding from the FBI. (Chapter Book)

The following books are out of print, but may be available at the local library.

Birds, Beasts, and Fish, by Anne Carter (Macmillan, 1991)
> A collection of animal poems from around the world.

Dead Man in Catfish Bay, by Mary Blount Christian (A. Whitman, 1985)
> A teenager visiting Catfish Cove is caught up in the tension between local fishermen and Vietnamese refugees.

Ellen and the Goldfish, by John Himmelman (Harper & Row, 1990)
> A young girl who loves to draw befriends a goldfish and uses her drawings to help him escape from a fisherman.

Fish and Flamingo, by Nancy White Carlstrom (Little, Brown, 1993)
> Two unlikely friends tell about their lives, help each other out, and enjoy their time together.

Jonah and the Great Fish, by Warwick Hutton (Antheneum, 1984)
> Retells the Biblical story of how Jonah was swallowed by a whale.

Lend Me Your Wings, by John Agard (Little, Brown, 1987)
> A fish who wants to fly and a bird that longs to swim trade fins and wings for a new look at life.

One Fish, Two Fish, Red Fish, Blue Fish, by Dr. Seuss (Random House, 1988)
> Dr. Seuss explores the world of the sea in his clever, rhyming way.

One Small Fish, by Joanne Ryder (Morrow Junior Books, 1993)
> A student watches a series of sea creatures move about the room as he sits in science class on Friday afternoons.

The Walking Catfish, by David Day (Macmillan, 1991)
> A tall tale about a Big Lie Contest where a tale about a giant catfish becomes true and swallows up its teller.

Whispering in the Park, by Fred Burstein (Bradbury Press, 1992)
> Two girls try a clever plan to call the goldfish in the park pond.

■ Science Activities

Freshwater/Saltwater Fish

Discuss as a class which fish are freshwater fish and which are saltwater fish. Together, find 10 examples of each. Ask the students which do we eat most often? Why do you think we eat more saltwater fish?

Math Practice

Bring in goldfish crackers for the students to use as manipulatives to practice math problems. Demonstrate grouping, addition, subtraction, multiplication, and so forth.

Research Project

Have students choose a particular type of fish (herring, seahorse, goldfish, shark, etc.) and research it thoroughly (have at least two outside sources plus an encyclopedia). Have students write a paper on and make a model of (or draw a detailed picture of) the fish they chose. The paper should include the following points:

name and detailed description of the fish

where the fish lives (if in the ocean, what zone)

what the fish eats

how the fish defends itself

how the fish contributes to its environment

Depending on the age of your students, this would be a good opportunity to teach them the proper steps to use in writing a paper. You can have them write an outline of what the paper will include, take notes from their sources, arrange the notes to follow their outline, write a rough draft, and write the finished product.

Teacher's note: The models of the students' fish can be made of fabric, papier-mâché, stuffed brown paper, clay, etc.

Hometown Research

Is there a lake, river, ocean, or creek near your school? Have the students do some research on it. Ask the students how they could find out if the quality of the water is clean or polluted. What kinds of fish live in it? Are they safe to eat? If possible, bring in a sample of water. Discuss that water safety cannot be assured by appearance alone. Water-testing kits are available from science suppliers. If possible, demonstrate how these kits work. Have the students write up their findings. If the water is polluted, have the class discuss what can be done to help the situation.

By the Sea

Fish live at different depths in the ocean. Why? Have the students research the characteristics of fish that live near the surface (e.g., they usually are smaller, they eat algae), fish that live in the middle depths (e.g., they are quick moving, they are predatory, they have streamlined bodies), and fish that live near the ocean's floor (e.g., they are slow moving, they eat food off the ocean floor, they are flat fish). Demonstrate this scenario by making a sea scene on the wall (or on a door). Cut out wavy strips of blue paper and tape them to the wall. Discuss the different types of fish and how far down they live in the ocean (twilight zone, midnight zone, etc.). Have the students design different fish out of paper and other materials they have at home. Place the fish in the proper area of your ocean. (You can enhance your ocean by placing the proper vegetation in your scene also.)

Fish to Eat

Check with local seafood restaurants or supermarkets to see if they conduct tours. Have the students list questions they can ask such as: What characteristics do they look for when buying fish? What should consumers look for when purchasing fish? Where do the different kinds of seafood offered in your city come from (e.g., lobster, mahi mahi, crab legs). How long does fish stay fresh? After your tour (or research) is completed, have the students write a consumer's guide for purchasing seafood.

The Fishing Industry

Have the students research five countries that depend on fishing. Students should consider these questions: What percent of their country's gross national product comes from the fishing industry? What percentage of their country's population is employed in the fishing industry? Are these countries considered rich or poor?

Caviar

Purchase some fish eggs or caviar to study. Examine them with a magnifying glass. Try to cut one in half. If you are using caviar, taste a small bite. Discuss as a class how these eggs compare to chicken eggs.

A Fish Story

After you have gone fishing and caught a "big one" (or after buying a fresh fish from your local market), look at some of its scales under a magnifying glass. Notice the rings on them. You can tell how old a fish is by counting these rings. Each year of a fish's life, an additional ring grows on its scales. (Does this remind you of any other dating system?)

A "Fish-Eye" View

- Cut out the bottom of an old plastic pail. Stretch a sheet of clear polyethylene across the bottom and up the sides of the pail. Attach the polyethylene by tightly tying a string or rope around the pail.
- Take the pail to a nearby pond or lake. Students can now view the underwater life of the pond or lake by holding the pail in the water and looking through the polyethylene.

A Fishing Adventure

Make a fishing pole by tying a magnet onto one end of a string and tying the other end of the string to a pencil or ruler. Draw several fish on different-colored paper and cut them out. Secure a paperclip to the mouth of each fish. Write a question or problem on each fish. These could include the following:

Math problems: Reinforce math skills by writing problems on the fish that the children can solve.

Geography: Put the names of the states on the fish. Students must name the capitals of the states.

History: Put the names of discoverers or famous people or events in history on the fish. Students must tell about the person or event.

Students can now "go fishing." Once a fish is caught, the student must answer the question on the fish to keep it. If the student cannot answer the question, it is thrown back. The student with the most fish at the end of the game is the "Fisher of the Day" and gets a special sticker or privilege.

Nesting Habits

Have the students choose two or three types of fish (salmon, shark, bluegill, bass, etc.) and research the nesting habits of each. Ask the students: Do all fish return each year to the same nesting place? How do different fish lay their eggs? What happens after the young fish hatch?

Sharks and Whales

- Divide the class into two groups: the "Whales" and the "Sharks." Have each group list the characteristics they possess. Compare the lists from both groups.
- Students can make a Venn Diagram to compare and contrast sharks and whales. Draw two intersecting circles on a piece of paper. In the area where the circles intersect, list similar characteristics of the shark and whale. In the section of the circle to the far left, list characteristics unique to the shark. In the section of the circle to the far right, list characteristics unique to the whale.
- Make other Venn Diagrams to compare and contrast other fish.

Plankton

Students can collect fresh pond, lake, creek, or sea water (not tap water) using the following instructions:
- Cut off the foot portion of an old, nylon stocking and fit it over the rim of a glass jar with a rubber band or cord.
- Weave a piece of wire through the toe end of the stocking and bend it into a circle about 8 inches across.
- Attach the ends of the wire to a small pole or stick using cord or duct tape.
- Pull the net and glass jar through the water, and pour what you collect into your "observation tank." (Directions for making a tank follow.)
  1. Take two pieces of stiff, clear plastic (about 4 inches by 4 inches).
  2. Join the two pieces of plastic together by pushing modeling clay along the side and bottom edges of the plastic, leaving about a 1/4-inch air space between them. Be sure to seal the edges tightly so that your water samples do not leak out.
  3. Pour the water that you collect into this observation tank.
  4. Use a magnifying glass to examine the plankton within the tank.

■ Creative Writing Activities

Following are instructions to give students for various writing activities.
- Write a paper explaining why you would like to live as a fish. Be sure to choose the type of fish you would like to be and where (what type of water) you would like to live. (You can rent the movie *The Incredible Mr. Limpet* before the exercise is completed to get ideas or afterwards to get another opinion on the issue.)
- Compose your own poem beginning with the line: "Down in the deep blue sea, sea, sea."
- Pretend you have been swallowed by a giant fish. Write a journal of your days inside the fish's belly. How do you live? How do you get out? Ideas for students who need some help: You find a ship inside that you live on, you send a note in a bottle to get help, if a whale, you climb up its spout hole to escape, you build a fire and smoke your way out. (*Jonah and the Great Fish* by Hutton)
- Write a letter to a pen pal describing a child in your neighborhood whom the other kids call "Fish Face." Why do they call him or her that? Is it all in fun, or does this hurt the child's feelings? How do you feel about the situation? (*Fish Face* by Giff)

- Write a petition to the city council giving reasons why an aquarium should be added to a public park near you. Present the petition to your class.
- Write a humorous story about a school of fish attending school. What are the subjects they study? What games do they play at recess? What does their school lunch consist of?
- Write an ABC's book of fish and make up poems to go with your illustrations (e.g., "A" is for Abalone, who likes to eat baloney).
- What is meant when it is said that a statement "sounds fishy"? Write a detective story in which the detective is investigating a character whose alibi "sounds fishy."
- Pretend you are a mermaid. Describe where you live and what your daily activities are. What is the biggest danger you face? What songs do you and your fellow mermaids sing as you go about your duties? Do you go to school? If so, what is it like?
- Write a story about what it would be like to take a ride on a seahorse. Where would you like to go? What adventures lie ahead?

■ Art Activities

Following are instructions to give the students for various art activities.
- Using crayons, draw a picture of a fish (press down hard on the crayon as you color to make the fish as dark as possible). Paint the entire piece of paper containing the fish with blue watercolor to simulate the water (make sure to paint over the top of the fish).
- Sponge paint a "sea" by dipping a dry sponge into a small dab of blue paint and pressing the sponge lightly onto paper several times. Repeat this process using some green or aqua paint. Cut out fish (from a magazine or that you have drawn) and glue them onto the paper sea.
- Make "hand" fish. Place your hand on a piece of paper, fingers together with your thumb sticking up on top. Draw around your hand with a pen, pencil, colored pencil, or crayon. Paint or color your "fish" as you like and add an eye and a mouth.
- Draw fish that look like their names. Some examples are angelfish, catfish, tiger shark, sailfish, lionfish, sawfish, hammerhead shark, needlefish, trumpet fish, and jewel fish.
- Make a 3-dimensional ocean scene. Wrap sandpaper around a can that has had the label removed and been cleaned. Glue or cement the sandpaper to the outside of the can. Cut out fish and other sea shapes from a magazine (or draw them yourself) and glue them to the sandpaper. Glue on small seashells and other artifacts you may have.
- Choose a specific fish and any other animal you want. Draw pictures of the fish and the animal as they really appear. Then draw a second picture giving each animal characteristics of the other (e.g., octopus and elephant: Give the octopus a trunk and big ears; give the elephant long skinny legs and no nose). (*Lend Me Your Wings* by Agard) Older students can draw a fish and then make a flip book. Cut out strips of paper (the width of the strips depends on the size of the fish you draw) and draw different noses on them. Staple these strips to the top of your original fish picture so that they hang down over the nose of the fish. You can then flip the strips of paper and see a strange fish with many funny noses.
- Design a poster for the "King of the Sea" dance to be held in your city.
- Make a picture of some fish. Using a hole punch, punch one hole (representing the eye) for each fish that you wish to have in your picture. Draw your fish around the hole in any shape and color that you want. You can draw your fish on any color paper you want. You can also mount your fish paper on a different color paper to give the fishes' eyes a contrasting color. (*Fish Eyes* by Ehlert)

- For those of you who are very adventuresome, try the Japanese art of fish printing (Gyota Ku). Wash a very flat fish with soap and water. Let it dry. Lay the fish on several layers of newspaper, being careful to spread out the tail and fins. Cover the fish with acrylic paint using a small brush. Paint against the grain of the scales, then smooth them out. Press a piece of paper, a plain T-shirt, or a piece of plain cloth on the fish and rub firmly (but gently). Peel off the paper slowly to avoid smudges. (Rice paper works well and would be more authentic.)

- If you have some budding artists in your midst, check out *Draw 50 Sharks, Whales, and Other Sea Creatures* by Lee J. Ames (Doubleday, 1989). Children will amuse themselves for hours drawing the many different sea creatures and creating scenes with them.

Chapter 5
Birds

■ Teaching Resources

Books containing experiment(s) relating to the subject matter are marked with a plus sign (+) before and after the title.

P   *Crinkleroot's Guide to Knowing the Birds,* by Jim Arnosky (Aladdin, 2000)
Introduction to birds that you might see in the woods. Written in storybook form.

P   *A First Look at Ducks, Geese and Swans,* by Millicent E. Selsam and Joyce Hunt (Walker, 1990)
Examines the similarities and differences among ducks, geese, and swans.

P   *Pigeons and Doves,* by Ray Nofsinger and Jim Hargrove (Children's Press, 1992)
Discusses the physical characteristics of pigeons and the talents of homing pigeons.

P   *The Puffins Are Back!,* by Gail Gibbons (HarperCollins, 1991)
A simple introduction to the characteristics, life cycle, and environment of the puffin.

P/I *Chickens,* by Mary Ann McDonald (Child's World, 1998)
An introduction to the physical characteristics, behavior, and life cycle of chickens.

P/I *Ducks,* by Mary Ann McDonald (Child's World, 1998)
An introduction to the physical characteristics, behavior, and life cycle of ducks.

P/I *+Owls,+* by Fern G. Brown (Franklin Watts, 1991)
Describes, in text and vivid photographs, the life cycle, habits and behavior, and species of the owl.

P/I *Woodpeckers,* by Mary Ann McDonald (Child's World, 1996)
An introduction to the physical characteristics, behavior, and life cycle of woodpeckers.

I   *Bird Migration,* by Liz Oram (Steck-Vaughn, 1992)
Discusses the migration patterns of many birds, including: pigeons, owls, penguins, and sparrows.

I   *The Goose Family Book,* by Sybille Kalas (North South Books, 2000)
Text and beautiful photographs discuss the physical characteristics and behavior of a family of goslings from the egg through adulthood.

I   *Ostriches and Other Flightless Birds,* by Caroline Arnold (Carolrhoda Books, 1990)
Discusses the physical characteristics, habits, and behavior of the ostrich and other flightless birds such as the rhea, emu, cassowary, and kiwi.

I *Ostriches, Emus, Rheas, Kiwis, and Cassowaries,* by Ann Elwood (Creative Education, 1990)
Discusses physical characteristics, habitats, and behavior of flightless birds.

I *Owls,* by Kevin Holmes (Bridgestone Books, 1998)
An introduction to owls, covering their physical characteristics, habits, prey, and relationship to humans.

I *Penguins,* by Kevin Holmes (Bridgestone Books, 1998)
An introduction to penguins, covering their physical characteristics, habits, prey, and relationship to humans.

I *Season of the White Stork,* by Heiderose Fischer-Nagel and Andreas Fischer-Nagel (Carolrhoda Books, 1986)
Describes the characteristics and behavior of the white stork as it raises its young.

I *Tiger with Wings: The Great Horned Owl,* by Barbara Juster Esbensen (Orchard Books, 1991)
Describes the physical characteristics, mating, nesting, and hunting techniques of the great horned owl.

I/U *Birds of Prey,* by Jill Bailey (Facts on File, 1988)
Through photographs, drawings, and text, describes the physical characteristics and behavior of various birds of prey.

I/U +*Eyewitness Books: Birds,*+ by David Burnie (DK Publishing, 2000)
A photographic essay on birds of the world that examines body construction, feathers and flight, feeding habits, nests and eggs, and birdwatching.

I/U *How Birds Fly,* by David Goodnow (Periwinkle Books, 1992)
Explains the mechanics of birds' wings and how they enable birds to fly.

■ Reading Selections

Books marked with an asterisk (*) before and after the title are related to activities in the activity sections of this chapter.

All My Little Ducklings, by Monica Wellington (E. P. Dutton, 1998)
   A group of ducklings enjoy their day in the water and on the shore.

The Chick and the Duckling, by Mirra Ginsburg (Econo-Clad, 1999)
   A chick learns that it has many similarities to a newly hatched duckling, but discovers one difference.

Chicken Little, by Sally Hobson (Aladdin, 2000)
   A retelling of a chicken's misconception that the sky is falling.

Child of the Owl, by Laurence Yep (Harper Trophy, 1990)
   A 12-year-old girl is sent to live with her grandmother in Chinatown and learns about her Chinese heritage. (Chapter Book)

Dancers in the Garden, by Joanne Ryder (Sierra Club, 1992)
   Follows the activities of a hummingbird and his mate in a garden on a sunny day.

Daniel's Duck, by Clyde Robert Bulla (Econo-Clad, 1999)
A wood-carver is temporarily depressed when the result of a winter's work is mocked.

The Dove's Letter, by Keith Baker (Harcourt Brace, 1993)
As a dove tries to deliver an unaddressed letter to its rightful owner, she brings great pleasure to those who read it.

Farmer Duck, by Martin Waddell (Candlewick Press, 1996)
Farmer Duck must do all the farm chores because the owner is too lazy to do them himself. But the owner gets his just deserts.

Feathers for Lunch, by Lois Ehlert (Voyager Picture Books, 1996)
A cat stalks several types of birds for lunch, but his bells warn the birds.

Five Little Ducks, by Raffi (Crown, 1999)
When five little ducks go out to play, they disappear one by one, causing Mother Duck to search for them.

Good Morning Chick, by Mirra Ginsburg (Greenwillow, 1997)
A newly hatched chick tries to imitate a rooster and falls into a puddle.

Good Night, Owl, by Pat Hutchins (Aladdin, 1990)
When all the other animals keep Owl from sleeping, he decides to take revenge.

Have You Seen Birds?, by Joanne Oppenheim (Scholastic, 1990)
The sounds and activities of several birds are simply described and illustrated.

If the Owl Calls Again, by Myra Cohn Livingston (McElderry Books, 1990)
A collection of poems about owls (by different authors).

Itchy, Itchy Chicken Pox, by Grace Maccarone (Scholastic, 1992)
A humorous look at having the chicken pox.

Jonathan Livingston Seagull, by Richard Bach (Macmillan, 1997)
Jonathan Livingston Seagull spends so much time trying to perfect his flying technique, and not finding food, that he is ostracized by the rest of the seagulls.

The Language of Doves, by Rosemary Wells (Dial Books for Young Readers, 1996)
For her sixth birthday, Julietta's grandfather tells her a story about how he raised and trained doves in Italy during the Great War, then gives her one of his doves as a present.

Little Penguin's Tale, by Audrey Wood (Econo-Clad, 1999)
A little penguin, who ignores the rules he's been taught and ventures out by himself, discovers that it is important to be careful.

The Little Red Hen, by Paul Galdone (Houghton Mifflin, 1985)
The Little Red Hen finds that none of her lazy friends wants to help make her cake, but all are willing to eat it.

Lorenzo, the Naughty Parrot, by Tony Johnston (Harcourt Brace Jovanovich, 1992)
Lorenzo, a cookie-loving parrot from Mexico, gets into all kinds of trouble as he tries to help his human family.

A Mother for Choco, by Keiko Kasza (G. P. Putnam's Sons, 1992)
Choco, a tiny, lonely bird, looks for its mother.

The Mountain That Loved a Bird, by Alice McLerran (Aladdin, 2000)
A barren mountain benefits by a beautiful bird.

Mr. Popper's Penguins, by Richard Atwater (Little, Brown, 1992)
>After receiving a penguin from the Antarctic, Mr. Popper's life and fortunes change dramatically. (Chapter Book)

Next Spring an Oriole, by Gloria Whelan (Econo-Clad, 1999)
>A 10-year-old girl and her family travel by covered wagon to the frontier, where they make a new home. (Chapter Book)

The Owl and the Pussycat, by Edward Lear (Atheneum, 1996)
>Owl and Pussycat take a courtship voyage for one year and a day and then are blissfully married.

Owl Moon, by Jane Yolen (Scholastic, 1987)
>The story of the adventures of a boy and his father when they go owling one night.

The Paper Crane, by Molly Bang (William Morrow, 1987)
>A paper crane is given as payment for dinner in a restaurant, and it magically comes to life.

Princess Penelope's Parrot, by Helen Lester (Houghton Mifflin, 1996)
>An arrogant and greedy princess loses her chance with a handsome prince when her parrot repeats to him all the rude comments the princess has made.

Rainbow Crow, by Nancy Van Laan (Econo-Clad, 1999)
>A legend of a crow who flies up to receive the gift of fire to save the animals from the threatening snow.

Rechenka's Eggs, by Patricia Polacco (Paper Star, 1996)
>An injured goose lays 13 beautifully colored eggs to replace the ones made for the Easter Festival that it broke.

The Story about Ping, by Marjorie Flack and Kurt Wiese (Viking, 1983)
>A little duck finds adventure on the Yangtze River when he is late in trying to board his master's boat one evening.

The Summer of the Swans, by Betsy Byars (Viking, 1996)
>When her mentally retarded brother gets lost, a young girl gains insight into herself and her family. (Chapter Book)

Tacky the Penguin, by Helen Lester (Houghton Mifflin, 1990)
>Tacky's behavior seems out of place, until it saves his and his friends' lives.

The Tale of the Mandarin Ducks, by Katherine Paterson (Puffin Books, 1995)
>A compassionate couple rescue a drake from an evil lord, who wants the duck for its beauty, and reunite it with its mate.

Trumpet of the Swan, by E. B. White (Econo-Clad, 1999)
>After learning to read and write, Louis, a voiceless Trumpeter Swan, is determined to learn to play a stolen trumpet.

Watch Out for the Chicken Feet in Your Soup, by Tomie de Paola (Econo-Clad, 1999)
>A young boy is dreading introducing his friend to his Italian grandmother and gains new respect for her when she and his friend get along wonderfully.

What the Parrot Told Alice, by Dale Smith (Deer Creek, 1996)
>Alice learns about the smuggling trade in rare birds and its consequences from her friend Bo Parrot. (Chapter Book)

The Winter Wren, by Brock Cole (Farrar, Straus & Giroux, 1988)
> When his village suffers from a hard winter, Simon goes in search of spring.

The Wizard, the Fairy, and the Magic Chicken, by Helen Lester (Houghton Mifflin, 1983)
> When three magicians try to outdo each other, they create a dilemma that can only be solved through cooperation.

The following books are out of print, but may be available at the local library.

Animals, Animals, by Eric Carle (Philomel Books, 1989)
> A collection of poems, by various authors, on pets, wild animals, and birds.

Birds, Beasts, and Fishes, by Anne Carter (Macmillan, 1991)
> A collection of animal poems from around the world.

The Black Falcon, by William Wise (Orchard Books, 1990)
> A peasant sacrifices his beloved falcon to honor the woman he loves.

Chicken Tricks, by Megan Lloyd (Harper & Row, 1983)
> Mischievous hens, expected to lay eggs, substitute innovative "eggs" for the real ones. When Christmas comes, the chickens see what the farmer has done with the eggs.

Dabble the Duckling, by Jane Burton (Random House, 1988)
> A story told in photos tells about the first months in the life of a duckling who was abandoned before it hatched and later adopted by a farmyard hen.

The Day the Goose Got Loose, by Reeve Lindbergh (Dial Books, 1990)
> It becomes chaotic on the farm when the goose gets loose.

The Duck and the Owl, by Hanna Johansen (Dutton Children's Books, 1991)
> Despite their differences, a duck and an owl decide to become friends.

Ducks, Ducks, Ducks, by Carolyn Otto (HarperCollins, 1991)
> Four young ducks from the country have an exciting time visiting their relatives who live in the city.

Egg Story, by Anca Hariton (Dutton Children's Books, 1992)
> The farm animals watch a new egg the hen has just laid. The book shows how an egg develops into a chick.

Flocks of Birds, by Charlotte Zolotow (Thomas Y. Crowell, 1981)
> The descriptions of birds flying across mountains, lakes, and cities soothes a youngster to sleep.

In Search of the Last Dodo, by Ann and Reg Cartwright (Little, Brown, 1990)
> A greedy king hurries to eat the rare dodo egg, only to have a change of heart.

Kenji and the Magic Geese, by Ryerson Johnson (Simon & Schuster, 1992)
> One of the geese in the picture on Kenji's wall flies off to join wild geese and then returns.

Nicholas, Where Have You Been?, by Leo Lionni (Alfred A. Knopf, 1987)
> A young mouse learns that birds aren't the horrible creatures he thought they were.

Nora's Duck, by Satomi Ichikawa (Philomel Books, 1991)
> Nora finds a duckling in the woods and takes it to Dr. John who provides love and care for many animals who are in trouble.

Owl at Night, by Ann Whitford Paul (General Publishing, 1985)
> An owl's nighttime activities are followed, describing his busy routine that occurs while people sleep.

Owl Lake, by Keizaburo Tejima (Philomel Books, 1987)
> As the sun sets and dusk approaches, Father Owl hunts to feed his hungry family.

Pigeon, Pigeon, by Caron Lee Cohen (Dutton Children's Books, 1992)
> A child and her parents view several different animals at the zoo.

Who Killed Cockatoo?, by W. A. Cawthorne (Farrar, Straus & Giroux, 1989)
> An Australian version of *Who Killed Cock Robin?*

Wings – A Tale of Two Chickens, by James Marshall (Viking Kestrel, 1990)
> Winnie, a chicken who never reads, is unaware of the potential dangers of traveling with a fox.

■ Science Activities

Bird Feeder

Students can make bird feeders out of "recyclables" using the following instructions:

- Cut windows out of a 2-liter plastic bottle, a plastic milk jug, or a bleach bottle. Place some birdseed in the bottom of the bottle and hang it with string or wire from a nearby tree.
- Spread peanut butter on a pinecone and roll it in birdseed. Hang it by a string or wire.
- Fill a mesh bag (such as the ones onions, oranges, or apples come in) with sunflower seeds. Hang it outside.

Use your imagination to feed the birds.

Paper Airplanes

Discuss the flight of birds and compare it to today's airplanes. Try folding paper to make different kinds of planes and see what style makes the best airplane. Have students experiment and then ask: Should it have large wings or short ones? Should the body be long or short? What shape should the plane be? See if your library has an experiments book showing how to make a variety of paper airplanes (or birds). Have the students try some of their designs. Discuss how these models compare to the ones the students made on their own.

Dissecting an Egg

Have the students crack a raw egg and separate the yolk from the white. Weigh the yolk first, then weigh the white. Discuss which weighs more. Notice that the white has two distinct sections, one thin and the other thicker. Notice the thin membrane along the shell. Research the purpose of each of these parts. Discuss which part of the egg contains cholesterol.

Shell-less Egg

As a class, make shell-less eggs. Place three or four eggs in a container and cover them with vinegar. Let the eggs and vinegar sit for two or three days until the shell dissolves. (To minimize the vinegar smell, cover the container.) The shell-less eggs can be held if students handle them gently.

Penguins

On a map, locate where the different species of penguins can be found. Each student can choose one type of penguin and write a diary detailing what its life is like on a day-to-day basis. Diary entries should describe what kind of environment the penguin lives in.

Nutrition

Have the students look up the nutritional data (i.e., calories, fat content, grams of protein, etc.) for 1 ounce of chicken and compare it to 1 ounce of pork, 1 ounce of beef, and 1 ounce of fish. Ask the students: How do they compare? Which are good for our bodies? Which should we eat in moderation?

Chicken Pox

Have the students try to find out how chicken pox got its name. As a group discuss: Did humans originally catch this disease from chickens? Can chickens (or birds) catch it? Do birds get sick? (*Itchy, Itchy Chicken Pox* by Maccarone) Students can create their own tales on how chicken pox got its name.

Bird Facts

Read *Feathers for Lunch* by Ehlert (or use an encyclopedia). Set up a graph and record data for some (or all) of the birds listed in the back of the book (or ones you find in the encyclopedia). Graph data such as:

- How many birds eat insects?
- How many birds live in Canada?
- How many birds are larger than 10 inches long?
- How many birds eat berries?

Have students decide which information that they would like to research and graph.

Feathers

Students can look at several different feathers under a magnifying glass or microscope. Ask the students: What do you see? Were the feathers from different birds alike? If not, how did they differ?

Feet Count

- Have the students make birds out of clay. (They can use pictures in an encyclopedia or in one of the books listed in the "Teaching Resources" section of this chapter as models.) Use wire to make the legs and feet. Make the toes on each bird a different length.
- Cut out various pieces of cardboard in the shape of lily pads.
- Fill a baking pan about three-quarters full with water and float the cardboard "lily pads" on the water. Each student should attempt to balance his or her clay bird on a lily pad.
- Ask the students: Which type of feet are best as far as the bird's balance is concerned? Which size bird balances more easily (a large one or a small one)? (The larger the toes, the better the bird can balance because its weight is more spread out.)

Birds of a Feather

If possible, go "feather hunting" as a class. Go for a walk in the woods, in a local park, or around your neighborhood. See how many bird feathers can be found on the ground or in bushes.

With the feathers that are collected, make a feather notebook. Have the students try to identify which bird the feathers came from and label each feather with the bird's name. Students can look up information about the bird and write a short summary about where it lives, what it eats, how it builds its nest, and so forth. (Always wash your hands after handling feathers.)

Nesting

As a class, research the types of nests that different birds make and the materials they each use. Have the students divide into several groups and choose a nest to duplicate. Locate materials and attempt to construct a nest. It is interesting to note different, special features of each bird's nest. Have students refrain from telling other groups which bird's nest they have made. See if students can identify the type of bird's nest each group has constructed by simply studying the finished products.

Picky-Picky

Ask the students: Did you know that birds are picky eaters, just like your younger brother or sister? To decide which types of birds would be attracted to a bird feeder, students must determine the right kinds of seeds to serve. The following seeds will attract given birds:

black oil sunflower: cardinals, chickadees, titmice, grosbeaks, and finches

striped sunflower: titmice, cardinals, jays, and grosbeaks

hulled sunflower: finches, cardinals, chickadees, and jays

safflower: doves, cardinals, and sparrows

thistle: finches

corn: sparrows, jays, and doves

Eat Like a Bird

Decorate the trees at school during the winter with food for the birds. (You can do this in warm weather also, but do not use fruit.) Give the students the following instructions:

- Make a garland by stringing cranberries on a doubled length of thread. You can add popcorn, too, if you like.
- Make a peanut garland by stringing together peanuts in their shells. Push a needle through the middle of the shells.
- Slice fruit, such as apple, kiwi, or an orange (cut crosswise in about 1/4-inch thickness).
- Loop a piece of cord (or double-strength string) through the edge of each slice and tie it around a branch.
- Find a pine cone and wrap a pipe cleaner around the top of it. Shape the pipe cleaner like a hook so it can be hung on a tree branch. Spread peanut butter on the pine cone and then sprinkle it with birdseed.

Nocturnal Animals

Some birds, such as owls, are nocturnal animals. Ask the students: What does it mean to be "nocturnal"? Why would it be beneficial to be awake at night? Can you name any other animals that are nocturnal? Students can research some of these animals and write a paper on the benefits and disadvantages of being a nocturnal animal. (Younger students can make a picture of the world of a nocturnal animal.)

Birdbath

- Construct your own school birdbath. As a class, get a drip pan from a plastic or ceramic flowerpot and cover the bottom with small, flat rocks. Pour no more than 3 inches of water into the pan, over the rocks.
- Place the birdbath on a tree stump, small pedestal, or deck railing near a bush or tree. You can also hang a plastic, 2-liter bottle filled with water and with a small hole punched in the bottom over the top of your birdbath. (Birds like the sound of running water.)
- Students will enjoy watching the birds that come to their birdbath. The class can chart the birds they see and study their drinking and bathing habits.

Pigeons

Pigeons are often considered a nuisance today, but that was not so long ago. At one time, the carrier pigeon served a beneficial purpose. As a class, research the carrier pigeon. What were carrier pigeons used for? Why aren't they used today? (In fact, they are extinct!)

■ Creative Writing Activities

Following are instructions to give the students for various writing activities.

- Imagine that you can fly; but only when you hold a special object. What would that object be? Where would you fly? Would you tell anyone else about your special object? Write a story about one of your adventures.
- Write a story about a goose and/or a gander using as many words as possible that begin with "g."
- If you could be any type of bird you wanted, what would you be? Write a story describing your day as a bird.
- Read the poems in *Animals, Animals* by Carle that are about birds, such as the chick, chickadee, owl, penguin, pigeon, sparrow, rooster, woodpecker, hawk, or eagle. Write your own poem about a favorite bird.
- Discuss preconceived ideas. Have you ever thought that you wouldn't like something before you even tried it or knew all the facts? Write a story about a time you thought one thing and then changed your mind. (*Nicolas, Where Have Your Been?* by Lionni)
- Write a letter to a special friend. Say something that will make them feel especially good or special. (*The Dove's Letter* by Baker)
- Write a story about a favorite picture in your house. Make a figure or object disappear from the picture. Explain why this happened (where it went; what happened to it; how it returned). (*Kenji and the Magic Geese* by Johnson)
- Write a letter to a friend about your experience of being lost in a large store and your search for your mother. (*A Mother for Choco* by Kasza)
- What does it mean when someone calls you a "bird brain?" How did this saying get started? Write a humorous story about a time when you did something that would qualify you for the title "bird brain." (We all have those moments!)
- Sometimes people refer to having "an albatross around their neck." What does this saying mean? Write your version of why an albatross would be considered "bad luck."
- What is a "bird of paradise?" Write a legend or tall tale about how this flower got its name. After you finish your story, research how the flower actually got its name and compare stories.

- Write a story about a town run by birds. What type of birds would have the different jobs in the town? Which birds would be mayor, postal carriers, librarians, police officers, and teachers?

- Write a story about an owl that wasn't so "wise." What happened? What lesson did the owl learn?

- Write a story entitled "The Great Egg Switch" in which eggs from several different animals (ostrich, eagle, snake, alligator, etc.) mysteriously get switched in the nest. What happens to each of the animals' babies after they hatch?

- Write a play about two very different birds (e.g., a penguin and a woodpecker) that meet each other for the first time. What activities do they share? How does their relationship develop? After the play is finished, make bird masks out of paper plates with popsicle stick handles and act out the play.

- If the stork is supposed to bring babies to human beings, how do storks get their babies? Write a silly story explaining the birth of baby storks.

■ Art Activities

Following are instructions to give the students for various art activities.

- Make a unique pencil holder out of a juice can and eggshells. Wash out some eggshells and let them dry. Crush the shells into small pieces. Spread some glue all over the juice can and then roll the can in the eggshells. The shells will stick to the glue. Let the glue dry and then paint the shells bright colors with tempera paints. (Tempera paints will adhere to the shells better than watercolors.)

- Collect feathers from your yard, the woods, or a nearby park. Use these feathers as the tails for birds that you draw.

- Tear or cut scraps of construction (or thin, colored) paper into small squares. Using these squares, make a mosaic picture of a brightly colored bird such as a parrot or toucan. (You can also cut up old magazines.)

- Use pine cones to make birds. The pine cone will serve as the body of the bird. Wings, a head, and a tail can be added using feathers, colored paper, scraps of cloth, ribbon, and so forth. You can paint the pine cone to match the accessories you have added or glue colored glitter to it.

- Go to your library and check out a book on origami. Follow the directions to make a paper crane. This is considered good luck. (*The Paper Crane* by Bang)

- In Mexico, Puerto Rico, and Brazil, artists often paint pictures of birds, trees, and flowers on the bark from trees. Get a scrap piece of wood (the rougher the better) and paint a brightly colored bird on it. (You can have it perched on a tree limb or near your favorite flower.)

- Draw a picture of a group of penguins dressed in funny clothes. Have the penguins participating in an unusual activity. (*Tacky the Penguin* by Lester)

- Think about a special image (a scene, an object, a person, or an animal) that helps you fall asleep at night. Draw or paint a picture of this image. You could frame this picture and hang it in your bedroom for those nights when it is hard to get to sleep. (*Flocks of Birds* by Zolotow)

- Make an edible bird's nest. Mix Chinese noodles and chocolate frosting together in a bowl. Place a mound of this mixture on a piece of waxed paper and have the students mold it into the shape of a bird's nest. Place jellybeans in the nest for bird eggs.

- Draw a design for your own bird using the parts of real birds that you especially like (the beak from a toucan, tail from a peacock, colors of the parrot, etc.).

- Make a bird mobile using a coat hanger. Cut the coat hanger into three segments. Tie the wires together in whatever design you want with strong string. Have the students draw and decorate birds to hang on the mobile. Birds can be made of a variety of materials: construction paper, tissue paper, egg cartons, feathers, and so forth. Be creative! When the birds are finished, punch a small hole in the back of each and tie them to the loose ends of the strings on your mobile.

- Make a bird silhouette. Place a piece of white paper into a 9-by-13-inch pan. Pour several different colors of paint, evenly spaced, on the paper (the paint spots should be approximately the size of a quarter). Place a marble or small ball in the pan and roll it around, going through the paint spots, thus spreading the paint across the white paper. (Use a paper towel to pick up the marble/ball when you have a satisfactory pattern on your paper.) Cut out a bird shape in the center of a piece of construction paper (any color you wish), being careful not to cut through the outside edge of the paper. Discard the bird, and save the paper with the bird-shaped hole in it. Glue or paste the construction paper over the painted paper so that you have a "framed" picture of a colorful bird.

Chapter 6
Mammals

■ Teaching Resources

Books containing experiment(s) relating to the subject matter are marked with a plus sign (+) before and after the title.

P   *Baby Animals: Chimpanzees,* by Kate Petty (Barron's Juveniles, 1992)
Discusses how chimpanzees are born and how they learn to find food and communicate with other chimpanzees.

P   *The Cousteau Society: Seals,* by the Cousteau Society (Simon & Schuster, 1992)
Introduces the harp seal through some text and beautiful photographs.

P   *Whales,* by Lesley A. DuTemple (Lerner, 1996)
Describes the physical and social characteristics of various whale species.

P   *Whales,* by Gail Gibbons (Holiday House, 1993)
A basic introduction to the different types of whales.

P/I   *Grizzlies,* by Mary Ann McDonald (Child's World, 1998)
An introduction to the physical characteristics, behavior, and life cycle of grizzly bears.

P/I   *Hippos,* by Beth Wagner Brust (Econo-Clad, 1999)
Describes different types of hippopotamuses, how they live, what they eat, and how they swim.

P/I   *Horses,* by Mary Ann McDonald (Child's World, 1998)
An introduction to the characteristics, behavior, and life cycle of horses.

P/I   *Kangaroos,* by Denise Burt (Carolrhoda Books, 2000)
Describes, through text and spectacular photographs, the habits, life cycle, and environment of the kangaroo.

P/I   *Whales,* by Kevin Holmes (Bridgestone Books, 1998)
An introduction to whales, covering their physical characteristics, habits, prey, and relationship to humans.

I   *Bats,* by Kevin Holmes (Bridgestone Books, 1998)
An introduction to bats covering their physical characteristics, habits, prey, and relationship to humans.

I   *Bats,* by Sharon Sigmond Shebar and Susan E. Shebar (Franklin Watts, 1990)
Describes, through text and vivid photographs, the anatomy, habits, flight abilities, and migration of the bat.

I   *Birth of a Foal,* by Hans-Heinrich Isenbart (Carolrhoda Books, 1987)
Details, in text and beautiful photographs, the birth and first few hours of a new foal.

I   *Dolphins,* by Kevin Holmes (Bridgestone Books, 1998)
An introduction to dolphins covering their physical characteristics, habits, prey, and relationship to humans.

I   *Elephant Seals,* by Sylvia A. Johnson (Lerner, 1989)
Discusses the characteristics, habits, and environment of the elephant seal.

I   *Giraffes,* by John Bonnett Wexo (Creative Education, 1990)
Describes the characteristics, habits, and habitat of the African giraffe.

I   *Guinea Pigs,* by Elvig Hansen (Carolrhoda Books, 1992)
Text and vivid photographs describe the characteristics, habitat, and life cycle of the guinea pig.

I   *Inside the Burrow: The Life of the Golden Hamster,* by Heiderose Fischer-Nagel and Andreas Fischer-Nagel (Carolrhoda Books, 1986)
Describes, in text and excellent photographs, characteristics and behavior of hamsters in the wild and in captivity. Also includes information on caring for pet hamsters.

I   *On the Trail of the Fox,* by Claudia Schnieper (Carolrhoda Books, 1986)
Discusses, through text and excellent photographs, the habits of the red fox, including birth, mating, hunting, fighting, and playing.

I   *Tasmanian Devil on Location,* by Kathy Darling (Lothrop, Lee & Shepard, 1992)
Describes the characteristics, behavior, and habits of the Tasmanian devil.

I   *Tule Elk,* by Caroline Arnold (Carolrhoda Books, 1989)
Describes the behavior and habitat of the tule elk through text and beautiful photographs.

I   *The Whales,* by Cynthia Rylant (Blue Sky Press, 1996)
Poetically describes the wonder of whales—what they look like, how they behave, and where they live.

I   *Whales,* by Amanda Harman (Benchmark Books, 1996)
Explores how whales live, why they are in danger, and what is being done to stop them from becoming extinct.

I   *Wild Boar,* by Darrel Nicholson (Carolrhoda Books, 1987)
Describes, in text and excellent photographs, the characteristics, habits, and natural environment of the wild boar.

I/U *Bears,* by Ian Stirling (Sierra Club Books for Children, 1990)
Text and excellent photographs describe the origins, adaptations, habitats, behavior, and life cycles of eight species of bears.

I/U *Walrus on Location,* by Kathy Darling (Lothrop, Lee & Shepard, 1991)
Discusses the characteristics, behavior, eating habits, and predators of the walrus.

U *Horses: History, Behavior, Breeds, Riding and Jumping,* by Jackie Budd (Kingfisher, 1995) History, behavior, breeds, riding, and jumping of horses are discussed.

U *Wolf Pack, Tracking Wolves in the Wild,* by Sylvia A. Johnson and Alice Aamodt (Lerner, 1985) Describes the interaction of wolves in a pack as they share the work of hunting, maintaining territory, and raising their young.

■ Reading Selections

Books marked with an asterisk (*) before and after the title are related to activities in the activity sections of this chapter.

Alaska's Three Bears, By Shelley Gill (Paws IV Publishing, 1990).
> A black bear, a brown bear, and a polar bear share an adventure in Alaska. Information about the bears is added to each page.

All Creatures Great and Small, by James Herriot (St. Martin's Press, 1998)
> Further adventures of the country veterinarian and the many animals he treats. (Other James Herriot books are available.) (Chapter Book)

All Things Bright and Beautiful, by James Herriot (Bantam Books, 1974)
> Recounts the experiences of a veterinarian in the English countryside. (Other James Herriot books are available.) (Chapter Book)

Along Came a Dog, by Meindert De Jong (Harper Trophy, 1980)
> A stray dog earns a home by protecting a hen and her chicks from a hawk. (Other De Jong books are available.) (Chapter Book)

Am I Beautiful?, by Else Holmelund Minarik (Greenwillow, 1992)
> A young hippo asks various families, "Am I beautiful?" and finally finds the answer he is looking for from his mother.

Androcles and the Lion, by Dennis Nolan (Harcourt Brace Jovanovich, 1997)
> The Aesop fable of Androcles and a wounded lion is retold.

Ape in a Cape, by Fritz Eichenberg (Harcourt Brace Jovanovich, 1952)
> An assortment of animals introduces the alphabet.

Ask Mr. Bear, by Marjorie Flack (Aladdin, 1986)
> A boy questions several animals about finding the perfect present for his mother's birthday. Only Mr. Bear suggests a gift that only Danny can give.

Baby Beluga, by Raffi Pike and Debi Pike (Crown, 1997)
> A little white whale frolics in the deep blue sea. (Based on the song "Baby Beluga" by Raffi.)

Bear, by John Schoenherr (Philomel, 1991)
> A young bear finds independence while searching for his mother.

The Bear's Toothache, by David McPhail (Econo-Clad, 1999)
> A little boy tries to help a bear remove an aching tooth.

Berlioz the Bear, by Jan Brett (G. P. Putnam's Sons, 1991)
> Berlioz and his musician friends are going to the town ball to play, when the mule refuses to pull their bandwagon.

The Biggest Bear, by Lynd Ward (Houghton Mifflin, 1973)
> Johnny wants to hang a bearskin of his own on the family barn, but he returns from a hunting trip with more than he bargained for.

The Bionic Bunny Show, by Marc Brown (Little, Brown, 1985)
> The reader views "behind the scenes" as an ordinary rabbit is transformed into a bionic bunny for television.

Black Beauty, by Anna Sewell (Dove Books, 1999)
> A horse in nineteenth-century England recounts his experiences with both good masters and bad ones. (Chapter Book)

The Black Stallion, by Walter Farley (Random House, 2000)
> A 17-year-old boy befriends a horse on a desert island, trains him, and rides him to victory in a race. (Other "Stallion" books are available.) (Chapter Book)

Born Free, by Joy Adamson (Schocken Books, 2000)
> The tale of Elsa the lioness's two lives, in the wild and in captivity. (Other "Elsa" books are available.) (Chapter Book)

Bread and Jam for Francis, by Russell Hoban (HarperCollins Juveniles, 1993)
> Frances sings about "Jam on Toast," the food she likes most, until she has it for the sixth meal in two days.

Brown Bear, Brown Bear, What Do You See?, by Bill Martin, Jr. (Henry Holt, 1996)
> A pattern book involving the reader and several colorful animals.

Bunnicula, by Deborah Howe and James Howe (Aladdin, 2000)
> Bunnicula seems to be a bit strange, but could he actually be a vampire bunny? (Chapter Book)

Burt Dow Deep-Water Man, by Robert McCloskey (Weston Woods, 1990)
> Burt accidentally hooks the tail of a whale and fixes the injury with a Band-aid. Now, as a friend, the whale protects Burt from a storm by temporarily swallowing his boat.

Can't You Sleep, Little Bear?, by Martin Waddell (Candlewick Press, 1994)
> Little Bear can't sleep with the darkness around. Big Bear lights up the cave little by little until they reach outside.

Caps for Sale, by Esphyr Slobodkina (Harper Trophy, 1987)
> A peddler takes time to nap, only to awaken to find a band of monkeys all wearing the hats he is selling.

The Cat in the Hat, by Dr. Seuss (Houghton Mifflin, 1957)
> Two children are put in quite a predicament when they are visited by a strange cat while their mother is not at home.

The Cat Who Wore a Pot on Her Head, by Jan Slepian and Ann Seidler (Econo-Clad, 1999)
> When Bendemolena misunderstands her mother's job assignments, the children do strange chores.

Cats Sleep Anywhere, by Eleanor Farjean (HarperCollins, 1996)
> A look around the house shows that the cats have many places to snooze.

Cecily G. & the 9 Monkeys, by H. A. Rey (Houghton Mifflin, 1989)
> A picture book about a lonely giraffe and his encounter with a homeless family of monkeys.

Charlie Needs a Cloak, by Tomie de Paola (Aladdin, 1988)
> A shepherd shears his sheep and, from the wool, makes cloth for a new red cloak.

Chester's Way, by Kevin Henkes (Mulberry Books, 1997)
> Two mice have very specific ways of doing things, until Lilly opens their eyes to new experiences.

The Church Mice at Bay, by Graham Oakley (McClelland & Stewart, 1995)
> The church mice, along with Sampson the cat, try to run the substitute vicar from the church.

Clifford, the Small Red Puppy, by Norman Bridwell (Scholastic, 1997)
> Tells the story of a tiny, sickly puppy who becomes larger than life because of a little girl's love. (Other "Clifford" books are available.)

The Clue at the Zoo, by Patricia Reilly Giff (Dell, 1990)
> Dawn and Jill look for clues to the owner of a mysterious notebook they find while visiting the zoo. (Chapter Book)

Curious George Goes to the Ice Cream Shop, by Margret Rey and H. A. Rey (Houghton Mifflin, 1989)
> George gets himself in trouble while waiting for the man with the yellow hat in an ice cream store. (Other "Curious George" books are available.)

Dandelion, by Don Freeman (Puffin Books, 1987)
> Dandelion is invited to a party, but when he overdresses, the hostess does not recognize him and turns him away.

Dragon's Fat Cat, by Dav Pilkey (Orchard, 1995)
> Dragon gets an unexpected surprise when he finds a fat cat and brings it home.

The Escape of Marvin the Ape, by Caralyn Buehner (Dial Books, 1992)
> Marvin escapes from the zoo and finds he can easily blend into city life.

Fantastic Mr. Fox, by Roald Dahl (Puffin Books, 1998)
> Three mean farmers declare war on a fox and his family.

Five Little Monkeys Jumping on the Bed, by Eileen Christelow (Clarion Books, 1989)
> One by one, the monkeys, who are jumping on the bed, fall and bump their heads.

Flossie and the Fox, by Patricia C. McKissack (E. P. Dutton, 1986)
> A notorious fox meets his match when a bold girl refuses to be frightened.

Frederick, by Leo Lionni (Econo-Clad, 1999)
> As the mice gather food for winter, Frederick collects a different type of "provisions."

Fritz and the Beautiful Horses, by Jan Brett (Houghton Mifflin, 1981)
> A horse is excluded when his appearance doesn't measure up, but when he saves the children, his skills and dependability earn him respect.

Gentle Ben, by Walt Morey (Puffin Books, 1992)
> Recounts the friendship between a boy and a bear in the Alaskan wilderness. (Chapter Book)

George and Martha One Fine Day, by James Marshall (Houghton Mifflin, 1978)

Two friends share experiences in five short stories.

A Giraffe and a Half, by Shel Silverstein (HarperCollins Juveniles, 1981)
A giraffe gets "transformed" into a giraffe and a half with many crazy accessories, and then the situation is reversed in a humorous way.

Gregory, the Terrible Eater, by Mitchell Sharmat (Four Winds Press, 1980)
As a very picky eater, Gregory prefers healthy foods, instead of the usual goat diet of shoes, tin cans, and junk.

The Happy Hedgehog Band, by Martin Waddell (Candlewick Press, 1994)
Happy hedgehogs playing drums soon recruit other woodland animals to join them in making music.

Have You Seen My Cat?, by Eric Carle (Franklin Watts, 1997)
A young boy searches for his cat and finds many other types of cats.

Horton Hatches the Egg, by Dr. Seuss (Random House, 1966)
Horton, the elephant, agrees to sit on the nest of a lazy bird that is tired of waiting for her egg to hatch.

Humphrey, the Lost Whale, by Wendy Tokudo and Richard Hall (Heian International Press, 1992)
A true story of a lost whale who enters San Francisco Bay.

*I Want a Dog,** by Dayal Kaur Khalsa (Crown, 1994)
May creates an imaginary dog out of a rollerskate when her parents won't let her get a real one.

If You Ever Meet a Whale, by Myra Cohn Livingston (Holiday House, 1992)
A collection of poems about whales.

If You Give a Mouse a Cookie, by Laura Joffe Numeroff (Harper & Row, 1985)
Recounts the cycle of requests a mouse makes after receiving a cookie; takes the reader through a young child's day.

Incident at Hawk's Hill, by A. W. Eckert (Little, Brown, 1995)
A shy, lonely six-year-old ends up in the Canadian prairie and is protected by a badger. (Chapter Book)

The Incredible Journey, by Sheila Burnford (Laurel Leaf, 1996)
A Siamese cat, a bull terrier, and a Labrador retriever travel together through the Canadian wilderness to find their families. (Chapter Book)

Is Your Mama a Llama?, by Deborah Guarino (Scholastic, 1997)
Baby llama Lloyd tries to guess what kind of animal everyone's mother is.

The Island Stallion, by Walter Farley (Random Library, 1998)
A boy and his friend find a hidden valley, underground tunnels, and a flame-colored stallion while visiting a desolate Caribbean island. (Other "Stallion" books are available.) (Chapter Book)

Jamberry, by Bruce Degen (Harper Festival, 1995)
A boy and a bear enjoy collecting all kinds of berries together.

Jesse Bear, What Will You Wear?, by Nancy White Carlstrom (Aladdin, 1996)
A rhyming story of a bear who changes clothes for different times of the day.

Julie of the Wolves, by Jean Craighead George (Harper Trophy, 1974)
A 13-year-old Eskimo, who is running away from home, is befriended by a pack of wolves. (Chapter Book)

Just So Stories, by Rudyard Kipling (William Morrow, 1996)
> Several short tales that explain how different members of the animal kingdom became as they are today.

The Lamb and the Butterfly, by Arnold Sundgaard (Orchard, 1988)
> A lamb and an adventurous butterfly compare lifestyles.

Lazy Lion, by Mwenye Hadithi (Polka Dot Press, 2000)
> A lazy lion demands that the animals of his kingdom build him a house before the Big Rain comes.

The Lion, the Witch, and the Wardrobe, by Clive Staples Lewis (HarperCollins Juveniles), 1994
> Four boys find a secret passage through the back of a wardrobe and assist the golden lion to triumph over the White Witch. (Chapter Book)

Little Bear, by Else Holmelund Minarik (Harper Trophy), 1978
> Four stories relate different events in the life of Little Bear. (Other "Little Bear" books are available.)

Little Gorilla, by Ruth Bornstein (Houghton Mifflin, 1986)
> A cute baby gorilla makes many friends, but will things change when he grows up and becomes big?

Little Polar Bear, by Hans de Beer (North South Books, 2000)
> A young polar bear gets separated from his father and drifts to a jungle, where a friendly hippo helps him out.

The Midnight Fox, by Betsy Byars (Econo-Clad, 1999)
> A city boy, visiting his aunt and uncle's farm, rescues a fox and her den. (Chapter Book)

Moby Dick, by Herman Melville (Bantam Classics, 1981)
> The adventures of Captain Ahab as he searches for the great white whale, Moby Dick. (Chapter Book)

The Monkey and the Crocodile, by Paul Goldone (Econo-Clad, 1999)
> A retelling of an Indian fable where, in the form of a monkey, Buddha outwits the crocodile who tries to capture him.

Monkey Island, by Paula Fox (Yearling Books, 1993)
> Abandoned by his mother, 11-year-old Clay is befriended by two men who help him survive. (Chapter Book)

Morris Goes to School, by Bernard Wiseman (Harper & Row, 1970)
> When Morris tries to buy some candy, he finds out that there is a lot he doesn't know, and he is encouraged to go to school to learn to read and count. (Other "Morris" books are available.)

The Mouse and the Motorcycle, by Beverly Cleary (William Morrow, 1965)
> A boy and a mischievous mouse make friends and discover the joys of motorcycling. (Chapter Book)

Mr. Brown Can Moo! Can You?, by Dr. Seuss (Random House, 1996)
> Mr. Brown is an expert at imitating all sorts of noises, including a cow, a bee, and even a hippopotamus.

My Friend Flicka, by Mary O'Hara (HarperCollins Juveniles, 1988)
> Recounts the experiences of a child and the horse who became best friends. (Chapter Book)

National Velvet, by Enid Bagnold (Camelot, 1999)
>A 14-year-old English girl wins a horse in a raffle and trains it to run in the Grand National steeplechase. (Chapter Book)

Newf, by Marie Killilea (Paper Star, 1996)
>A large Newfoundland dog meets a small white kitten in a deserted house. The two become good friends, with Newf saving the kitten on more than one occasion.

Noah's Ark, by Heinz Janisch (North South Books, 1997)
>Retells the story of the great flood in which Noah, his family, and the animals of the world were saved.

Noah's Ark, by Peter Spier (Yearling Books, 1992)
>A wordless picture book depicting the many joys and struggles of collecting all of the various animals and keeping them in the ark for such a long time.

Noisy Nora, by Rosemary Wells (Puffin Books, 2000)
>Nora feels neglected and tries to capture the attention of her parents by making more and more noise.

Nuts to You, by Lois Ehlert (Harcourt Brace Jovanovich, 1993)
>A squirrel finds himself in an apartment and has quite an adventure.

Oh Kojo! How Could You?, by Verna Aardema (Econo-Clad, 1999)
>Kojo finally gets the best of the mischievous Anansi.

Old Bear, by Jane Hissey (Philomel, 1998)
>The toy animals try to rescue Old Bear from the confines of the attic.

Old Yeller, by Fred Gipson (Harper & Row, 1956)
>The story of a boy and his dog living in Texas in the 1860s. (Chapter Book)

Polar Bear, Polar Bear, What Do You Hear?, by Bill Martin, Jr. (Henry Holt, 1997)
>Zoo animals make their distinctive sounds for each other, while children try to imitate them.

A Porcupine Named Fluffy, by Helen Lester (Houghton Mifflin, 1986)
>A misnamed porcupine is unhappy until he meets a misnamed rhinoceros.

Possum Come a-Knockin', by Nancy Van Laan (Dragonfly Books, 1992)
>A rhythmic story of a mountain family and a possum who comes visiting.

Puss in Boots, by Charles Perrault and Paul Galdone (Houghton Mifflin, 1993)
>When his cat outwits a giant, a poor man gains fortune and meets a beautiful princess.

Puss in Boots, by Lincoln Kirstein (Little, Brown, 1994)
>A retelling of the French tale wherein a clever cat wins his master a fortune and the hand of a princess.

R-T, Margaret and the Rats of NIMH, by Jane Conly (HarperCollins Juveniles, 1991)
>The survival of a community lies in the hands of two young children and the super-intelligent rats of NIMH. (Other "NIMH" books are available.) (Chapter Book)

Raccoons and Ripe Corn, by Jim Arnosky (Econo-Clad, 1999)
>At night, the hungry raccoons feast on the ripe corn they find in the field.

Rascal, by Sterling North (Puffin Books, 1990)
> The tale of a mischievous raccoon and the mishaps that befall him. (Other "Rascal" books are available.) (Chapter Book)

The Right Number of Elephants, by Jeff Sheppard (HarperCollins Juveniles, 1992)
> A counting book about a girl who needs the right number of elephants to do various activities.

The Runaway Bunny, by Margaret Wise Brown (Harper Festival, 1991)
> A mother rabbit assures her little bunny that wherever he goes, she will be nearby.

Seven Blind Mice, by Ed Young (Philomel, 1992)
> Retells the Indian legend in which seven blind people (depicted as mice) argue over the appearance of an elephant.

17 Kings and 42 Elephants, by Margaret Mahy (Dial Books, 1987)
> A group of kings and elephants encounter a variety of animals as they journey through the jungle.

Shadrach, by Meindert De Jong (Harper Trophy, 1980)
> The story of Davie, a Dutch boy, and the joy and trepidation he experiences when his grandfather gives him a real rabbit. (Other De Jong books are available.) (Chapter Book)

Sheep in a Jeep, by Nancy Shaw (Houghton Mifflin, 1997)
> A group of sheep go for an adventure in a jeep. (Other Nancy Shaw "Sheep" books are available.)

Sheep in a Shop, by Nancy Shaw (Sandpiper Press, 1994)
> While shopping for a birthday present, sheep find the day does not go as planned. (Other Nancy Shaw "Sheep" books are available.)

Sleepy Bear, by Lydia Dabcovich (Puffin Books, 1985)
> A story of an expressive bear who prepares for a winter's nap and then wakes up at the signs of spring.

The Story of Babar, the Little Elephant, by Jean de Brunhoff (MK Productions, 1995)
> An orphaned elephant goes to the city to live with an old lady who gives him everything he could ever want. Eventually, however, he returns to the forest and is crowned king of the elephants. (Other "Babar" books are available.)

The Story of Doctor Doolittle, by H. Lofting (William Morrow, 1997)
> The introduction to Doctor Doolittle's world of animals. (Other "Doctor Doolittle" books are available.) (Chapter Book)

The Story of Ferdinand, by Munro Leaf (Viking, 1987)
> The story of Ferdinand, an unusual bull, who doesn't fit in with the rest of his friends.

Sylvester and the Magic Pebble, by William Steig (Aladdin, 1987)
> In a panic situation, Sylvester, a donkey, asks the magic pebble to turn him into a rock, and then cannot hold the pebble to return himself back to normal.

The Teddy Bears' Picnic, by Jimmy Kennedy (Aladdin, 2000)
> Teddy bears from all over gather for the annual picnic, but what will happen if humans try to join the fun?

The Three Billy Goats Gruff, by Janet Stevens (Harcourt Brace Jovanovich, 1990)
> Three billy goats must outsmart a troll to cross a bridge.

The Three Little Pigs, by James Marshall (Dial Books, 1989)
> The classic story of three pigs and a wolf who tries to outsmart them.

The True Story of the Three Little Pigs, by Jon Scieszka (Puffin Books, 1996)
> The wolf gives his version of what happened the day he visited the three pigs.

The Valentine Bears, by Eve Bunting (Clarion Books, 1983)
> A surprise Valentine celebration is planned for Mr. Bear, despite the fact that it's hibernating time.

The Velveteen Rabbit, by Margery Williams (Camelot, 1996)
> The story of a toy bunny who learns what it is like to become "real."

The Walrus and the Carpenter, by Lewis Carroll (Boyd Mills Press, 1998)
> A walrus and a carpenter take a walk on the beach and discover a mutual fondness for oysters.

The Way Home, by Judith Richardson (Econo-Clad, 1999)
> When baby elephant doesn't want to leave the beach, mother elephant finds another method to show him the way home.

We're Going on a Bear Hunt, by Michael Rosen (Macmillan, 1989)
> The tale of a bear hunt is retold, with the hunters encountering grass, the river, mud, a forest, and other obstacles.

Whales' Song, by Dyan Sheldon (Scholastic, 1991)
> After hearing her grandmother's stories of the singing of whales when they're left a special gift, Lilly leaves a present at the shore and waits.

What Do You Do with a Kangaroo?, by Mercer Mayer (Econo-Clad, 1999)
> A little girl manages several demanding animals.

When Sheep Cannot Sleep, by Satoshi Kitamura (Farrar, Straus & Giroux, 1988)
> A counting book involving a sheep who has trouble falling asleep.

Where's My Teddy?, by Jez Alborough (Candlewick Press, 1994)
> When a small boy searches for his lost teddy bear in the woods, he encounters a gigantic bear with a similar problem.

Where's Spot?, by Eric Hill (Putnam, 1990)
> A mother dog finds many other animals hiding throughout the house before she finds her lost puppy. (Other "Spot" books are available.)

The White Stallion, by Elizabeth Shub (Bantam Books, 1996)
> A little girl, who is carried away from her wagon train in Texas in 1845, is befriended by a white stallion. (Chapter Book)

Who Wants a Cheap Rhinoceros?, by Shel Silverstein (Macmillan, 1983)
> A rhinoceros can be very useful, if you use your imagination!

Whose Mouse Are You?, by Robert Kraus (Aladdin, 1986)
> A mouse reunites his family and is surrounded by love.

The Wind in the Willows, by Kenneth Graham (Simon & Schuster, 1989)
> The adventures of Toad, Mole, Rat, and Badger, four friends who live in the English countryside. (Chapter Book)

The Winged Cat, by Deborah Nourse Lattimore (Harper Trophy, 1995)
> A young servant girl in ancient Egypt works with a High Priest to find the correct magic spells that open the 12 gates of the Netherworld. This is done to determine who is telling the truth regarding the death of her cat.

The Yearling, by Marjorie K. Rawlings (Aladdin, 1988)
> A boy from the backwoods of Florida must decide the fate of a fawn he has raised as a pet. (Chapter Book)

The following books are out of print, but may be available at the local library.

All About Arthur (An Absolutely Absurd Ape), by Eric Carle (Franklin Watts, 1974)
> A lonely ape travels from city to city meeting other animals.

Animals, Animals, by Eric Carle (Philomel Books, 1989)
> A collection of poems describing domestic and wild animals.

The Badger and the Magic Fan, by Tony Johnston (G. P. Putnam's Sons, 1990)
> A badger makes a fortune by stealing a magic fan and making a rich girl's nose grow.

Big Time Bears, by Stephen Krensky (Little, Brown, 1989)
> Time measurements such as minute, hour, day, and year are demonstrated by the bear family.

The Bear's Toothache, by David McPhail (Little, Brown, 1972)
> A little boy tries to help a bear remove an aching tooth.

Fierce the Lion, by Evaline Ness (Holiday House, 1980)
> Fierce, the lion, wants to leave the circus in search of a new job.

Fox Went Out on a Chilly Night, by Wendy Watson (Lothrop, Lee & Shepard, 1994)
> An illustrated version of the folk song in which a fox travels many miles to get dinner for his wife and ten cubs.

Greedy Zebra, by Mwenye Hadithi (Little, Brown, 1984)
> A zebra's stripes are explained through the legend of a greedy zebra.

Haircuts for the Woolseys, by Tomie de Paola (G. P. Putnam's Sons, 1989)
> A family of sheep gets spring haircuts, only to be surprised by a snowstorm. Luckily, Granny has planned ahead.

The Happy Lion, by Louise Fatio (McGraw-Hill, 1954)
> A lion is visited often at the zoo by happy, friendly people who view the lion differently when he is loose and goes to visit the people.

Jack, the Seal, and the Sea, by Joanne Fink (Silver Burdett, 1988)
> Jack ignores the fact that the fish he is catching are sickly, until he meets an ailing seal and realizes how polluted the water is. (Video cassette by Great Plains National, 1990)

Little Tricker the Squirrel Meets Big Double the Bear, by Ken Kesey (Viking Penguin, 1990)
> Big Double, the bear, terrorizes the woodland animals until a tricky squirrel gets even.

Need a House? Call Ms. Mouse, by George Mendoza (Grosset & Dunlap, 1981)
> Henrietta Mouse custom-designs homes for her animal friends.

Nicholas, Where Have You Been? by Leo Lionni (Alfred A. Knopf, 1987)
> A young mouse learns that birds are not the enemy, as he thought, after he spends time with a bird and gets to know him.

Nobody's Cat, by Barbara Joosse (Harper Collins, 1992)
> A stray cat finds homes for her kittens and herself, with the help of a disabled boy.

Pig Pig and the Magic Photo Album, by David McPhail (E. P. Dutton, 1986)
> While waiting for the photographer, Pig Pig practices saying "cheese" and looks through a photo album. In doing so, he encounters many surprises. (Other "Pig Pig" books available.)

The Pigs' Wedding, by Helme Heine (Macmillan, 1978)
> The guests at the pigs' wedding have a great time painting on clothes, eating a big feast, and wallowing in the mud.

Red Fox, by Hannah Giffard (Dial Books, 1991)
> After searching all night for food, Red Fox finds a surprise back in his den.

Tail, Toes, Eyes, Ears, Nose, by Marilee Robin Burton (Harper & Row, 1989)
> Body parts of animals are presented for the reader to determine what the whole animal is.

The Tapestry Cats, by Ann Turnbull (Little, Brown, 1992)
> A lonely princess lives just as the Queen wishes until her Fairy Godmother grants her wish for "Gold" and "Silver".

Tillie and Mert, by Ida Luttrell (Harper & Row, 1985)
> Tillie and Mert share many experiences such as going to garage sales, opening their own grocery store, and telling fortunes.

Two Foolish Cats, by Yoshiko Uchida (McElderry Books, 1987)
> Two foolish cats try to settle their quarrel by visiting the old monkey of the mountain.

Valentine Foxes, by Clyde Watson (Orchard Books, 1989)
> Four little foxes plan a surprise for their parents, while the parents plan surprises, too.

When Panda Came to Our House, by Helen Zane Jensen (Dial Books, 1985)
> A panda bear visits a little girl and shares his Chinese customs with her.

■ Science Activities

Scientific Names

Animals are often labeled by the name of their genus and species. Have students try to identify: What is a *Canis familiaris* (dog), a *Canis latrans* (coyote), or a *Canis lupus* (wolf)? What are the characteristics of the canis genus? Let each child choose an animal and research its scientific name. Begin with the kingdom it is in (animal) and work down through phylum, class, order, family, genus, and finally, species.

Carnivores versus Herbivores

Have the students investigate which animals are carnivores (meateaters) and which animals are herbivores (vegetarians). Divide a sheet of paper in half (lengthwise) and list the carnivores on one side and the herbivores on the other side. Beneath this list of names, write down the characteristics shared by the carnivores and the characteristics shared by the herbivores. Discuss and compare these characteristics. Also discuss characteristics of omnivores (who eat both types of food) from each of the lists.

What is a Mammal?

Have the students list animals that are mammals. Discuss the characteristics that mammals have in common (have backbones, have large brains, are warm-blooded, are usually born alive, have body hair, suckle milk from milk glands). Did the students list humans? Ask them questions about humans, such as: What kingdom and classification do humans belong to? What characteristics do people and animals have in common? Even though humans are considered mammals, there are three major biological characteristics that separate them from other animals. Can you name them? (Humans have a complex brain and reasoning power, a well-developed voice box, and hand control that allows them to use tools.)

Products

What products do we get from animals? As a class, make a chart listing some of the contributions we get from animals (food, clothing, protection, research, work, etc.).

Folk Tales

Share a few folk tales involving animals. Often, folk tales give animals human traits such as the ability to talk. Aesop's fables are good examples of such stories involving animals, with moral values added. Discuss why authors such as Aesop decided to use animals as their characters rather than people. As a class, examine the traits that particular animals consistently receive in these stories (e.g., the fox is crafty, the owl is wise, the lion is brave). What animal characteristics might create these ideas in authors' minds?

Felines

Wild Cats

Have the students research the different kinds of "wild" cats. This would be a great time to use the Internet. Ask the students: What types can be found in the United States? Are there any cats in the United States that are considered "endangered" animals? Which states are home to the wild cats of the United States? Why?

Panthers

A panther looks like it is solid black, but in actuality it has black spots. Research the panther to find out where it lives and how it survives. Can you find another cat that is closely related to the panther? (Jaguar.)

Domestic Cats

As a class, look at the different types of domestic cats. If possible, have students bring in photos of their cats. Discuss what characteristics they have in common. How do they differ? Ask the students if they could choose any cat to have as a pet, which one would they choose. Why?

Canines

A Service Breed

Discuss some of the services dogs can provide. Discussion questions can include: What types of dogs make the best watchdogs? Which dogs are used in Alaska to pull sleds? Which dogs are usually trained to be seeing-eye dogs? Which dogs are used by police to locate drugs? Which dogs are good hunters? List the different services dogs can provide (don't forget companionship), and give three dog types that would be good for each purpose. Older students can research how dogs are trained as seeing-eye dogs or as members of Alaskan dog sled teams.

Obedience

Contact a local dog training school and see if they will allow you to attend a class or if they would be willing to come to you. Discuss why it is important for a dog to be trained. Have the students each make a list of five commands that they think would be important for a dog to be taught.

Bats

Animal Sonar

Bats use their hearing ("sonar") to guide them as they fly in dark caves. Have students close their eyes and listen to the sounds in their house. Have them draw a map of their home (they can also map out their front and back yards or neighborhood), using sounds as the landmarks.

Blind as a Bat

Demonstrate how sound waves bounce off of objects by having the students follow these instructions:

- Make a tray out of aluminum foil (about 14 inches wide) by folding up the edges of the foil and bending them over twice.
- Shape a piece of modeling clay that is approximately 5 inches long to form a wall. Flatten its sides and put it on the tray about 4 inches from the end that is farthest from you.
- Put the tray on a flat surface and have a light shining on it from the far end. (You'll get a better effect with the lampshade off.)
- Fill the tray with about 2 inches of water. (Be careful not to splash water on the lamp, and don't touch the light bulb!)
- Push the sides of the tray out until they are sloped enough to barely keep the water inside.
- Touch the surface of the water with one fingertip at the end of the tray that is nearest to you. Then pick up your finger and watch the water ripple as it flows away in every direction.
- The ripples will come back toward you after they have "bounced off" the wall at the end of the tray. These small waves represent the echoes of sound that a bat can detect that tell it where objects are. This is the bat's only way of "seeing."

Skunks

Have the students find out more about skunks. Ask them: What types of foods do skunks eat? What do they use their spraying abilities for? How are they de-scented? Which state has the largest population of skunks? Are they really related to cats, as they are portrayed in cartoons?

Rabbits for Food

As a class, research the different types of rabbits. Which types are raised for food? What other purposes are rabbits raised for? Research which countries eat rabbit. Is it eaten more often in some countries than in others? Which ones? When cooking small animals such as rabbits, squirrels, or wild birds, the cook will usually stew or boil the meat. If you are adventurous, find a recipe for rabbit stew and prepare it.

Beavers

The beaver's lodge is unique in that the entrance is underwater. Discuss what purpose this serves. Call a local park and inquire as to where you would find the nearest beaver lodges. Plan a trip to the area to watch the beavers and observe their lodges. After seeing a real beaver lodge, have the students make their own for a snack. Use Chinese noodles mixed with chocolate frosting. Give children a small mound of this mixture and have them mold it into the shape of a beaver lodge. Afterwards they can eat it.

Bears

Smokey Bear

Have the students research the story of Smokey Bear. Was there really a bear that was named Smokey? What happened to him? How did a bear come to represent fire safety in the forest? Afterwards, each student can create a poster reminding people to practice fire safety.

Types of Bears

As a class, make up a chart listing the different types of bears (polar, kodiak, grizzly, brown, sloth, etc.). Together, read *Alaska's Three Bears* by Gill. What characteristics do bears have in common? How do they differ? (Consider facts such as what they eat, what environment they live in, their size, their personalities, and their skills.) Are any bears considered endangered?

Teddy Bear Day

- Have a Teddy Bear Day. Read *The Teddy Bears' Picnic* by Kennedy, *Who Wants an Old Teddy Bear?* by Hofmann, or one of the Corduroy Bear or Winnie-the-Pooh books. (If you can't decide, read all of them!) Afterwards, use a bear-shaped cookie cutter to make bear sandwiches for your own picnic lunch. For dessert, have ice cream Winnie-the-Pooh style, with honey on top! (Don't forget to set a place for your teddy bear.)

- Have the students write a letter to his or her teddy bear. Tell the teddy bear why you are happy to have him or her for your own. Draw a picture of your picnic to hang in your room. Take your teddy bear for a walk, a ride in a stroller, or a ride on your bike. Does your teddy need a bath? (Check with Mom for cleaning instructions.) Don't forget to tuck your bear into bed with you at the end of the day!

Pandas

Students can do research on the panda. Ask the students: Where do they live (include both the countries where they are found and the environment they need to survive)? Are all pandas found in China? Are pandas truly bears? If not, what type of mammal are they? What other animals are found in China?

Sheep

Baa, Baa, Black Sheep

Have students speculate as to whether there really is such a thing as a black sheep. Research sheep and try to find out. After they discover that black sheep do exist, have them discover if black sheep are predominant in a particular species of sheep, or are they present in several different types? Have them write their findings and other interesting information on a chart. Include any facts you can find about where the black sheep came from and if it is used for any special purposes.

Sheep Shearing

Contact the local county extension office and find out if there is someone who does sheep shearing nearby. (If not, ask about any exhibits at nearby museums or get a detailed book from the library.) Contact the shearer to see if the class can watch a demonstration. Document the process that takes wool from a sheep and turns it into cloth for clothes.

Kosher Foods

Have the students research Jewish beliefs and customs to find out what kosher foods are and why the Jewish people eat them. Discuss what types of food they avoid. Students can use several sources for information and write an essay explaining this custom and its basis.

Sausage

Make homemade sausage in your own classroom. Get 1–2 pounds of pork scraps from the butcher. The teacher can demonstrate how to grind the pork in a meat grinder or food processor. Students can then add 1 tablespoon of sage and 1 teaspoon of pepper to the ground pork. They can form the mixture into patties and fry them. (Be sure that the patties are well done before eating them.) You may want to discuss where pork comes from while you are cooking it. You can also use the recipe to strengthen mathematical skills.

What are Marsupials?

Introduce marsupials. Have the students research answers to these questions: What characteristics make an animal a marsupial? Where are most marsupials found? (Pay special attention to the reproduction and development of the marsupial.) What purpose does the "pouch" serve? What marsupial lives in North America?

Kangaroos

The most common marsupial is the kangaroo. Write each of the following questions on an index card. On a bulletin board, or a poster board, place a library card pocket for each question. Place one card into each of the pockets. As students discover the answer to the question, remove the card and staple or glue the question and the answer to the bulletin board or poster board. How fast can kangaroos travel? How do they compare in speed to other animals? Do the hind legs serve any other purpose besides hopping? What would happen if the front legs were the longer legs on a kangaroo? How do kangaroos defend themselves? Do they really kick with their hind legs, as is often portrayed?

Elephants

Compare Asian and African elephants. What characteristics do they have in common? How do they differ? Why does the African elephant have larger ears than the Asian elephant?

On Safari

Perhaps the students can transform one of the rooms in their houses into an African jungle by using green and brown construction paper or cardboard to make trees, vines, grass, etc. They can twist bulletin board paper to make vines and die cut leaves. Hang the jungle on the walls and from the ceiling. Fill it with the mammals who should inhabit it. Use stuffed or plastic toys or pictures from magazines, or make models of favorite animals. This is a good project to work on throughout the "Mammals" chapter. Put the jungle together piece-by-piece so that it is finished when the chapter is finished. You can also add any appropriate insects, reptiles, and birds that you have studied.

Beasts of Burden

Define the term "beast of burden" and decide, as a class, which mammals qualify for this label. Make a chart listing each animal, what country uses it, and what type of services the beast provides. Discuss what the characteristics are that these mammals share. Do any of them have unique features that specifically suit them to the task they are used for?

Rhinoceros

Read *Who Wants a Cheap Rhinoceros?* by Silverstein. Have the students make their own "For Sale" sign listing the animal of choice to sell, their name and telephone number, and a price that they want to sell it for. On the back of the "For Sale" sign, list as many ways they can think in which their animal might be helpful to its new owner. (You might even have the students write out a little sales pitch that they would give to prospective buyers who call to inquire about the animal for sale.)

Animals in Groups

- What are different groups of animals called? It depends on the animal. What do you call a group of: elephants, geese, gorillas, pigs, fish, horses, cats, ducks, lions, cattle, foxes, kangaroos, peacocks, bees, turkeys, sheep, whales, and gnats? (Answers: herd, gaggle, band, litter, school, team, clowder, brace, pride, drove, skulk, troop, muster, swarm, rafter, flock, pod, horde.)
- Make up flash cards with the name of the animal on one side and the name of the animal group on the other. (Let the students decorate the cards, if you like.) Have them use the flash cards to drill each other on the different group names. Let the students make up their own games based on the flash cards.

Monkey Business

As a class, compare the different animals (other than humans) considered to be "primates." Ask the students: How are monkeys, chimpanzees, apes, gorillas, and orangutans different from each other? Do they eat the same foods? Where do they live? How large do they get? Make up a chart to compare primates' similarities and differences. Write the characteristics they choose to research across the top of the chart. (You can include the questions listed above and add information that your students are interested in researching. This can include physical characteristics of the different primates.) List the primates the students will research down the side of the chart. You can also have students draw a picture of each primate next to its name, or check the Internet for photos.

Whales as Mammals

Discuss what characteristics of a whale make it a mammal and not a fish. Have each student divide a piece of paper or cardboard into two sections. Draw a picture of a whale on one half and a picture of a shark on the other half. (You can have the students cut out pictures from a magazine and glue them on the paper.) Label the parts of each animal that can be seen that make it a mammal or a fish. List below the pictures any other characteristics that cannot readily be seen.

Animal Research

Animals, such as mice, monkeys, and rabbits, are often used in medical and product research. Discuss as a class the pros and cons of using animals for this purpose. Ask the students to consider if they were in the government and were expected to vote on this issue, would they vote in favor of or opposition to animal research. Students can write a speech that they would give on the Senate or House floor that incorporates the pros or cons that they prepared. Students could also send a copy of their speech to their state and federal representatives.

Animal Classifications

As a class, make a list of certain animals that don't quite fit their classifications. For example, an echidna is a mammal, but it lays eggs like a bird. A platypus gives milk like other mammals but also lays eggs. After reviewing the list of such animals, have students debate what category each animal should fit into. If opinions differ from its present classification, write a short essay backing up opinions with facts.

Peaceful Co-Existence

There are many animals that live peacefully side-by-side that you might think would be natural enemies. Some examples of this are the tickbirds that are permitted to eat insects off a rhinoceros's back and the water dikkops that eat insects that bother crocodiles and are permitted to lay their eggs alongside the crocodiles' eggs. This is called "mutualism" or a "symbiotic relationship." Have students investigate other examples of mutualism in the animal kingdom. They can write ways in which people might be able to learn from these animals.

Cool It

Ask the students to try this experiment at home: Place one sock in warm water. Put a dry sock on one foot and put the wet sock on the other foot. After a few minutes, observe if one foot feels colder than the other. This short experiment demonstrates the important part that water and the effects of evaporation play in keeping an animal's body cool in a hot, dry environment.

Camels

Camels are often called "Ships of the Desert." Discuss what features camels have that make them adaptable to the desert. What role has the camel played in the history of the desert regions of the world? Are they used in the same ways today as they were in earlier periods of history?

Horses

Horses have served many purposes throughout history. Ask the students to research the following questions.
- What roles do horses play in our society? Research the history of the horse.
- Who domesticated the horse?
- What have been different uses of horses throughout history?
- How did horses come to the New World (the American continent)?
- How did hunting and transportation change since the domestication of the horse?

■ Creative Writing Activities

Following are instructions to give the students for various writing activities.
- Cut out pictures of animals from magazines. For each animal, write a short poem. Make a book of animal poems, using the cut-out pictures as illustrations. (*Animals, Animals* by Carle)
- Read or recite some nursery rhymes that involve animals ("Three Blind Mice"; "Hickory, Dickory, Dock"; "Farmer in the Dell"; "Little Boy Blue"; etc.). Make a book by writing these rhymes on separate pages, illustrating them, and then binding the pages together with ribbon. (You can also make a cover for the book with old wallpaper or by illustrating one yourself.)

- Write a story similar to *The Cat in the Hat* by Seuss. Some possibilities are "A Dog in a Log," "A Mouse in a House," or "A Pig in a Wig."

- It is often said that a cat has "nine lives." If you could live nine different lives as nine different people, what lives would you like to live? Why?

- Write to the University of Kentucky asking for information about their mascot, the wildcat. Why do they call themselves the "Wildcats?" What type of cat do they use to represent their school? Do they actually have a cat on campus? If so, how do they care for their mascot?

- Read *The Happy Lion* by Fatio. Write an adventure story about the time that Happy Lion visited your town.

- Plan a pretend party to which you will invite your favorite animals. Write out invitations to each guest. Include information in the invitations on what the "theme" of the party will be and what activities will take place. (You can also decorate the invitations in accordance with the theme of the party.) What type of animals would you invite to your party? What foods would your guests prefer? (*Dandelion* by Freeman)

- Some cats have long hair, while others have short hair. What do you think animals with short hair (mice, pigs, cows, horses, etc.) would look like with long hair? How would long-haired animals (St. Bernard dogs, rabbits, hamsters, etc.) look like with short hair? Write a story about an animal who wants to have a new hairdo.

- An old fable tells of a "boy who cried wolf." What does that phrase mean? What was the moral of the story? Write a story that would teach the same lesson.

- Dogs have been labeled as "man's best friend." Why? Write a story about a person whose best friend is a dog. Why are they such good friends? What do they do together?

- A wolf is usually cast as the "bad guy" in fairy tales (*The Three Little Pigs, Little Red Riding Hood*, etc.). Write a story in which a wolf saves the day.

- In the *Valentine Foxes* by Watson, each member of the family does something to make Valentine's Day special for the others. What is your family's favorite holiday? What do the members of your family do to make it special? Write down things that you plan to do on the next holiday to make it a memorable day for your family. Write an invitation asking someone who is lonely to join your family's celebration. (Mailing this invitation to someone real would make this activity even more meaningful.)

- Write a story about a little girl or boy who pretends that a favorite toy is a real, live pet. (*I Want a Dog* by Khalsa)

- Write a suspense story with a scene in it that requires the lead character to be "as quiet as a mouse."

- Write a letter to a friend describing a terrible toothache that you had and how the dentist helped make it feel better. (*The Bear's Toothache* by McPhail)

- Read *Brown Bear, Brown Bear, What Do You See?* and *Polar Bear, Polar Bear, What Do You Hear?* by Bill Martin, Jr. Make a similar book using your favorite animals and colors. Illustrate the book. If possible, laminate the book when it is finished and save it to read to younger family members and friends.

- Make a list of goals that you would like to accomplish in one hour, in one day, in one month, and in one year. Keep this list and use it as a checklist to keep track of how many of your goals you do accomplish. (*Big Time Bears* by Krensky)

- Read *Sheep in a Jeep* by Shaw. Write your own story about another type of mammal taking an unusual trip.

- People are sometimes labeled as the "black sheep" of the family because their ideas don't quite fit in with the rest of the family's. Write a story about someone who didn't fit in but who became someone special in the end.
- Write a tall tale explaining why the pig's tail is curly. (You can alter this exercise to include any animal with an unusual characteristic—elephant/trunk, rhinoceros/horn, giraffe/neck, etc.) (*Greedy Zebra* by Hadithi)
- Write a fan letter to Miss Piggy, Porky Pig, or Hampton Pig. Tell your character why you are such a fan. You could also request a photograph for your room.
- Develop a menu of exotic pork dishes. Name each dish and give a short description of what it contains (e.g., Pork with Marshmallow Sauce: two lean pork chops baked to a golden brown, smothered in marshmallow sauce and topped with a cherry).
- Read *The Three Little Pigs* by Marshall and *The True Story of the Three Little Pigs* by Scieszka. Choose another story you know and rewrite it from the "bad guy's" point of view.
- Pretend you are a kangaroo. What items would you keep in your pouch? Why? Write a story about your adventures as a kangaroo and how the items in your pouch came to be there.
- A "Bill of Rights" lists the things that people have a right to do or possess. Write a "Bill of Rights" for monkeys. What things do you think monkeys would like to have a guaranteed right to?
- Pretend you are Curious George. Where would you like to visit? What would you hope to see there? Write a story about your adventures. What kind of trouble would you get into as a result of being so curious? (*Curious George Goes to the Ice Cream Shop* by Rey)
- There is a gorilla named Koko who was taught by Dr. Penny Patterson to communicate by using sign language. Find out more about her. Learn some of the signs that she was taught. How has she responded to some of the questions asked her? What would you say to Koko if you met her? (Sign it!) If you were Dr. Patterson, what signs would you have taught Koko?
- List some of the activities that zookeepers must do to maintain the health of the animals under their care (e.g., bathing elephants, cutting rhinoceros's toenails, checking an alligator's teeth). Where does a zookeeper go to learn such skills? What type of training and experience do you think a zookeeper would need to perform this job effectively? Write a job description for the classified want ads in the newspaper. You are the director of a zoo who has a vacancy to fill. Decide what animal this new employee would be taking care of and what qualifications you feel the person who takes this job must have.

■ Art Activities

Following are instructions to give the students for various art activities.

- Think of animals that are used in advertising (Elsie the Cow, Smokey Bear, Tony the Tiger, McGruff the Anti-Crime Dog, Woodsy the Anti-Pollution Owl, etc.). Choose an animal and design an advertisement around it.
- It is sometimes said, "It's raining cats and dogs." Draw a picture to illustrate this saying.
- Make a lion using a paper plate. Draw a picture of a lion's face on the center section of the plate. Add a mane made out of yellow, brown, or tan construction paper that has been cut into 1-by-4-inch and 1-by-8-inch strips. (You can mix the colors of construction paper, too.) Curl the strips by wrapping them around a pencil. Glue the strips to the outer rim of the paper plate with the shorter curls inside the row of longer curls.
- Have each student draw a picture of an animal on a sheet of paper. On separate sheets of paper, draw the animal's tail, toes, eyes, ears, and nose, labeling each part by writing its name next to

the picture. Make a book with the parts of the animals first and the picture of the whole animal immediately following. See if other children can guess what animal each is by looking at the body parts one at a time. (*Tail, Toes, Eyes, Ears, Nose* by Burton)

- Sometimes it is said that owners look like their pets, or vice versa. Draw a picture of three people and their dogs. Make the owner and dog look like each other.

- Look at the dogs in the comic strips. Make your own comic strip involving one of the dogs you like. (You can also create your own comic strip dog.)

- Read *The Pigs' Wedding* by Heine. Draw a picture of another animal wedding.

- Cut fabric into varying shapes and sizes. Arrange these scraps of fabric to make animal shapes. How many different animals can you make?

- Make a paper plate bunny. Fold a paper plate in half. Add a cotton ball on one end and add ears, eyes, and a mouth (made out of fabric, construction paper, etc.) to the other end. Use some cardboard or construction paper to put feet on your bunny.

- What is your favorite animal TV star? Draw a picture of the animal in a favorite scene from one of its TV shows. (*The Bionic Bunny Show* by Brown)

- Design a home for yourself as if you lived in the woods. Your home can be inside a hollow tree, a tree house, a cottage in the woods, and so forth. (*Need A House? Call Ms. Mouse!* by Mendoza)

- Read *Bread and Jam for Frances* by Hoban. On a paper plate, glue pictures of healthy foods and plan a meal for Frances.

- Make a book of pig phrases and illustrate it. Phrases could include "Your room looks like a pigsty"; "He made such a pig of himself at dinner"; "My mom brings home the bacon at our house"; "Don't be so pig-headed!"; or "That's a bunch of hogwash."

- Make an elephant hat out of cardboard or poster board and a paper grocery bag. Make a headband out of the cardboard. Cut two large ears out of the bag and staple or tape them to the sides of the headband. Cut a 4-by-24-inch strip out of the bag. Fold the strip in half lengthwise and then cut slits in both sides of the folded strip. Unfold and staple on the headband to make a long trunk.

- Listen to a recording of the elephant movement of "Carnival of the Animals" by Saint Sans. How does the music give you the impression of an elephant? Can you picture the other animals portrayed in this piece of music? How do the different elements of music (tempo, pitch, rhythm) help portray the animals?

- Pretend you are a fortune-teller. What fortune would you predict for your best friend? Dress up like a fortune-teller and put on a performance giving predictions to friends and family. (*Tillie and Mert* by Luttrell)

- Draw a picture of a whale. Decorate its tail with a bandage (*Burt Dow Deep-Water Man* by McCloskey); by painting designs on it; or by gluing glitter, colored tissue paper, or something similar to it.

- Make a "pig" placemat for a special occasion. You will need poster board in three different colors, a 10-inch plate, glue, a craft knife, and a marker. Use the plate to draw a circle for the face on one of the pieces of poster board. Leave room at the top to draw in two ears. Cut out the face. Use the other pieces of poster board to draw and cut out pieces for the nose, eyes, mouth, and any other features you would like to add to the face. Glue these pieces in place. You may even draw a curly tail and attach it to the lower right-hand side of the face. You can use the leftover poster board to make name cards and/or napkin rings decorated with small pig faces or curly tails to give your table an even more festive look.

- Draw a poster of a winter scene that shows not only the above ground scenery but also what is happening underground. Include various animals and their hibernation environments in your picture. Give your poster some dimension by gluing on sticks, dried leaves, and grass where appropriate.
- Create a large mural of Noah's Ark by first painting the ark and a background on a large piece of cardboard. Cut out pictures of animals from magazines (or draw them) and add the animals to your picture.

Chapter 7
Dinosaurs

■ Teaching Resources

Books containing experiment(s) relating to the subject matter are marked with a plus sign (+) before and after the title.

P   *Dinosaur Babies,* by Lucille Recht Penner (Random House, 1992)
Discusses the characteristics and behavior of baby dinosaurs.

P   *Dinosaurs,* by Gail Gibbons (Holiday House, 1987)
Introduces the characteristics and habits of a variety of dinosaurs. Written in simple text.

P   *My Visit to the Dinosaurs,* by Aliki (Thomas Y. Crowell, 1985)
A little boy receives an introduction to the habits, characteristics, and habitats of 14 kinds of dinosaurs during a visit to the natural history museum.

P   *Strange Creatures That Really Lived,* by Millicent Selsam (Scholastic, 1987)
Describes some animals that lived millions of years ago, such as the giant sloth, camelus, huge roaches, and unitatherium.

P   *Wild and Woolly Mammoths,* by Aliki (HarperCollins Juveniles, 1998)
Describes the woolly mammoth that roamed the northern areas of the Earth thousands of years ago.

P/I *Dinosaur Bones,* by Aliki (Harper Trophy, 1990)
Explains how scientists who study fossils provide information about how dinosaurs lived millions of years ago.

P/I *Dinosaur Days,* by Joyce Milton (Random House, 1985)
A brief and simple discussion of the different kinds of dinosaurs that inhabited the Earth millions of years ago.

P/I *Dinosaurs and Other First Animals,* by Dean Morris (Raintree Books, 1990)
A discussion of various prehistoric animals and their relationship to present-day species.

P/I *Dinosaurs Are Different,* by Aliki (Harper Trophy, 1986)
Explains how the different orders and suborders of dinosaurs were similar and how they were different in structure and appearance.

I   *+Be a Dinosaur Detective,+* by Dougal Dixon (First Avenue Editions, 1988)
Explores what dinosaurs were like and how they lived, based on clues found in fossils. Includes questions/answers sections and instructions for making your own dinosaurs and other activities.

I *Dinosaurs and Their Young,* by Russell Freedman (Holiday House, 1983)
Discusses the recent discovery of the fossilized remains of duckbill dinosaur eggs and the young that hatched from them. Delves into the subject of whether some dinosaurs cared for their young.

I *Discovering Dinosaur Babies,* by Miriam Schlein (Bookwright Press, 1991)
Discusses what scientists have been able to determine about how dinosaurs cared for their young.

I *Living with Dinosaurs,* by Patricia Lauber (Aladdin, 1999)
Attempts to recreate what it would be like if we had lived at the time of the dinosaurs in North America.

I *The News about Dinosaurs,* by Patricia Lauber (Aladdin, 1994)
Discusses, through text and detailed pictures, the latest scientific thinking about the dinosaurs.

I/U *Dinosaur and Other Prehistoric Animal Factfinder,* by Michael Benton (Kingfisher Books, 1992)
An alphabetical guide to 200 dinosaurs and other prehistoric animals.

I/U *Dinosaurs and Other Archosaurs,* by Peter Zallinger (Random House, 1999)
Describes many individual species of dinosaurs and the smaller prehistoric reptiles.

I/U *Eyewitness Books: Dinosaur,* by David Norman, Ph.D., and Angela Milner, Ph.D. (DK Publishing, 2000)
Text and photographs describe the structure of the dinosaurs, their eggs, and fossils.

U *Dinosaur Mountain, Graveyard of the Past,* by Caroline Arnold (Clarion Books, 1989)
Discusses, in text and excellent photographs, the discoveries made at Dinosaur National Monument in Utah and the work scientists are doing to learn about dinosaurs.

U *The Rise and Fall of the Dinosaur,* by Joseph Wallace (David & Charles, 1989)
Discusses the life and world of the dinosaur millions of years ago through in-depth text and excellent artists' depictions.

■ Reading Selections

Books marked with an asterisk (*) before and after the title are related to activities in the activity sections of this chapter.

The Berenstain Bears and the Missing Dinosaur Bone, by Stan Berenstain and Jan Berenstain (Beginner Books, 1980)
> The Berenstain Bears search for the missing dinosaur bone. Written in a rhyming format.

Bones, Bones, Dinosaur Bones, by Byron Barton (Thomas Y. Crowell, 1990)
> A group of friends search for dinosaur bones and, when they find some, they try to assemble them.

Danny and the Dinosaur, by Syd Hoff (Harper Festival, 1999)
> On Danny's trip to the museum, he finds a live dinosaur who spends the day with him.

Derek, the Knitting Dinosaur, by Mary Blackwood (Carolrhoda Books, 1990)
>Derek doesn't want to act ferocious like his brothers and prefers to stay home and knit. When cold weather arrives, his knitting becomes useful.

Dinosaur Bob and His Adventures with the Family Lazardo, by William Joyce (HarperCollins Juveniles, 1995)
>The Lazardo family vacation in Africa and bring a friendly dinosaur back with them that becomes the talk of the town.

Dinosaur Days, by Linda Manning (Bridgewater Books, 1994)
>Each day of the week, a different dinosaur appears at a girl's house to engage in some kind of mischief.

A Dinosaur for Gerald, by Helena Clare Pittman (Carolrhoda Books, 1990)
>Mom and Dad find a way to make Gerald happy when he wants a real dinosaur for his birthday.

Dinosaur Garden, by Liza Donnelly (Scholastic, 1991)
>Rex plants a garden to attract dinosaurs and gets some unexpected results.

The Dinosaur Mystery, by Gertrude Chandler Warner (Whitman, 1995)
>A series of mysterious happenings hampers the Aldens' work as they try to assist with the opening of a dinosaur exhibit at the Pickering Natural History Museum. (Chapter Book)

The Dinosaur Princess and Other Prehistoric Riddles, by David Adler (Holiday House, 1988)
>A collection of jokes and riddles about dinosaurs and cave dwellers.

Dinosaur Roar!, by Paul Stickland and Henrietta Stickland (Dutton Children's Books, 1997)
>Sweet, grumpy, spiky, and lumpy dinosaurs are presented through illustrations and rhyming text.

How I Captured a Dinosaur, by Henry Schwartz (Orchard, 1993)
>Liz finds a living dinosaur on a camping trip and brings it home.

If You Are a Hunter of Fossils, by Byrd Baylor (Aladdin, 1984)
>A fossil hunter describes how the Earth may have appeared in prehistoric times.

Prehistoric Pinkerton, by Steven Kellogg (Pied Piper Paperbacks, 1991)
>A dog's natural instinct to chew on things while teething causes problems while it is visiting a museum's dinosaur collection.

Rosie and the Dance of the Dinosaurs, by Betty Ren Wright (Holiday House, 1989)
>Rosie finds that the challenge of an upcoming piano recital is actually made easier by having only nine fingers (Chapter Book)

The Trouble with Tyrannosaurus Rex, by Lorinda Bryan Cauley (Harcourt Brace Jovanovich, 1988)
>The other dinosaurs come up with a plan to outwit Tyrannosaurus Rex.

Tyrannosaurus Tex, by Betty G. Birney (Houghton Mifflin, 1996)
>A dinosaur cowboy helps Cookie and Pete put out a prairie fire and scares away some cattle rustlers.

Tyrone the Double Dirty Rotten Cheater, by Hans Wilhelm (Scholastic, 1991)
> Boland has to decide how to handle problems with Tyrone, the school bully, when he cheats at games played during an outing to Swamp Island. (Other "Boland" books are available.)

Tyrone the Horrible, by Hans Wilhelm (Scholastic, 1992)
> A little dinosaur named Boland tries several different ways to deal with Tyrone, the biggest bully in the forest, until he finally finds a way.

The following books are out of print, but may be available in the library.

Dinosaur Dances, by Jane Yolen (Putnam, 1990)
> Whimsical poems feature allosaurus, stegosaurus, tyrannosaurus, and other dancing dinosaurs.

*Dinosaur Dos and Don'ts,** by Jean Burt Polhamus (Prentice-Hall, 1975)
> A group of dinosaurs discuss good behavior and manners in a poetic manner.

Dinosaur Dream, by Dennis Nolan (Macmillan, 1990)
> Wilbur finds a baby dinosaur outside his bedroom window and travels back in time to return it to its home.

Dinosaur Dress Up, by Allen L. Sirois (Tambourine Books, 1992)
> Professor Saurus describes another possible explanation for the disappearance of the dinosaurs – their obsession with fashion and their clothing habits.

The Dinosaur That Followed Me Home, by Bruce Coville (Pocket Books, 1990)
> While at Camp Haunted Hills, Stuart and his friends get more than they bargained for when they travel back to the time of the dinosaurs. (Chapter Book)

Mrs. Toggle and the Dinosaur, by Robin Pulver (Macmillan, 1991)
> Mrs. Toggle and her class expect a dinosaur to be coming in as the new student.

*Oliver Dibbs and the Dinosaur Cause,** by Barbara Steiner (Four Winds Press, 1986)
> Oliver campaigns to make the stegosaurus the Colorado state fossil, and soon encounters an interfering bully. (Chapter Book)

*What Do You Feed a Dinosaur for Breakfast?,** by Della Cohen (Marvel Entertainment, 1987)
> Grandpa tells Jeremy a bedtime story about when he was a boy and had a dinosaur come home to spend the night with him.

■ Science Activities

Dinosaur Eggs

As a class, research what dinosaur eggs really looked like, then make your own. (Let the students do any measuring that is required and use this activity as an opportunity for a short math lesson also.)

- Hard-boil one egg for each student. Tap the shells of the hard-boiled eggs gently on a table or counter until the shell is cracked all over. (DO NOT REMOVE THE SHELLS.)
- Mix 3 cups of cool water with one envelope of unsweetened soft drink mix (pick any color, or use more than one color) in a small bowl. Place the cracked eggs in the colored water.
- Put a piece of plastic wrap over the bowl and put it in the refrigerator for a couple of days.
- Take the bowl out of the refrigerator, remove the eggs from the colored water, and peel off the cracked shells. You may think that your dinosaur eggs are too pretty to eat!

Dinosaur Bones

Different types of dinosaur bones have been found in different states. Have the students research a specific area of the United States to find out what types of dinosaurs are thought to have lived there. Locate the important dinosaur digs that are located in this country. Determine what these dinosaurs' particular characteristics were and discuss why they would have chosen that part of the continent to live in.

Time Line

As a class, make a time line of the different dinosaur periods. On a chart (or on the wall) make a long line and divide it into the five prehistoric periods (Cenozoic, Mesozoic, Paleozoic, Proterozoic, and Archaeozoic). Along the line (above and below) record the different plants and animals that are believed to have lived during that period. Have your children illustrate the time line.

Comparing Dinosaurs

Ask the students to compare and contrast two species of dinosaurs from two different prehistoric periods by answering the following questions:
- How many legs did they walk on?
- What did they eat?
- What area of the world did they live in?
- What type of communities did they live in?
- What was the structure of their family unit, and how did they care for their young?

Lesser-Known Dinosaurs

Have the students pick one of the lesser-known dinosaurs listed below (or one they would like to know more about) and do a research project on it. Students can write an outline determining what information they want their research papers to contain (where the dinosaur lived, what it ate, whether it was peaceful or warlike, what its family unit was like, etc.). Gather books and encyclopedias that contain information on dinosaurs. Students can make a model of the dinosaur they chose. (The model can be made out of any type of material.)

Some lesser-known dinosaurs are

Ankylosaurus

Apatosaurus

Camptosaurus

Ceratosaurus

Corythosaurus

Deinonychus

Diplodocus

Elasmosaurus

Euparkeria

Hypsilophodon

Orinitholestes

Pachycephalo

Polacathus

Psittacosaurus

Spinosaurus

Struthiomimus

Paleontologist versus Archeologist

Ask the students: What is a *paleontologist*? How does that compare with an *archeologist*? As a class, research what is involved with these two occupations and where paleontology and archeology are currently being practiced.

Be an Archeologist

Before class, make fossils and have the students work as archeologists. Take approximately ½ cup of clay and flatten it on a paper plate. Repeat 8 to 10 times. Press an everyday item into each mound of clay. Have the students guess what the items are. Be sure to have magnifying glasses available. Examples of objects that make interesting fossils are:

a craft stick on its side

a rubber band that has been twisted

a sponge

a penny, or any coin

a spoon turned over making part of the fossil deeper than the other part

a piece of yarn

scissors

a pencil, but insert only the eraser

To make this activity more challenging, only press a portion of the item into the clay.

Afterward, discuss that "real" archeologists do not have someone to tell them if they have identified a fossil correctly. It is very fortunate to find a fossil that has not been broken or has parts missing. Speculate as to what other challenges an archeologist might face.

■ Creative Writing Activities

Following are instructions to give the students for various writing activities.

- You have made friends with a dinosaur. What would you and your friend do together? How could its large size be of benefit? How would it be a hindrance? Write a story about a day you spent with your very special friend. (*What Do You Feed a Dinosaur for Breakfast?* by Cohen)

- Imagine you are a cave dweller living during the period of the dinosaurs. You have not learned how to write using an alphabet, but you do use symbols to tell a story. Write a simple story using symbols.

- Write a story about life in the time of the dinosaurs, only with a twist. Pretend many of the inventions that we have today existed in that long-ago time, only in a different form, and that people also lived at that time. What would a car look like? How about a vacuum cleaner? Write a story about a "typical" day in the life of a cave dweller with these "modern" conveniences. (You could also illustrate your favorite part or illustrate the entire story and make it into a book to keep.)

- Write a poem about the proper way to act when you go out to dinner and a movie with friends. Be sure to stress good manners in your poem. (*Dinosaur Dos and Don'ts* by Polhamus)

- Write and illustrate a story that has you in the starring role living in prehistoric times. What type of situation will you put yourself in? (*If You Are a Hunter of Fossils* by Baylor)

- Choose a dinosaur that would make a good state symbol for your state. Make up a letter convincing the governor that your choice is a perfect representative for your state. (*Oliver Dibbs and the Dinosaur Cause* by Steiner)

- You are planning a dinosaur picnic and are responsible for organizing the food. What types of food would you serve? Remember that some of your guests prefer plants and others eat meat. As a twist on this assignment, have your child plan a dinosaur theme picnic for friends or family. What type of "dinosaur" food and drinks would be served? What types of games could the children play? What type of decorations would be used? Have your child create an invitation to this picnic. (You can choose to actually have the picnic or just make up an imaginary picnic.)

- Over the years, bones of dinosaurs have been found throughout the world, and scientists have determined the "shape" of the different dinosaurs based on these finds. However, there is still some controversy over the "skin" of these animals. Usually dinosaurs are depicted as having brown or green-colored skin, but some scientists believe that they may have been brightly colored, too. Study the bright color combinations of some of the birds and reptiles of today. Write an editorial to a science magazine stating your views on the question of the dinosaurs' skin colors and the reasons that support your view.

■ Art Activities

Following are instructions to give the students for various art activities.

- Make a dinosaur skeleton out of pipe cleaners. Twist two pipe cleaners together to make a strong backbone. Connect four legs by twisting a pipe cleaner around the backbone at the base of the neck and another at the top of the tail. You can twist two pipe cleaners together before attaching the legs to the backbone to give your dinosaur extra strength for standing. Use four "single-strength" pipe cleaners, cut in varying lengths, to make the dinosaur's ribs. Twist each pipe cleaner around the backbone, in the stomach area, and bend it down in a "U" shape to form ribs. Try making different kinds of dinosaurs of your own design.

- Make a dinosaur puppet out of old household items. Cut a strip of four paper egg carton cups. Decorate the strip any way you want to. Cut another strip of two egg carton cups. Draw eyes on the two cups. Slip your arm inside an old sock. Lay the four-cup egg carton strip on your arm right below your wrist. Have an adult put one rubber band around your arm and between the third and fourth cups of the strip. Place another rubber band between the first and second cups. This makes the dinosaur's back and secures it to your puppet. Tape the eyes to the sock near the toe between the knuckles and joints of your fingers. Pick your favorite dinosaur story and put on a play using your new puppet as one of the characters.

- Draw a picture of your favorite dinosaur on a piece of cardboard or heavy white paper. Cut it out. Dab small amounts of glue randomly over the dinosaur's body and stick small stones, bits of Styrofoam, or other small objects to it. You can also use raisins or small pieces of candy. Paint or color the rest of the dinosaur's body. You can also paint the decorations you glued onto the dinosaur.

- Draw a picture of a dinosaur on a piece of cardboard or cut a picture out of a magazine and mount it on a piece of cardboard and cut out the cardboard to make a dinosaur stencil. Using colored chalk, color heavily on the edges of your stencil. Tape the stencil onto a piece of paper. Have students brush the chalk off the stencil and onto the piece of paper with their fingers or a small paintbrush. Remove the stencil, and you will have the silhouette of your dinosaur surrounded by a halo of colored chalk.

- Make dinosaur fossils. Use the following recipe to make the fossil material:

1/2 cup corn starch
1 cup baking soda
5/8 cup water

Makes four or five fossils. Cook this mixture over medium heat until it is thick. Let the mixture cool. While the mixture is cooling, look for items around the house whose impressions would look like dinosaur fossils (shells, bones, marbles, etc.). When the mixture is cool, flatten a ball of it between two pieces of waxed paper. Press the item(s) that you found into the mixture and let dry completely. You have made your own dinosaur fossil!

- Construct a dinosaur headpiece. Fold four paper plates in half lengthwise. Decorate these plates in any way you want to. Lay three of the paper plates side-by-side (lengthwise) so that they overlap each other about 1 inch. Make sure the folded edges are all on the same side. Staple the three plates together on the folded edge where they overlap. Slide the fourth plate 1 inch over one of the end plates (perpendicular to the stapled plates—the hat will resemble the number "7"). Staple the fourth plate in place. This is the headpiece. Poke a hole in each side of the fourth plate about halfway down on the open edge. Pull a piece of yarn through each hole. Tie a knot at the end of the yarn to secure it in the hole. Tie the yarn under your chin to hold your hat on your head.

- Make a dinosaur snout using a Styrofoam cup. Cut out the bottom of the cup, then, cut an upside-down "V" shape up from the bottom of the cup, on two sides, to within about 1 inch of the upper rim of the cup. This makes the dinosaur's mouth. Tape rickrack to the outer edges of the "V" shapes to make teeth. Color or decorate the rest of the snout any way you want. Tie a piece of yarn to each corner of the mouth for use in tying the snout over your mouth and nose. You can also make a tongue out of red felt or paper and let it hang out of your dinosaur mouth.

- Make dinosaurs out of salt dough. Mix together:

---

2 cups flour
1 cup salt
1 cup water

Shape into different dinosaurs. Bake at 250 degrees for two or three hours. Shellac or paint with acrylic paints. You can use these dinosaurs in your diorama (see next activity).

- Make a diorama of prehistoric times using a shoebox. Cut a small peephole in one end of the box. Cut out the other end of the box and cover the opening with colored plastic wrap. Remove the lid of the shoebox and arrange pictures of dinosaurs, or your salt dough dinosaurs from above, vegetation, rocks, and so forth, to make a prehistoric scene. You can mount pictures of dinosaurs, jungles, mountains, and other features on pieces of cardboard and then tape them to the sides and bottom of the box. You can also tape things to the shoebox lid. Place the shoebox lid back on the box and view your scene through the peephole.

Additional Resources

■ Experiment Books

More Mudpies to Magnets, Science for Young Children, by Elizabeth A. Sherwood, Robert A. Williams, and Robert E. Rockwell (Gryphon House, 1991)
> Gives instructions for experiments involving plants, animals, and space.

Papercraft Projects with One Piece of Paper, by Michael Grater (Dover, 1988)
> Introduces techniques for making animals out of paper.

Pets in a Jar, by Seymour Simon (Puffin Books, 1988)
> Explains how to catch and keep many small animals, such as butterflies, earthworms, crickets, and tadpoles.

Science in Your Backyard, by William R. Wellnitz, Ph.D (TAB Books, 1992)
> Includes experiments involving plants, animals, and earth sciences that can be done close to home and that encourage the development of observation and measurement skills.

■ Horses

American Donkey and Mule Society
Rt. 5, Box 65
Denton, TX 76201

Appaloosa Horse Club
P.O. Box 8403
Moscow, ID 83843
(official Appaloosa club)

Belgian Draft Horse Corporation
of America
P.O. Box 335
Wabash, IN 46992

Clydesdale Breeders of the United States
Rt. 1, Box 131
Pecatonica, IL 61063

International Arabian Horse Association
224 E. Olive Ave.
P.O. Box 4502
Burbank, CA 91503

Horse Publications

Arabian Horse Journal
P.O. Box 181
Odessa, MO 64076

Arabian Horse World
2650 E. Bayshore Rd.
Palo Alto, CA 94303

The Draft Horse Journal
P.O. Box 670
Waverly, IA 50677

Small Farmer's Journal
3890 Stewart St.
Eugene, OR 97402

■ Chimpanzees

Jane Goodall Institute for Wildlife Research, Education, and Conservation
P.O. Box 26846
Tucson, AZ 85726

■ Dinosaurs

When writing to the addresses listed below, please explain exactly what you want to know about dinosaurs and include your full name and address with your request.

Field Museum of Natural History
Roosevelt Rd. @ Lake Shore Dr.
Chicago, IL 60605

The University of Kansas
Museum of Natural History
Lawrence, KS 66045

■ Magazines

Dolphin Log
The Cousteau Society
8440 Santa Monica Blvd.
Los Angeles, CA 90069

Wildlife Conservation Magazine
New York Zoological Park
Bronx, NY 10460

National Geographic World
National Geographic Society
Washington, DC 20036

Your Big Backyard (preschool)
National Wildlife Federation
8925 Leesburg Pike
Vienna, VA 22184-0001

Owl & Chickadee
The Young Naturalist Foundation
255 Great Arrow Ave.
Buffalo, NY 14207-3082

Zoo Books Magazine
Wildlife Education, Ltd.
3590 Kettner Blvd.
San Diego, CA 92101

Ranger Rick (ages 6-12)
National Wildlife Federation
8925 Leesburg Pike
Vienna, VA 22184-0001

Listed below are books that deal with specialized areas within the "animals" category. These books can be used to study an area of interest more thoroughly or to add creativity to your approach to the subject of animals.

■ Questions and Answers/Fun Fact

Animal Fact/Animal Fable, by Seymour Simon (New York: Crown, 1979)

Elephants Can't Jump and Other Freaky Facts about Animals, by Barbara Seuling (New York: E. P. Dutton, 1985)

Lies People Believe about Animals, by Susan Sussman and Robert James (Niles, IL: Whitman, 1987)

Mysteries of Nature: Explained and Unexplained, by Roger Caras. (New York: Harcourt Brace Jovanovich, 1979)

Why Do Cat's Eyes Glow in the Dark? and Other Questions Kids Ask about Animals, by Joanne Settel and Nancy Baggett (New York: Atheneum, 1988).

■ At the Zoo

Behind the Scenes at the Zoo, by David Paige (Toronto: Whitman, 1978)

Maybe You Belong in a Zoo, by Karen O'Connor (New York: Dodd, Mead, 1982)

New Zoos, by Madelyn Klein Anderson (New York: Franklin Watts, 1987)

A Visit to the Zoo, by Sylvia Root Tester (Chicago: Children's Press, 1987)

Zoo, by Gail Gibbons (New York: Thomas Y. Crowell, 1987)

Zoo Clues—Making the Most of Your Visit to the Zoo, by Sheldon L. Gerstenfeld, U.M.D. (New York: Viking, 1991)

Zoo Year, by Alice Schick (New York: J. B. Lippincott, 1978)

■ Unusual Animals

Amazing Science: Armadillos and Other Unusual Animals, by Q. L. Pearce (Englewood Cliffs, NJ: Messner, 1989)

Animal Olympians, by David Taylor (Minneapolis, MN: Lerner, 1989)

Big and Small, Short and Tall, by Ron Roy (New York: Clarion Books, 1986)

Giants of Land, Sea, and Air: Past and Present, by David Peters (New York: Alfred A. Knopf, 1986)

Little Giants, by Seymour Simon (New York: William Morrow, 1983)

Rare and Unusual Animals, by Nina Leen (New York: Holt, Rinehart & Winston, 1981)

Strange Creatures, by Seymour Simon (New York: Four Winds Press, 1981)

The View from the Oak, by Judith Kohl and Herbert Kohl (Boston: Sierra Club Books, Little, Brown, 1977)

■ Miscellaneous

Animal Behavior: Hibernation, by John Stidworthy (New York: Gloucester Press, 1991)

Animal Communication, by Jacci Cole (San Diego: Greenhaven Press, 1989)

Animal Fathers, by Russell Freedman (New York: Holiday House, 1976)

Animals Keeping Clean, by Jane Burton (New York: Random House, 1989)

Animals Keeping Cool, by Jane Burton (New York: Random House, 1989)

Animals Keeping Warm, by Jane Burton (New York: Random House, 1989)

Animals of the Night, by Lionel Bender (New York: Gloucester Press, 1989)

Getting Born, by Russell Freedman (New York: Holiday House, 1978)

John James Audubon, by Jan Gleiter and Kathleen Thompson (Milwaukee, WI: Raintree Children's Books, 1988)

Leeches, Lampreys, and Other Cold-Blooded Bloodsuckers, by Gail LaBonte (New York: Franklin Watts, 1991)

Making Soft Dinos: A Dinosaur Craft Book, by Linda Bourke (New York: Harvey House, 1980)

State Birds, by Arthur Singer and Alan Singer (New York: E. P. Dutton, 1986)

Whose Baby?, by Masayaki Yabuuchi (New York: Philomel, 1985)

■ Videos

Fish (Dorling Kindersley, 1997)
> Take the plunge from dazzling coral reefs to the darkest depths to meet fish.

The Octopus; The Crayfish; The Crab (Diamond Entertainment Corp., 1996)
> Three videos provide factual information about the octopus, the crayfish, and the crab.

■ Web Sites

The following Web sites reference several other Web sites about each topic. These Web sites were created especially for children. All sites were accessed in February 2001 and were active at that time.

Arachnids: http://www.yahooligans.com/science_and_oddities/Living_things/Animals/Arachnids
Birds: http://www.yahooligans.com/science_and_oddities/Living_things/Animals/birds
Insects: http://www.yahooligans.com/science_and_oddities/Living_things/Animals/Insects
Mammals: http://www.yahooligans.com/science_and_oddities/Living_things/Animals/Mammals
Marine life: http://www.yahooligans.com/science_and_oddities/Living_things/Animals/Marine_life
Reptiles and amphibians: http://www.yahooligans.com/science_and_oddities/Living_things/Animals/Reptiles_and_amphibians
Worms: http://www.yahooligans.com/science_and_oddities/Living_things/animals/worms
Zoos: http://www.yahooligans.com/science_and_oddities/Living_things/animals/zoos

The following Web sites discuss a specific topic related to animals:

Bats: www.batcon.org/
Bee information: http://www.billybee.com/
Bears: http://www.nature-net.com/bears
Bird information: http://theaviary.com
A Butterfly Garden: http://www.butterflies.com/guide.html
Butterfly information: http://mgfx.com/butterflies/
Cats: http://www.wildaboutcats.org
Chameleons: http://www.skypoint.com/members/mikefry/chams2.html
Dinosaur Exhibit: http://www.hcc.hawaii.edu/dinos/dinos.1.html
Dinosaur Society: http://www.dinosociety.org/
Fish information: http://www.wh.whoi.edu/homepage/faq.html
Froggy Page: http://www.cs.yale.edu./html/yale/CS/Hyplans/loosemore.sandra/froggy/html

The Gater Hole: http://magicnet.net/~mgodwin/

Heatherk's Gecko Page: http://wwwgeckoworld.com/~gecko/

Hummingbirds: http://www.hummingbirds.net

Interactive frog dissection: http://curry.edschool.Virginia.EDU/go/frog

Mammal information: http://edx1.educ.monash.edu/e-zoo.html

Marine mammals: http://www.tmmc.org/

Marsupials: http://www.koala.net/

Monkeys and primates: http://www.selu.com/~bio/PrimateGallery

Octopus information: http://is.dal.ca/~ceph/TCP/index.html

Penguins: http://www.vni.net/~kwelch/penguins

Pet bird information: http://www.petbirdpage.com

Raccoons: http://www.loomcom.com/raccoons

Sea urchins: http://seaurchin.org/

Spiders: http://www.jasonproject.org

Turtles: http://www.turtles.org/

Water dragons: http://www.icomm.ca/dragon/

Whales: http://curry.edschool.Virginia.EDU/go/whales

HABITATS

- Key Concepts

- Comprehensive Teaching Resources

- Chapter 1: Sea Life

- Chapter 2: Deserts

- Chapter 3: Polar Regions

- Chapter 4: Tropical Rain Forests

- Chapter 5: Grasslands

- Chapter 6: Woodlands and Ponds

- Additional Resources

Key Concepts

■ Primary Concepts

Students will be able to:

1. Be aware that animals live in various habitats (i.e., oceans, deserts, rain forests, woods, ponds, grasslands, polar regions, etc.) (Chapters 1–6).

2. Identify the coverings of various animals (mammals, reptiles, birds, amphibians, fish, insects) and understand that they differ between habitats (Chapters 1–6).

3. Recognize that animals and plants have special characteristics that enable them to survive in a particular habitat (Chapters 1–6).

4. Name various plants and animals that live in an ocean habitat and explain the interactions among them (Chapter 1).

5. Name various plants and animals that live in a desert habitat and explain the interactions among them (Chapter 2).

6. Name various plants and animals that live in a woodland habitat and explain the interactions among them (Chapter 6).

7. Name various plants and animals that live in a pond habitat and explain the interactions among them (Chapter 6).

8. Explain the effects of the changing seasons on plants and animals within each habitat (Chapters 1–6).

■ Intermediate Concepts

Students will be able to:

1. Name the various plants and animals that live in a polar region habitat and explain the interactions among them (Chapter 3).

2. Name the various plants and animals that live in a tundra habitat and explain the interactions among them (Chapter 3).

3. Name the various plants and animals that live in a tropical forest habitat and explain the interactions among them (Chapter 4).

4. Name the various plants and animals that live in a grassland habitat and explain the interactions among them (Chapter 5).

5. Discuss various plant and animal features that are aids to survival in each unique habitat (Chapters 1–6).

6. Classify animals as herbivores, carnivores, or omnivores, according to the food they eat (Chapters 1–6).

7. Distinguish between consumers and producers of food (Chapters 1–6).

8. Diagram a food web or a food chain that exists in a particular habitat and summarize its importance in that community (Chapters 1–6).

9. Explain how the following factors can affect the size of a population in an ecosystem: birth rate, amount of food available, and number of predators (Chapters 1–6).

■ Upper Concepts

Students will be able to:

1. Do the following in relation to oceanic animal life (Chapter 1):

    Explain the characteristics of various deep-water ocean animals.

    Sketch and label the main parts of most fish: mouth, eyes, nostril, scales, lateral line, dorsal fins (spiny and soft), caudal fin, anal fin, pectoral and pelvic fins, gill opening, and cover.

2. Divide the ocean into life zones according to the amount of light each zone receives (Chapter 1).

3. Illustrate the oceanic food chain, including plankton and its role in this cycle (Chapter 1).

4. Do the following in relation to oceanic plant life (Chapter 1):

    Research several oceanic plants and discuss their methods of food intake and individual habitats.

    Define and discuss the importance of algae.

    Explain common uses of seaweed.

5. Research and discuss the contributions of Jacques Cousteau (Chapter 1).

6. Describe the interactions among plants, animals, and natural resources in a given habitat (Chapters 1–6).

7. Predict the results of upsetting the plant/animal balance in any ecosystem (Chapters 1–6).

Comprehensive Teaching Resources

Listed in the table are books that cover a wide range of topics in the area of habitats. One of these could serve as your main teaching guide while studying this unit. Each book is listed with a short summary, and the chapters it covers are noted. The books are listed by degree of difficulty, easiest to most difficult.

BOOK AND SUMMARY	AUTHOR	CHAPTERS					
		1	2	3	4	5	6
The Ocean World of Jacques Cousteau (World Publishing) Twenty-volume set of resource books thoroughly covering life in the oceans and in the arctic.	Jacques-Yves Cousteau, (1985)	X		X			
The Usborne Book of Earth (Usborne Publishing) Includes detailed information on deserts, oceans, and the arctic.	Fiona Watt, (1994)	X	X	X			

Each chapter in this section lists reference books that focus on the specific habitat being addressed. These books can be used to complement and expand upon the basic information provided in the comprehensive resource books listed in the table.

The reference books in each chapter have been classified by age level to help you select those that best fit the needs and interests of the students.

Chapter 1
Sea Life

■ Teaching Resources

Books containing experiment(s) relating to the subject matter are marked with a plus sign (+) before and after the title.

P   *Ocean Day,* by Shelley Rotner and Ken Kreisler (Macmillan, 1993)
Photo essays, nicely done, depicting tides, dunes, tide pools, animal life, and waves.

P   *What's under the Ocean,* by Janet Craig (Troll, 1989)
Animals and plants that live in the ocean are introduced with brief text and simple illustrations.

P/I   *Coral Reef,* by Barbara Taylor (DK Publishing, 2000)
Enlarged pictures and brief text describe life found on coral reefs.

P/I   *At Home in the Coral Reef,* by Katy Muzik (Charlesbridge, 1995)
An introduction to life on the coral reef.

P/I   *At Home in the Tide Pool,* by Alexandra Wright (Charlesbridge, 1999)
Simplistic text and pictures look at tide pool creatures in this book written by a 12-year-old girl.

P/I   *Life in the Oceans,* by Lucy Baker (Scholastic, 1993)
Concise text with nice illustrations looking at plant and animal life and natural resources in the ocean. Brings to light the destruction we are causing to the oceans.

P/I   *Look Inside the Ocean,* by Laura Crema (Grosset & Dunlap, 1998)
Uses a question-and-answer format, with enjoyable illustrations, to tell about ocean life.

P/I   *World Book Looks at the Sea and Its Marvels,* by Brian Williams and Brenda Williams (World Book, 1997)
Presents information about the sea and the plants and animals living there.

P/I/U   *Coral Reef Images,* by Michael George (Creative Editions, 1995)
Beautiful, full-color pages, with brief text overlaid, describing coral reef formations and animals that live there.

P/I/U   *Seashores: A Guide to Animals and Plants Along the Beaches,* by Herbert S. Zim, Ph.D. and Lester Ingle, Ph.D. (Golden Books, 1989)
A handy pocket book full of seashore information about animals, plants, and especially shells.

I *The Magic School Bus on the Ocean Floor,* by Joanna Cole (Scholastic, 1994)
Ms. Frizzle leads her class on an ocean tour, explaining it and the creatures who live there.

I *Oceans,* by Seymour Simon (Mulberry Books, 1997)
Brilliant photos with brief text describe the physical characteristics, life, and fragility of the world's oceans.

I/U *Incredible Facts about the Ocean: Volumes I & II,* by W. Wright Robinson (Dillon, 1990)
Question-and-answer books that cover all possible aspects of ocean life, with easy-to-understand text and helpful illustrations.

U *The Great Barrier Reef: A Living Laboratory,* by Rebecca Johnson (Lerner, 1991)
Nice photographs accompany the text about research projects covering plants and animals on Australia's Great Barrier Reef.

■ Reading Selections

Books marked with an asterisk (*) before and after the title are related to activities in the activity sections of this chapter.

Ahoy There, Little Polar Bear, by Hans de Beer (North South Books, 1999)
> Nemo, the cat, helps rescue Lars from a fishnet and get him back home where he belongs.

All I See, by Cynthia Rylant (Orchard, 1994)
> A painter, who sets up on the shore of a lake, paints the imaginary whales that he sees there.

Amos and Boris, by William Steig (Sunburst, 1992)
> After being rescued at sea by a friendly whale, Amos, the mouse, finds a way to reciprocate.

Baby Beluga, by Raffi (Crown, 1997)
> This text beautifully illustrates the song about a little white whale in the sea.

The Black Pearl, by Scott O'Dell (Yearling Books, 1996)
> Ramon finds a giant pearl in a sea creature's cave as he learns the family art of pearl diving. (Chapter Book)

The Book of Jonah, by Peter Spier (Baker Book House, 2000)
> The story of Jonah, who spends three days and nights in the belly of a great fish.

Burt Dow Deep-Water Man, by Robert McCloskey (Weston Woods, 1990)
> Burt catches a whale on his fishing hook, lets it go, and bandages the whale's tail. In return, the whale swallows Burt's boat to protect it during a raging storm.

Curious George Goes to the Aquarium, by Margret Rey and Alan J. Shalleck (Houghton Mifflin, 1984)
> George decides to feed the seals while on a trip to the aquarium and ends up doing tricks in the seal tank.

Cyrus the Unsinkable Sea Serpent, by Bill Peet (Houghton Mifflin, 1982)
> Cyrus decides he is tired of wandering the seas all day long and wants to have some fun. Instead of having fun, however, Cyrus ends up helping a ship full of people have a safe voyage across the sea to a new land.

Fish Face, by Patricia Reilly Giff (Yearling Books, 1984)
> One in a series of books centered around the Kids of the Polk Street School. (Chapter Book)

The Fish of Gold, by the Brothers Grimm, adapted by M. Eulalia Valeri (Silver Burdett, 1985)
> A poor fisherman catches a fish of gold that promises to grant any wish the fisherman may have if he will set it free.

Herman the Helper, by Robert Kraus (Aladdin, 1987)
> Herman, the octopus, is always willing to help anyone who needs him.

Humphrey the Lost Whale, by Wendy Tokuda (Heian International, 1992)
> The true story of how people around the San Francisco area helped save a beached whale.

If You Ever Meet a Whale, by Myra Cohn Livingston (Holiday House, 1992)
> A collection of poems about whales.

Is This a House for Hermit Crab?, by Megan McDonald (Orchard, 1990)
> Hermit Crab must search for a new house when he outgrows the one he has.

Jimmy's Boa and the Big Splash Birthday Bash, by Trinka Hakes Noble (Dial Books for Young Readers, 1989)
> At Jimmy's birthday party at Sealand, everyone ends up taking a dip in the big tank!

Kermit the Hermit, by Bill Peet (Houghton Mifflin), 1980
> Kermit, the crab, works hard to repay a young boy who saves him from disaster.

The Little Whale, by Ann McGovern (Four Winds Press), 1979
> Describes the life of a humpback whale from birth to adulthood.

Look Again! The Second Ultimate Spot-the-Difference Book, by April Wilson (Dial Books for Young Readers, 1992)
> Find different plants and animals that use camouflage to hide in 12 habitats.

The Magic Fish, by Freya Littledale (Scholastic, 1989)
> The fisherman's greedy wife is never satisfied with the wishes granted her by an enchanted fish.

The Major, the Poacher, and the Wonderful One-Trout River, by Dayton O. Hyde (Boyds Mills Press, 1998)
> The Major, who wants to raise a record-breaking trout, has to deal with a 14-year-old poacher. (Chapter Book)

McElligot's Pool, by Dr. Seuss (Random House, 1966)
> A little boy daydreams about how he just might catch a fish in McElligot's pool.

Moby Dick, by Herman Melville (Bantam Classics, 1981)
> The adventures of Captain Ahab as he searches for the great white whale, Moby Dick. (Chapter Book)

Penguin Pete, by Marcus Pfister (North South Books, 1997)
> Pete plays on land with his friends and learns how to swim in the sea.

Penguin Pete and Pat, by Marcus Pfister (North South Books, 1989)
> Penguin Pete meets a beautiful, blue-beaked girl penguin who changes his life.

Sea Squares, by Joy N. Hulme (Hyperion Press, 1993)
Various sea creatures are used, along with rhyming text, to practice counting and squaring numbers.

The Seashore Book, by Charlotte Zolotow (Harper Trophy, 1994)
A young boy who has never seen the sea listens to his mother describe a day at the beach.

Secret of the Seal, by Deborah Davis (Random House, 1994)
Kyo, an Eskimo boy, must make a difficult choice between his family loyalty and his friendship with a seal. (Chapter Book)

Shark Beneath the Reef, by J. C. George (HarperCollins Juvenile, 1991)
On the island of Coronado, a young Mexican fisherman becomes aware of the politics and corruption around him. (Chapter Book)

The Smallest Turtle, by Lynley Dodd (Gareth Stevens, 2000)
A newborn turtle must make the dangerous journey across the beach to the sea.

Stina, by Lena Anderson (Greenwillow, 1989)
Every summer, Stina would go to visit her grandfather at his house by the sea and collect treasures on the beach. This summer a tremendous storm sends her a present she will never forget.

Stringbean's Trip to the Shining Sea, by Vera Williams (Scholastic, 1991)
Stringbean describes his trip to the Pacific Ocean through a series of postcards.

Swimmy, by Leo Lionni (Econo-Clad, 1999)
Swimmy, the only black fish in the school and the fastest swimmer, is the only one to escape the jaws of a large tuna. Swimmy discovers the wonders of the ocean as he searches for a new school to belong to.

The Two-Thousand-Pound Goldfish, by Betsy Byars (Harper Trophy, 2000)
Warren escapes into movie fantasies while he awaits the return of his mother, who is hiding from the FBI. (Chapter Book)

Whales' Song, by Dyan Sheldon (Scholastic, 1991)
After hearing her grandmother's stories of the singing of whales when they are left a special gift, Lilly leaves a present at the shore and waits.

Winter Whale, by Joanne Ryder (Morrow Junior Books, 1991)
A child experiences life in the ocean when he is turned into a humpback whale.

The following books are out of print, but may be available from the local library.

Danger on the Arctic Ice, by Elizabeth Sackett (Little, Brown, 1991)
As summer approaches, a small harp seal encounters danger from hunters and animals alike. (Chapter Book)

The Girl Who Danced With Dolphins, by Frank DeSaix (Farrar Straus Giroux, 1991)
After Adrianne is rescued from a shark by a dolphin, she has a beautiful dream about this heroic animal.

Go Fish, by Lucy Dickens (Viking Press, 1991)
Herbert needs to test out the waters after all of his food sources desert him.

Greyling, by Jane Yolen (Philomel Books, 1991)
A magical selchie becomes a boy on land to bring happiness to a fisherman and his wife, but returns to the sea to save a drowning man.

Hansy's Mermaid, by Trinka Hakes Noble (Dial Press, 1983)

> After a Dutch family finds a mermaid and puts her to work for them, their youngest son tries to help her return to the sea.

John Tabor's Ride, by Edward C. Day (Alfred A. Knopf, 1989)

> John is not excited about his first whaling voyage until he ends up going on an extraordinary journey.

Jonah and the Big Fish, by Sekiya Miyoshi (Abingdon, 1982)

> God speaks to Jonah through a giant rainbow fish and orders him to travel to a faraway city to warn them of their ultimate destruction if they do not change their evil ways.

The Seal Mother, by Mordicai Gerstein (Dial Books for Young Readers, 1986)

> Based on a Scottish folk tale, a fisherman tricks a seal-turned-woman into staying with him for seven years.

The Seashell Song, by Susie Jenkin-Pearce and Claire Fletcher (Lothrop, Lee & Shepard, 1992)

> A young girl listens to the song of a seashell and wonders about all of the hidden treasures of the sea.

Very Last First Time, by Jan Andrews (Atheneum, 1985)

> Eva, an Inuit girl, gets to go down under the ice to search for mussels along the bottom of the seabed.

■ Science Activities

Submarine

Obtain a large cardboard box (similar to a refrigerator box) and make a class submarine. Turn the box on its side and cut out peepholes. Paint and decorate the box to your liking and fill it with books and information about oceans, sea life, and submarines. Students can make fish to hang around the box to give it an underwater atmosphere.

Research Project

Have students choose a particular type of fish or sea animal (octopus, seahorse, goldfish, shark, etc.), research it thoroughly, then write a paper and make a model of (or draw a detailed picture of) the fish they have chosen. The model can be made of fabric, papier-mâché, stuffed brown paper, clay, etc. (But try to make it easy enough so that they can do most of the model on their own.) The paper should include the following points:

- name and detailed description of the fish
- where the fish lives (in what zone of the ocean)
- what the fish eats
- how it defends itself
- how the fish contributes to its environment

Depending on the age of your students, this would be a good opportunity to teach them the proper steps to use in writing a paper. Have them write an outline of what the paper will include, take notes from their sources, arrange the notes to follow their outlines, write a rough draft, and write the finished product.

Fish Shelters

Ask the students: What do fish use as shelter? Which fish carry their shelters around with them? Which depend on coral or other shelters provided by the ocean? Which fish are predatory and worry little about shelter? Have students research different varieties of fish and what they use for "homes." Make a chart dividing the fish into categories depending on their use of shelter.

Coral

As a class, research different types of coral and have the students create their own reference books. Have the students draw a picture of each type of coral they find on one page of the book and write the name and a brief summary of the coral on the adjacent page. Create covers for the books using old wallpaper, construction paper, or fabric.

By the Sea

Fish live at different depths in the ocean. Why? Have the students research the characteristics of fish that live near the surface (e.g., they usually are smaller, they eat algae), fish that live in the middle depths (e.g., they are quick moving, they are predatory, they have streamlined bodies), and fish that live near the ocean's floor (they are slow moving, they eat food off the ocean floor, they are flat fish).

Demonstrate this scenario by taping together several sheets of blue construction paper (changing shades as you move from one zone to the next). Discuss the different types of fish and how far down they live in the ocean. Have the students design different fish out of paper and other available materials and place these fish in the proper place in your ocean. You can also place drawings of the proper vegetation in your scene.

Aquarium

If possible, set up a real aquarium. You can get a small tank and two or three fish for $20.00–$25.00. If you cannot set up an aquarium, discuss what items go into an aquarium. Use facts about aquariums as a math quiz: How many quarts of water can a 20-gallon tank hold? If each fish requires 5 gallons of water, how many fish can live in a 200-gallon tank? If each fish needs two plants, how many plants will you need for seven fish? Students can also keep a journal of the activity they see going on inside the aquarium.

Fish/Whales

Have the students compare fish and whales. Use a Venn Diagram with two large, overlapping circles. In the center section (the parts of the circle that overlap) list the characteristics that fish and whales have in common. In one outer circle, list characteristics that pertain only to fish. In the other outer circle, list characteristics that pertain only to whales. Older students could do a three-way diagram or chart that includes dolphins, whales, and fish.

Blue Whale

The largest animal in the ocean is the blue whale. The smallest animals are called plankton. Have students draw a chart of an ocean food chain that starts with plankton and ends with the blue whale. (*Hint:* Start with what the blue whale eats and work backwards.) You can also use a measuring tape to map out the length of the blue whale on the playground, in the classroom, or in your yard. Determine the sizes of a variety of other fish, map them out, and compare them to the blue whale. Older students can make a bar graph showing the sizes of the different fish you mapped out.

Whaling

As a class, discuss and research why whaling has been outlawed throughout most of the world. Ask the students: What would be possible reasons why some people still feel that whaling should be legal? What industries depend on whaling? Which cultures have a strong tie with the whaling industry? After the students' research is complete, each student should decide where he or she stands on this issue. Have the students write letters to their representative or senator outlining their views, giving reasons to support their opinions.

Symmetry

The animals of the sea come in many different shapes. As a class, collect pictures of several different sea creatures (starfish, octopus, fish, clams, etc.) from nature magazines. Determine which creatures look symmetrical (if divided in half, the halves are mirror images of each other). Draw lines of symmetry on the different animals and see if your guesses were correct. (*Note:* The direction in which you draw the line can determine if the object is symmetrical. Humans would be symmetrical if a vertical line were drawn, but not if a horizontal line were drawn! You may want to try different ways to "divide" the animals to check for symmetry.)

At the Bottom of the Sea

Scientists believe that many deep-sea creatures have yet to be discovered. Have the students research some sea creatures that live at the very bottom of the ocean. Have them notice the special adaptations that the creatures have to exist in their deep, dark environment. Students can draw a picture of one of the creatures they learned about in their research. Discuss what special features it has, and how it uses them. Students can prepare a report on this creature to present to fellow students. They can explain where the creature is found and present other interesting facts about it.

Food Chains

Have the students illustrate five food chains that involve sea creatures. Ask the students: Are only sea creatures dependent on sea life for food? Which animals eat sea creatures? Which animals eat fish? Which sea creatures eat land animals? Which animals live and eat both in and out of the water?

Shell Animals

Gather a variety of shells and let the students examine them. Number the shells and have the students write down which sea creature they think once inhabited each shell. Have books available to verify the correct answers and to provide the students with more information about the animal that lived in the shell. Use these same shells for math exercises (addition, subtraction, etc.). You can also sort the shells while studying size, shape, and color.

Regeneration

A starfish is able to regenerate an appendage if it is bitten off by a predator or lost in some other way. Discuss whether there are other sea animals who have this same ability. Research animals that can regenerate parts of their bodies. Discuss how life would be different for human beings if we had this ability.

Aquatic Scavenger Hunt

Plan a visit to a local aquarium (many zoos include excellent aquariums as part of their exhibits). Before you take your trip, compile a list of items for the children to find while at the aquarium. Give each child a copy of the list of items. Leave enough space after each item for the students to write down exactly what they saw and where they saw it. Following are some suggestions:

an animal that lives in water but breathes air

an animal that uses camouflage for protection

an animal that looks like a flower (or resembles a land animal)

an animal whose teeth are easily visible

an animal that stays on the bottom of the aquarium

■ Creative Writing Activities

Following are instructions to give the students for various writing activities.

- Cut out two large outlines of fish. On one fish, write a story about a fish that wanted to walk, fly, or talk. Decorate the other fish and use it as a cover for your story.

- Write a story about a time when you were nervous or afraid to do something, but after you completed the event, you felt proud. (*Very Last First Time* by Andrews)

- Compare several different versions of the Grimm Brothers' tale about an enchanted fish that grants a fisherman several wishes. What is the same about each story? How do they differ? Why do you think so many versions of this story were written? (*The Fish of Gold by* Valeri; *The Magic Fish* by Littledale) Take a piece of paper and divide it into sections based on how many different versions of the story you are comparing. List similarities and differences of each story in a column with the name of the story at the top. (Write similarities in blue ink, differences in red.) Choose your favorite version of the stories you have compared and write down the reasons for your choice.

- Create a magazine that discusses your recent scuba diving trip. Write several different articles detailing the trip from several different angles. Outline the preparations you made for the trip; explain the technical aspects of the trip—what equipment you used, how deep you went, how long you could stay under, and any problems you encountered; and describe what you saw and how it felt. Illustrate your magazine articles with pictures from your adventure and of the animal life that you saw. Design a cover for your magazine.

- If you could be any sea creature, what would you be? Write a story about your new life as this animal.

- What would it be like to live in a submarine? If you were going on a three-week submarine mission, what items would you take with you? What would you enjoy most? What would you miss most? Write a letter home telling your family about your trip.

- Have you ever seen someone sad or unjustly treated and tried to help? Describe the situation and what you did to help. What was the outcome? How did it make you feel? Were you glad you intervened? (*Hansy's Mermaid* by Noble)

- Write a story about a creature that you discovered on your last deep-sea expedition. What special features does it have, and how does it use them? Name your creature and draw a picture of it to go along with your story. Be sure to explain where you found your creature and how you discovered it.

- You are a newborn turtle just hatching out of your shell. Write an essay describing your experiences and feelings as you come out of your shell and make your way across the beach to the sea. (*The Smallest Turtle* by Dodd)

- Imagine you are a dolphin who has been changed into a human. You must remain in human form for one year and then you can decide whether to return to the sea or remain on land. Make a list of pros and cons for each way of life to help you make your decision. You will need to determine what type of life you are living as a human and research life as a dolphin before making your choice. Write a short essay stating your choice and the reasons for it. (*The Seal Mother* by Gerstein; *Hansy's Mermaid* by Noble; *Greyling* by Yolen)

■ Art Activities

Following are instructions to give the students for various art activities.

- Read *Jonah and the Big Fish* by Miyoshi. Make a chalk drawing, similar to the illustrations found in the book, depicting Jonah and the fish.

- Make a poster showing the different types of animals that live at different depths of the sea. Decorate your poster to look like the actual zone of the ocean by putting in the proper plant life and coloring the background in an appropriate color. (*Sea Squares* by Hulme)

- Tie dye an old sheet using blue and green dyes to make it look like an ocean. On your ocean, add different examples of fish, coral, plants, and other objects you might find in the sea. Make these objects out of felt, fabric, and iron-on patches, or paint them on with fabric paint. To tie dye, gather a small handful of material from the sheet. Approximately 2 to 4 inches down from the top of the gather, wrap a rubber band tightly around the fabric. Repeat this process until you have as many gathered sections as you wish. Dip the fabric into fabric dye and hold it there until it has attained the desired color. It is advisable to wear rubber gloves during this procedure. After the dying is complete, rinse the fabric thoroughly according to the manufacturer's instructions and remove rubber bands.

- Using a shoebox, make a diorama of the sea. Cut out one short end of the shoebox and cover the opening with colored plastic wrap. Cut a small peephole in the opposite short end of the shoebox. You could paint the sides of the inside of the box to resemble water, glue sand to the bottom inside the box, make coral and plants out of construction and tissue paper, hang fish from the inside of the lid, and so forth. When you have finished, hold the box up to the light and look through the peephole at your seascape.

- Design your own sea creature. Use "recyclables" (egg cartons, milk cartons, straws, and a variety of papers and fabrics) to make your underwater creature. (*Cyrus the Unsinkable Sea Serpent* by Peet)

- Use a 3-by-5-foot piece of paper (or poster board) to create an underwater scene. Using crayons, draw animals and plant life that you would see in the ocean. When you are finished, paint over the entire scene with blue tempera paint or blue watercolors. This is a good project to do in small groups.

- Research the artist Homer Winslow. What type of art is he famous for? Compare several of his works. What feeling or point do you think he is trying to convey through his work?

- Make your own coral. Shape hardening clay into the desired coral shape. Use a pencil or toothpick to make small indentations in your coral. You can attach the clay to a rock to make it look as if it is actually coral in the ocean. Paint it when it is dry.

- Think of your favorite song about the sea or a sea creature. Write the words of the song on separate pages like a book. Make illustrations to go along with the words on each page. Design a cover for your "song book." (*Baby Beluga* by Raffi)

- Make an ocean scene inside a sealable plastic bag. Place colored aquarium stones in the bottom of your bag and then fill the bag three-quarters full with water. Put two or three drops of blue food coloring in the water and mix it up (for effect). Make a sea creature out of clay to live at the bottom of your ocean. Make coral and sea life out of different colors of flat foam (available at craft stores). When you have completed your scene, push in on the sides of the bag to put your ocean in motion.

- Design an ocean scene as seen through the porthole of a submarine. Cut a large circle out of the center of a piece of construction paper. Be careful not to cut through the edge of the paper. Discard the circle and retain the piece of paper with the hole cut out of the center. Tape a piece of blue plastic wrap over the hole to resemble water and decorate around the hole on the construction paper to resemble a porthole. On a white piece of paper, draw or paint an ocean scene. Tape your scene to the back of the construction paper so that the scene shows through the plastic wrap and the porthole.

- Use packing peanuts to make sea creatures. Glue (or sew) eight peanuts together at the tips to make an octopus. Glue (or sew) other pieces together to make coral structures or your own sea creatures. Make a starfish or squid. Be creative! Decorate your creations using paint, glitter, sequins, or markers.

- Make an underwater scene that looks like a fish tank. Use a box that has a clear acetate top (like the ones Christmas cards come in). Cover the bottom and the sides of the box with blue construction paper to resemble water. Cut out pictures of coral and seaweed (or draw your own on colored construction paper) and glue them to the blue paper. Then draw or cut out sea creatures and place them in your scene. Put the acetate cover back on the box and glue it in place. You can glue some of your sea creatures or sea plants onto the acetate cover before you put it over the box, if you like. Glue a piece of string or yarn to the back of your box so you can hang your ocean fish tank on your wall.

- Make an octopus from an old egg carton (cardboard cartons work best). Cut out two-cup sections from the egg carton and paint them black, gray, or whatever color you want your octopus to be. While the cups are drying, cut eight pieces of yarn. Each piece should be about 5 inches long. Tie a knot in one end of each piece of yarn. These will be used for the octopus's legs. After the cups have dried, poke eight small holes in the bottom of one of the cups. Feed a piece of yarn through each hole. The knot will hold it in place. You can also knot the ends of the legs that stick out of the cups after you have fed the yarn through the holes. Place one painted cup on top of the other cup (open ends together) and glue them in place. Make a mouth and eyes out of white and colored paper and glue them in place.

- Make a sea turtle. Cut off the edges of a piece of green construction paper so that they are rounded and the paper is an oblong shape. Cut three 3-inch-long slits at the two oblong ends going toward the center of the paper. Overlap the paper at these slits and staple it together so that the paper takes on a 3-D shape that resembles a turtle's shell. Place your shell in the center of a larger, brown sheet of paper and trace the outer edge of the shell. Remove your shell and draw the outline of a head and four legs in the proper place on the shell you traced. Cut out your drawing. Staple the cutout to the bottom edge of your shell. The face and legs will stick out. Decorate your shell with paints, markers, or glitter. Put eyes on the head, and your turtle is complete.

- Make poke-and-sew cards in marine life designs. Draw your favorite sea creature on a piece of Styrofoam (e.g., a clean meat tray) or on a heavy piece of cardboard. After your drawing is complete, poke holes in the Styrofoam or cardboard around the outline of the animal you drew. Sew yarn through the holes to outline your animal in the colors you choose.

- Make a fish mobile out of small (lunch-bag sized) paper bags. For each fish you make, place a paper bag flat on your working surface. To make the face, fold the upper corner of the closed end of the bag toward the center of the bag and glue or tape it in place. Repeat this process with the lower corner. You will have formed a pointed "face" at the closed end of the bag. Color or paint the designs you want on each of your fish. You can draw an eye on either side of the face or glue eyes you have bought in place. Stuff the bag with bits of newspaper until it is as plump as you want it. Tie a string around the open end of the bag (about 2 inches from the end) to form the tail. Poke or punch a hole in the top of the head of each fish. Feed string or ribbon through the hole and attach each fish to a coat hanger to form your mobile.

- Try your hand at the ancient Japanese art of Gyota Ku. Obtain a fresh fish and clean it well with soap and water. Dry the fish carefully with paper towels. Place the fish on several layers of newspaper. Be sure to spread out the fins (you may want to secure them in place) so that they will show up in your picture. Paint the surface of one side of the fish with acrylic or tempera paint using a small brush. Paint against the grain of the scales and then gently smooth them down. Press a piece of paper, a plain T-shirt, or a piece of plain cloth against the fish, gently but firmly. Peel off the paper or cloth slowly to avoid smudges. You will have a beautiful fish print. You can add touches like eyes to your print.

- Make your own rendition of a coral reef. Wrap a piece of sandpaper around an empty can that has been cleaned and dried. (An empty soup, vegetable, or nut can will do nicely.) Glue the sandpaper in place. Cut out pictures of coral, shells, plant life, and small fish from a magazine. Glue the pictures in place to make your scene.

- Make a fish windsock. On a large piece of paper (approximately 12 by 18 inches), draw the outline of a fish head. Allow about a 2-inch margin in front of the head (where the mouth is). This margin will be used to secure the fish to a coat hanger. Decorate the fish head however you wish. Glue multicolored tissue streamers to the back end of the fish head. Then fold 1 inch of the 2-inch margin over the bottom of a coat hanger and tape it in place.

- Make a 3-dimensional fish. Draw your fish shape on a piece of paper at least 8 1/2 by 11 inches in size. (It can be bigger.) As you draw the inside design on the fish, be sure to include seven curved lines (like scales), approximately 1/2 to 3/4 inch apart, and all the same length. Begin the lines about 1/2 inch from the top of the fish and draw them to within 1 inch of the bottom of the fish. Paint the entire fish. Trace all of the lines you drew with black magic marker. Cut out the fish. Then cut slits in the body of the face where the seven lines are. Weave a tube from an empty roll of paper towels through the slits in the body of the fish to give it a 3-D look. You might want to paint the outside of the paper towel roll before inserting it in your fish.

- Read *Stringbean's Trip to the Shining Sea* by Williams. Design your own postcard showing a place you have visited or read about. Write a message from this place to a friend, describing where you are.

Chapter 2
Deserts

■ Teaching Resources

Books containing experiment(s) relating to the subject matter are marked with a plus sign (+) before and after.

P/I *Cactus Hotel,* by Brenda Z. Guiberson (Henry Holt, 1991)
Describes the life cycle of the saguaro cactus and other desert animals that call it home.

P/I *Desert Giant, the World of the Saguaro Cactus,* by Barbara Bash (Little, Brown, 1990)
Looks at the saguaro cactus's life cycle and ecosystem, with nice watercolor illustrations and brief text.

P/I *Wonders of the Desert,* by Louis Sabin (Troll, 1989)
Describes the plants and animals of the desert, with watercolor illustrations.

P/I/U *Deserts,* by Michael George (Creative Education, 1992)
Wonderful, full-page photographs, with brief overlaying text; discusses the deserts' characteristics and the life found there.

I/U *Deserts,* by Lynn Hassler Kaufman and Kenn Kaufman (Houghton Mifflin, 1993)
Peterson Field Guide coloring book loaded with information on desert plant and animal life in North America.

I *Deserts,* by Seymour Simon (Mulberry Books, 1997)
Has descriptions of deserts, their nature and characteristics, locations, and formation.

I *This Place Is Dry,* by Vicki Cobb (Walker, 1993)
A nicely done book on Arizona's Sonora Desert describing its people and animals. Includes information on Hoover Dam.

■ Reading Selections

Books marked with an asterisk (*) before and after the title are related to activities in the activity sections of this chapter.

The Adventures of Ali Baba Bernstein, by Johanna Hurwitz (William Morrow, 1985)
David is convinced that his life will be more exciting if he changes his name to Ali Baba. (Chapter Book) (Other "Ali Baba Bernstein" books are available.)

Ali Baba and the Forty Thieves, by Walter McVitty (Abrams, 1989)
The story of Ali Baba, who must deal with the thieves who are pillaging Baghdad. (Chapter Book)

Clean Enough, by Kevin Henkes (Greenwillow, 1982)
    A little boy finds more to enjoy in the bath than just getting clean.

The Desert Is Theirs, by Byrd Baylor (Macmillan, 1975)
    The plant and animal life of the desert is described in poetic verse.

Desert Voices, by Byrd Baylor (Scribner, 1981)
    A variety of inhabitants of the desert describe the beauty of their home. (Chapter Book)

Gila Monsters Meet You at the Airport, by Marjorie Weinman Sharmat (Econo-Clad, 1999)
    A little boy is nervous about his move from New York City to a city in the West because of ideas he has about what it will be like there.

Happy Birthday, Dear Duck, by Eve Bunting (Houghton Mifflin, 1990)
    All of duck's birthday presents require water for use, which presents a problem, except for his last and best one.

How the Camel Got His Hump, by Rudyard Kipling (Rabbit Ear Books, 1995)
    A tall tale explaining how the camel received his hump after saying, "Humph!" once too often.

The Legend of the Indian Paintbrush, by Tomie de Paola (G. P. Putnam's Sons, 1988)
    A legend explaining the beautiful colors of the Indian Paintbrush.

Look Again! The Second Ultimate Spot-the-Difference Book, by April Wilson (Dial Books for Young Readers, 1992)
    Find different plants and animals that use camouflage to hide in 12 habitats.

Mojave, by Diane Siebert (HarperCollins Juvenile, 1992)
    The land and inhabitants of the desert are described in poetic text.

Pamela Camel, by Bill Peet (Houghton Mifflin, 1986)
    A circus camel who does not have the qualities to perform in the big top runs away and proves that she is far from ordinary.

The Pueblo, by Charlotte Yue and David Yue (Houghton Mifflin, 1990)
    Tells the story of the special relationship to the land shared by the Pueblo people.

Secret of the Missing Camel, by Page McBrier (Troll, 1987)
    Oliver's pet-care service faces a dilemma when a camel he is watching gets loose. (Chapter Book)

Shabanu, Daughter of the Wind, by Suzanne Fisher Staples (Random House, 1989)
    An 11-year-old daughter of a nomad must marry an older man who can bring prestige to the family, or risk the consequences of defying her father's wishes and the customs of the area. (Chapter Book)

This House Is Made of Mud, by Ken Buchanan (Northland Publishing, 1991)
    Follows the actions of a family as they build an adobe house in the desert.

The Trek, by Ann Jonas (Mulberry Books, 1989)
    A little girl tells of her trip across the desert on her way to school.

The following books are out of print, but may be available from the local library.

Coyote Dreams, by Susan Nunes (Atheneum, 1988)
> When evening falls, coyotes come to a suburban garden and bring with them dreams of their special desert world.

Desert December, by Dorian Haarhoff (Clarion Books, 1992)
> An African boy journeys through the desert to be reunited with his parents and to see his new sister. (Chapter Book)

Nadia the Willful, by Sue Alexander (Pantheon Books, 1983)
> Nadia will not let her favorite brother be forgotten after he disappears in the desert.

Sister Yessa's Story, by Karen Greenfield (Laura Geringer, 1992)
> Yessa, the storyteller, tells the animals the story of how they were all deposited on the Earth in the areas that they now consider their homes.

Wind, Sand, and Sky, by Rebecca Caudill (E. P. Dutton, 1976)
> A collection of poetry with desert themes. (Chapter Book)

■ Science Activities

Plant Adaptations

Even in very arid climates, some plants have adapted to survive. Have the students research the following plants and list some characteristics of each. Discuss what common characteristics the plants have and how these features help them survive.

> saguaro cactus (Cereus giganteus)
>
> prickly pear (Opuntia ficus-indica)
>
> Welwitschia (Welwitschia mirabilis)
>
> night-blooming cereus (Selenicereus spp)
>
> agave (Agave americana)
>
> ocotillo (Fouquieria splendens)
>
> blue Kleinia (Senecio articulatus)

Some characteristics include the ability to store water for long periods; waxy coatings to retard water loss; a shallow, but wide-spreading, root system; small leaves; and spines to protect them from animals. Bring in a small cactus and a broad-leaf plant. Dissect both of the plants and have the students compare them.

Nomads

Many nomads still exist today who spend their lives constantly moving from place to place. As a class, compare and contrast their lives to the life you live. Ask the students: Why do they move around? How does their way of dressing differ from yours, and why? What provisions would they depend on obtaining from an oasis? What provisions do you depend on getting from the grocery store? Why do you think someone would choose to live this kind of life? How do nomads make their money? Students can write a short play depicting what it would be like to be a child traveling with a nomadic family.

Animal and Plant Life

As a class, study the animals and plants that inhabit the desert regions. Discuss what special features they have that allow them to adapt to the desert's climate. Have the students pick a particular animal and one particular plant and list the adaptations they possess that allow them to survive in the desert.

Habitation

People who live in the desert must protect themselves from both extremely high and very low temperatures that are encountered there. Have the students research the various types of housing and clothing that desert dwellers use to provide insulation from the heat and cold.

Pyramids

Have the students look into the history of the pyramids. Ask them: Why were they constructed? Who was the "Sphinx" created for? Was there a real King Tutankhamen? Why are archeologists interested in the pyramids? What types of articles are found inside a pyramid? As a class, research one particular pyramid. Make a drawing or model of it. Have the students write a research paper that includes the following points:

- When was the pyramid built?
- Where was it built?
- Who was it built for? Find out as much as you can about this person and his or her background.
- Are there any legends surrounding this pyramid?
- Have archeologists studied this pyramid? What have they found in it? What theories do they have about the inhabitants?

Australia

One-third of Australia is desert. Have the students research the animal life of Australia. An excellent Web site for studying Australian animals is *http://ausinternet.com/ettamogah*. (This site was accessed in February 2001 and was active at that time.) A fun activity to do with this Web site is a scavenger hunt. Download the photos of some of the different Australian animals and give copies to the students. They can search the Australian map for these animals, read the Web site information, and then write one fact (or one paragraph) about that animal. Ask the students: What animals are unique to Australia? Which animals live in the desert there? What are marsupials? What unique feature do marsupials have? What marsupial do we have in the United States (the opossum)?

Camels

Have the students research the camel to find out what makes it so perfectly suited to life in the desert. Students can make a diagram of a camel and label the various parts of its anatomy that help it withstand life in the desert. Discuss whether camels exist in Australia. If so, what part do they play in the Australian economy?

Pueblo Indians

As a class, research the lives and culture of the Pueblo Indians. Ask the students: What were their religious beliefs? How did these beliefs affect their everyday lives? How did they construct their homes? Have the students construct a Pueblo village. (A good group activity.) Villages can be made by painting used cereal boxes or brown paper lunch bags. If using lunch bags, stuff them with crumpled newspaper after they are painted. Make roofs for the buildings by drawing designs on construction paper and attaching it to the top of the buildings. Use the research they did on the Indians to make the villages authentic.

Rainfall

Chart the amount of rainfall in a U.S. desert. As a class, compare the rainfall with two nearby cities. Choose a coastal city and add its rainfall figure to the chart. Discuss the results the class has charted.

Resources

Ask the students: What resources do we get from the desert? Look into the plants that grow in the desert and the animals that live there. What everyday products do we get from these sources (oil, petroleum jelly, figs, olives, olive oil, aloe, dates)?

Cacti

To someone living outside of the desert, a cactus may seem to be a somewhat useless plant. Have the students research the uses of various cactus plants (industrial, for animals, etc.). Discuss the different types of cacti. Have the students research how to care for a cactus. Purchase one for the classroom, if that is possible. Does your cactus require different care than your other plants?

Desertification

Older students can research the causes of desert expansion (desertification). Ask the students: What are the results of desert expansion? What areas of the world have been affected by it? Are any steps being taken to prevent further desertification?

To Be or Not To Be a Desert

Not all scientists agree on the definition of a desert. Some think that a desert is any region in which the amount of moisture lost each year is more than the precipitation that falls. Other scientists think that the type of soil and plant life that exist there are the determining factors. There are even regions near the North and South poles that some scientists consider desert regions. Have the students consult various resources and decide which definition of a desert they agree with. Have them support their opinion with as many facts as possible. On a world map, color in the desert regions that fit that definition.

Sand

Collect sand from different areas. This takes some preplanning—ask students and friends to collect some over the summer. Have the students compare the colors and grain size of the different sands. Have them try to determine from what substance each type of sand is made (e.g., black beaches are made from lava) and research where they would find white beaches, black beaches, and pink beaches.

■ Creative Writing Activities

Following are instructions to give the students for various writing activities.

- You are traveling across the desert when, suddenly, you are hit by a sandstorm. Using your five senses, describe the sandstorm. What does it look like, feel like, and so forth? Compare your ability to withstand the forces of the storm with that of the camel you are riding. (*The Trek* by Jonas)
- A nomad has sold you a magic carpet and a magic lamp. Where would you go on your carpet? Write an adventure story about your travels. What three wishes would you make with your lamp? Describe your wishes and the results they bring.

- You are on a trip to Egypt and have toured the pyramids. Write a letter home describing your experiences on the tour. Be sure to include historical facts about the pyramids that you learned on your tour.

- Read *Sister Yessa's Story* by Greenfield. Pretend you are the one who must decide where each animal of the world should live. Write a humorous memorandum to your staff telling them where you want the animals placed and why. Be imaginative! The decision is yours!

- Pretend you are an Indian in the U.S. Southwest in the 1800s. Describe how you get your food.

- You are a cactus, and no animal will come near you because of your prickly needles. If you could be transformed into another desert plant, what would you become? Why? Would you want to be transformed? If not, why not?

- You are moving from your city home to a small town in a desert region. What changes would you expect? What sports will be popular? What activities might be available to you? Will the people be different? Write a letter to a friend describing your feelings, your expectations, and what you found in your new home. (*Gila Monsters Meet You at the Airport* by Sharmat)

- Write a story about a hungry rattlesnake who must set up a trap to capture its food.

- Think about the animals that make their homes in the desert. Write a poem about these animals, how they live, the sounds they make, and the feel of the desert. (*Coyote Dreams* by Nunes)

- During the month of July, Bombay, India, receives 24 inches of rainfall. July is also the peak time for Arab tourism in Bombay. Write a decisive argument for why you, an Arab tourist, would want to visit Bombay during this time of the year.

■ Art Activities

Following are instructions to give the students for various art activities.

- Make a sand painting. To color sand, mix dry sand (enough sand to fill whatever container you have chosen) with liquid tempera paint (make sand in several different colors) and allow it to dry. Layer the different-colored sand in a clear container (with a lid) using a spoon. Heap some layers high against the sides of the container. Push depressions into other layers by using a toothpick to push one color down into a lower-level color. Use your imagination to create the pattern you want. After your container is filled, put the lid on tightly so nothing disturbs your artwork. You can also place about 4 inches of soil on top of your artwork and plant a small cactus in it.

- Find a picture of the Taj Mahal in an encyclopedia or book about India. Draw your own version of an Indian palace.

- Plan an Arabian music festival. Students can listen to music such as the "Sabre Dance" or other songs from this region. Students can make finger cymbals and try belly dancing, or simply let the music direct their dancing. Finger cymbals can be made out of bottle caps or milk jug lids taped onto elastic. Make snake armbands by winding different-colored pipe cleaners together and wrapping them around your upper arm. (*Ali Baba and the Forty Thieves* by McVitty; *Wind, Sand, and Sky* by Caudill)

- Using colored sand (see instructions in first art activity), make a textured scene. Draw a desert picture including any objects that come to mind. Then color your sand in the shades you want to use on your picture. Put glue on the areas of your picture that you want to add sand to and then sprinkle the colored sand on top of the glue. Pat down the sand gently with your fingertips. After the glue has dried, shake off any excess sand.

- Paint a desert scene on a piece of sandpaper. Use tempera paints for the best effect. You can also cut out a frame of colored construction paper, wallpaper scraps, or wrapping paper and paste the paper around the outside edges of your sandpaper artwork. (*Mojave* by Siebert)

- Make a desert evening scene using colored chalk. Choose your colors to coincide with colors found in the desert at sunset. Smear the chalk you use for the sky to make your sunset look realistic. (*Legend of the Indian Paintbrush* by de Paola)

- Pretend you are a snake charmer. Make your own turban out of a towel wrapped around your head. Create a basket out of papier-mâché using one of the following sets of ingredients:

> 3 cups water
> 1 cup flour
>
> 1 cup wallpaper paste
> 3 cups water
>
> 2 cups glue
> 1 cup water
>
> Depending on which ingredients you choose, stir the water into the flour, paste, or glue until the mixture is smooth and creamy. Tear sheets of newspaper into strips about 1 inch wide and 13 1/2 inches long. Cover the strips with the papier-mâché mixture by pulling each strip through the mixture you prepared. To make your basket, start with a coffee can or similar sized can (or small bowl). Wrap one layer of newspaper strips around your can in one direction. Smooth down the strips and then wrap another layer of newspaper strips around your can in the opposite direction. Continue this process, varying your wrapping style, until you have achieved the shape that you desire. Allow your object to dry in an open area for two or more days (or, under adult supervision, dry it in an oven set at 150 degrees Fahrenheit (65 degrees Celsius), checking it periodically). You can paint your basket after it has dried,. Use an old tie stuffed with rags or newspaper, a piece of rope, or a plastic toy for your snake. Investigate the history of snake charmers. Prepare a short play or pantomime that tells the story of the snake charmer.

- Make a picture cube of desert scenes. Draw five desert scenes, cut five desert pictures out of magazines, or use five photographs of a trip you took to the desert. Draw the pictures on poster board or mount the magazine pictures or photographs on poster board. Cut each picture and the poster board into a 5- or 6-inch square. Lay four of the squares side by side and tape them together (on the outside) with colored tape. Fold the strip of squares to form a cube and tape the first picture to the fourth one. Tape the fifth picture to the top of the cube. The bottom can be just a plain piece of poster board or a piece of poster board with felt glued on it. Attach the bottom of your cube and you have a desert photo-square.

- In some areas, such as parts of Mexico, large cactus plants are decorated at Christmastime. Children make brightly colored ornaments and hang them from the cactus plants. These ornaments are geometrical or striped and are not based on "Christmas" colors or symbols. Design an ornament to hang on a Christmas cactus. You can even make a large cutout of a cactus and hang your ornaments on it.

- Make your own desert snake out of an old tie. Sew the small end of a tie closed. Choose a tie with colors that remind you of the desert. Stuff the snake with fiberfill. You may need a long stick or rod to push the fiberfill inside. Cut out a square piece of felt that matches the size of the large end of the tie. Sew the square to the back side of the wide end of the tie to close the opening. Put a face on your snake by adding eyes, a tongue, fangs, and so forth, using sequins, pom-poms, and felt.

- Make a desert diorama. Cut off the short end of a shoebox and cover it with a piece of colored plastic wrap. Cut a peephole in the other short end of the shoebox. Use plastic straws, toothpicks, or modeling clay to make a desert scene inside your shoebox (facing the peephole). Put the lid on the shoebox and view your scene through the peephole.

Chapter 3
Polar Regions

■ Teaching Resources

Books containing experiment(s) relating to the subject matter are marked with a plus sign (+) before and after the title.

I   *Life in the Polar Lands,* by Monica Byles (Econo-Clad, 1990)
Looks at the survival of humans, plants, and animals at the North and South poles, the effects of industrial activity there, and how world weather changes affect the poles.

I   *One Day in the Alpine Tundra,* by Jean Craighead George (Thomas Y. Crowell, 1984)
Details a boy's adventure alone on the tundra during a stormy day, with pencil illustrations.

I   *This Place Is Cold,* by Vicki Cobb (Walker, 1991)
Describes the land, animals, plants, and climate of Alaska, with well-done illustrations.

I/U +*Arctic National Wildlife Refuge,*+ by Alexandra Siy (Dillon, 1991)
Describes plant and animal life on the Alaskan tundra, with helpful photographs.

■ Reading Selections

Books marked with an asterisk (*) before and after the title are related to activities in the activity sections of this chapter.

Ahoy There, Little Polar Bear, by Hans de Beer (North South Books, 1989)
Nemo, the cat, helps rescue Lars from a fishnet and get him back home where he belongs.

Arctic Memories, by Normee Ekoomiak (Owlet, 1992)
Describes a life that no longer exists for the Inuit people. Contains text in both English and Inuktitut. (Chapter Book)

Black Star, Bright Dawn, by Scott O'Dell (Juniper, 1990)
Bright Dawn faces the challenge of the Iditarod race alone when her father is injured. (Chapter Book)

A Caribou Alphabet, by Mary Beth Owens (Sunburst, 1990)
The characteristics and habits of the caribou are depicted in this alphabet book.

Dogteam, by Gary Paulsen (Yearling Books, 1995)
Shows the beauty, excitement, and danger of a night run of a dog team.

Here Is the Arctic Winter, by Madeleine Dunphy (Hyperion Books for Children, 1993)
A cumulative book introducing the animals of the cold white world.

Julie of the Wolves, by Jean Craighead George (Harper Trophy, 1973)
>An Eskimo girl gets lost on the North Slope of Alaska while running away from home and is befriended by a pack of wolves. (Chapter Book)

Little Penguin's Tale, by Audrey Wood (Harcourt Brace, 1993)
>Little Penguin is looking for fun and finds it in several spots in his polar world.

Look Again! The Second Ultimate Spot-the-Difference Book, by April Wilson (Dial Books for Young Readers, 1992)
>Find different plants and animals that use camouflage to hide in 12 habitats.

*Mama, Do You Love Me?,** by Barbara Joosse (Chronicle Books, 1991)
>A child who lives in the Arctic finds out that a mother's love is unconditional.

Maroo of the Winter Caves, by Ann Turnbull (Clarion Books, 1990)
>Maroo must take charge and lead her family to the winter camp before a blizzard strikes. (Chapter Book)

Nessa's Fish, by Nancy Luenn (Aladdin, 1997)
>Nessa protects her grandmother and the fish caught for the Eskimo village from a fox, a pack of wolves, and a bear.

Penguin Pete, by Marcus Pfister (North South Books, 1997)
>Pete plays on land with his friends and learns how to swim in the sea.

Penguin Pete and Pat, by Marcus Pfister (North South Books, 1996)
>Penguin Pete meets a lovely, blue-beaked girl penguin who changes his life.

Penguin Pete's New Friends, by Marcus Pfister (North South Books, 1995)
>Because Pete is not big enough to go on the fishing trip with the other penguins, he decides to take a trip of his own.

The Polar Express, by Chris Van Allsburg (Houghton Mifflin, 1985)
>A Caldecott Medal Book about a magical train ride that a boy takes on Christmas Eve to the North Pole to receive the first gift of Christmas from Santa himself.

Salty Takes Off, by Gloria Rand (Henry Holt, 1991)
>Salty, a dog, falls from an airplane over Alaska and must learn to survive until he can be rescued.

Secret of the Seal, by Deborah Davis (Random House Children's Books, 1994)
>Kyo, an Eskimo boy, must make a difficult choice between his family loyalty and his friendship with a seal. (Chapter Book)

The Stranger, by Chris Van Allsburg (Houghton Mifflin, 1986)
>Farmer Bailey brings home a stranger whom he inadvertently hit with his truck. The stranger's recovery seems to be linked closely with weather conditions. Could he be Jack Frost?

Tacky the Penguin, by Helen Lester (Houghton Mifflin, 1990)
>Tacky, a rather unusual penguin, shows that you don't have to fit in to be useful.

Tundra Mouse: A Storyknife Book, by Megan McDonald (Orchard, 1997)
>Two Eskimo sisters share a story about the mouse that made a nest out of tinsel from the Christmas tree.

Water Sky, by Jean Craighead George (Harper Trophy, 1989)
> A boy living with an Eskimo family learns the importance of whaling to their culture. (Chapter Book)

Woodsong, by Gary Paulsen (Bradbury Press, 1990)
> Tells the tale of a man and his family's life in the wilds of northern Minnesota with wolves, deer, and the sled dogs that make their life possible.

The following books are out of print, but may be available at the local library.

Arctic Spring, by Sue Vyner (Viking Press, 1993)
> As spring approaches, most of the Arctic animals venture out, except for a polar bear who has good reason to stay close to the den.

The Bear on the Moon, by Joanne Ryder (Morrow Junior Books, 1991)
> Relates how the polar bears came to live at the top of the world on all of the ice and snow.

The Boy Who Found the Light, by Dale Dearmond (Sierra Club Books, 1990)
> A collection of Eskimo folk tales beautifully illustrated. (Chapter Book)

Brrr!, by James Stevenson (Greenwillow Books, 1991)
> Grandpa tells Mary Ann and Louie about a really cold winter when they begin to complain about how cold it is outside.

Danger on the Arctic Ice, by Elizabeth Sackett (Little, Brown, 1991)
> As summer approaches, a small harp seal encounters danger from hunters and animals alike. (Chapter Book)

The Haunted Igloom, by Bonnie Turner (Houghton Mifflin, 1991)
> Jean-Paul becomes trapped in an igloo in the Northwest Territory and spends a terrifying time in the dark and close-to-freezing weather.

A Hunter Comes Home, by Ann Turner (Crown Publishers, 1980)
> An Eskimo boy spends the summer learning old ways from his grandfather after a year spent away at a white man's boarding school. (Chapter Book)

Ice Warrior, by Ruth Riddell (Macmillan, 1992)
> Rob hopes that iceboating will be his way of proving himself to his new stepfather. (Chapter Book)

Ralph's Frozen Tale, by Elise Primavera (G. P. Putnam's Sons, 1991)
> A friendly polar bear helps a fearless explorer on his journey to the North Pole.

Tale of Antarctica, by Ulco Glimmerveen (Scholastic, 1989)
> The story of penguins in Antarctica demonstrates how their environment is being threatened by the pollution from man's presence.

Tobias Goes Ice Fishing, by Ole Hertz (Carolrhoda Books, 1984)
> Tobias and his father fish through the ice that covers the inlet.

Very Last First Time, by Jan Andrews (Atheneum, 1985)
> Eva, an Inuit girl, gets to go down under the ice to search for mussels along the bottom of the seabed.

■ Science Activities

South Pole

Several explorers tried to be the first to reach the South Pole (Roald Amundsen, James Cook, Richard Byrd, Robert Scott, Lincoln Ellsworth, Charles Wilkes). Have the students research the explorers to discover when the different expeditions took place. Make a time line ranging from 1800 to 2000 and, for each explorer, make a line that depicts when his expedition(s) took place. Ask the students: Who was the first to reach the South Pole? Were all expeditions successful?

Penguins

As a class, research different types of penguins. Ask the students: What species live at the North Pole? (None!) How tall can the emperor penguins get? What do they eat? Have each student cut five penguin outlines out of white paper. Have them write one penguin fact on each of the birds and color the wings black. Make a mobile by hanging the five penguins from a coat hanger.

The Antarctica Treaty

The Antarctica Treaty was signed by 12 countries. It declares that Antarctica is to be used only for scientific research and exploration. Which 12 countries signed this agreement? Have the students research what resources are protected and what other stipulations are contained in this treaty. (There is no mining of coal or metal ore, no oil exploration, no military bases or nuclear weapons, and no disposal of radioactive materials, and the plants and animals are protected.) Discuss what makes this treaty so important in today's world.

Antarctica

Few animals can survive the harsh weather at the South Pole, but many can survive "the icy waters" surrounding Antarctica. Have the students research the eating habits of some of the animals that inhabit the southern polar region (penguins, whales, krill, fish, birds). Students can then develop a food chain for these animals.

What's Below the Surface?

The continent of Antarctica is covered by ice with an approximate thickness of 6,600 feet (2,000 meters; more than a mile!). The ice is thinner near the coast. Often, bits of the ice break off and make icebergs that float away. Icebergs are dangerous to ships because most of the ice is below the water line. To demonstrate this fact, create an iceberg by filling a large plastic bowl with water and then freezing it. Float the iceberg in a tub of water. Notice that more than three-quarters of the ice is below the water. Research the *Titanic* and its fateful voyage in 1912 to discover how dangerous icebergs can be. Prepare a report detailing any precautions that could have been taken to avert the disaster. What laws and safety measures have taken effect to protect travelers from this type of disaster happening again?

Frost

As a class, make frost. Fill a can with ice cubes. Cover the cubes with water. Add 1–2 tablespoons of salt and stir for four or five minutes. A layer of frost will form on the outside of the can.

Snowflake Math

Create a math snowflake game for the students. Cut a snowflake out of white paper and hide it in a room. On slips of paper, write eight to ten clues that describe the hidden snowflake's location. Cut out additional strips of paper (2 by 8 inches) and fold them in half. On the outside of the folded strips, write a math problem. On the inside of the strips, write a question pertaining to the polar regions. Students must first answer the math problem correctly to see the science question. If students can answer both questions correctly, they are given a clue to find the snowflake. Read the clue aloud to the class. The student who finds the snowflake is the winner. (Hide several snowflakes for an extended game and review.)

Water and Ice

Have the students discover the volume and density of water and ice. Before class, mark the outside of several paper cups at about the two-thirds line. Have the students fill the cups to that line with water. Weigh the cups with the water in them. Then place the paper cups in the freezer and leave there until the water freezes. As a class, predict whether they think the cups and water will have the same weight and volume when the water turns to ice. When the water has frozen, weigh the paper cups and ice. Ask the students: Did the weight change? Why or why not? Did the volume change? How could you tell?

Have the students place an ice cube in a glass and add water until the glass is filled to the rim. Ask the students: What will happen when the ice melts? Will the cup overflow? Have them write down their predictions. (The level of water will stay about the same. The water from the melted ice takes up less space than the ice.)

Freezing Water

One of the many difficulties explorers and travelers face at the South Pole is keeping fresh water available for drinking (it often freezes while they travel). Discuss as a class, that other than having access to fire or heat to warm up and melt the frozen water every time they want a drink, what other solutions can you think of to this problem?

Have the students perform some experiments by adding various ingredients to water to attempt to slow down the freezing process. Make sure any ingredient they add is something they would want to drink (e.g., food coloring, coffee crystals, tea, powdered drink mix). Place the mixtures in a freezer and compare the time it takes to freeze to the time it takes to freeze plain water. Ask the students: Did any of the ingredients you tried actually slow down the freezing process? Why? Would eating snow be a good alternative source of water?

Eskimo Culture

Have the students research how the arrival of European whalers and fur traders changed the way of life of the Eskimos during the 1800s. (The introduction of rifles and the destruction of many animals due to hunting had impacts on the Eskimo culture.)

Before this time, Eskimos lived in traditional cultural groups. These groups were governed by "rules of conduct" that required each person to assist the others and help provide necessities for those who did not have what they needed. Discuss these rules and other ways of life within this cultural group. (Many different Eskimo cultural groups existed, depending on the region in which they lived. Focus on one group, or contrast the practices of different ones.)

■ Creative Writing Activities

Following are instructions to give the students for various writing activities.

- You have been asked to accompany a group of researchers to the South Pole. It is a very dangerous expedition. Do you go? Why or why not? Write a letter to the scientists accepting or declining their invitation and giving the reasons for your decision. (*Ralph's Frozen Tale* by Primavera)

- Investigate the techniques used in ice fishing. What equipment is required? What safety rules need to be followed? You are going on an ice fishing expedition. Keep a journal of your trip and experiences. (*Tobias Goes Ice Fishing* by Hertz)

- Have students in your school ever made fun of another child just because he dressed, looked, or acted differently from the majority of children? Write an article for a children's newspaper making a case for the right of "individuality" and telling how it benefits everyone. (*Tacky the Penguin* by Lester)

- Many people's moods or health are affected by the weather. Do you feel happier or healthier on a bright, sunny day than on a cold, cloudy one? Or is it the other way around? Write a story in which a sudden change in weather changes the way you feel (for better or worse) physically and/or emotionally. (*The Stranger* by Van Allsburg)

- The majority of people enjoy warm, sunny weather on a continual basis more than ice and snow for their day-to-day weather. But there are people who love the cold, snowy weather and seek out arctic regions in which to make their homes. Read up on what life in Alaska or northern Canada is like. Write an essay detailing what causes some people to love life in arctic areas.

- The Iditarod dogsled race is the most famous cold-weather event of our times. Find out all you can about this race (when it is held, what the requirements are, who can participate, what prize is awarded). Prepare a flyer advertising the Iditarod to prospective participants. Make it as informative as possible. (*Black Star, Bright Dawn* by O'Dell; *Dogteam* by Paulsen)

- Write a story giving your impressions of what an Eskimo's (or Inuit's) life was like before civilization (airplanes, telephones, automobiles) came to the arctic regions. After your story is complete, look up facts about the early life of the Eskimo. Compare these facts with your story. (*A Hunter Comes Home* by Turner)

- Exposure to severe cold for an extended period of time can be very dangerous. Interview professionals, such as doctors or nurses, who are versed in procedures to follow to protect yourself from extreme cold (how to dress, how long to stay out in cold weather, what to do if you suspect frostbite, what to do if you are trapped outside in extreme cold). Write a pamphlet outlining safety procedures for extreme cold weather.

- Find information on the sport of iceboating (how it is done, what equipment is required). Put together a brochure explaining the wonders of iceboating and describing a vacation spot that caters to iceboaters. (*Ice Warrior* by Riddell)

- You have been assigned the job of managing the Antarctica Travel Bureau. It is your responsibility to design a travel brochure that describes the many sights of this region in an attempt to lure tourists to the area. Design a brochure that shows the many wonders Antarctica has to offer.

- Eskimos call themselves by various words, all of which mean "people" in their language: Inuit in Canada, Yuit in Siberia and St. Lawrence Island, Inupiat and Yupik in Alaska. Choose a word from your native tongue. Use different forms of this word (real or made up by you) to describe the people in the different sections of the United States (East Coast, Southeast, Southwest, West Coast, North, and Midwest).

■ Art Activities

Following are instructions to give the students for various art activities.

- Make a frost-covered window. On dark construction paper, draw snowflakes using white crayons or paint. Cut black strips and glue them across the paper, one vertically and one horizontally, to make the windowpanes. Cut fabric scraps to resemble curtains and glue the "window." (*BRRR!* by Stevenson)

- Draw a picture of Jack Frost. Use a piece of black or dark blue construction paper and draw or paint your figure with white crayons, chalk, or tempera paint. Draw or paint an entire "white" scene around your figure of Jack Frost.

- Make a suitcase by folding a sheet of paper in half and adding a paper handle. Inside your suitcase, draw the items you would pack if you were going on an expedition to the North or South pole. Remember that there's no electricity, food, or shelter! Students can also make a suitcase out of a shirt box. Tape the lid to the box bottom on one long side of the box. Punch two holes (about 3 inches apart) in the other long side of the lid and thread a ribbon or pipe cleaner through the holes to make a handle. Students can go through a catalog and cut out pictures of the things they would take with them on their trip. These pictures can then be pasted inside their box suitcases.

- Discuss the importance of hunting and how certain animals are used for meeting the basic needs of food, shelter, and clothing. Have the students create an advertisement for a food, article of clothing, or shelter that would appeal to an Eskimo.

- Discuss the Eskimos' use of animal parts for making decorations and tools. Discuss how scrimshaw is made from walrus tusks or other pieces of ivory. Make a scrimshaw carving using a bar of white soap, a sharp pencil to "carve" with, and black shoe polish to brush into the carvings. Have students bring in examples of scrimshaw, if possible.

- Show illustrations of the Northern Lights and discuss when they appear. Using watercolors, have the students paint a scene that includes the Northern Lights.

- Make Eskimo "dance rings." Using embroidery hoops (or other similar size rings), feathers, and ribbons. Decorate your hoops to represent "dance rings." Sing a simple song, accompanied by a drum, and have the students dance waving their rings around in the air. Repeat the song three times, playing it faster each time.

- Make a totally white, 3-dimensional picture. Use a white Styrofoam tray or plate for the background. Find as many white items as possible to use in your creation (cotton balls, paper straws, packing peanuts, white yarn, white tissue paper, even egg shells). Glue the different items on your tray or plate to make a 3-dimensional blizzard scene.

- Draw a scene using crayons. Use firm strokes. Using white paint, "wash" the entire picture by lightly applying the paint over the picture. The wax from the crayons will resist the paint.

- Do some snow painting! Fill several plastic spray bottles (or squirt guns) with water. Add drops of food coloring to make the water in each bottle a different color. Go outside on a snowy day and draw a picture by squirting the different- colored water in patterns on the snow. If you cannot go out in the snow, or if you do not usually have snow where you live, use a large piece of white paper to represent the snow. Fill small squirt guns with the different-colored water and create your "snow art" indoors.

- Discuss the games and activities of the Eskimos (string games, sled races, outdoor contests, blanket tossing, storytelling, etc.). Make a diorama that depicts a scene of Eskimos participating in one of the events you discussed. (*Arctic Memories* by Ekoomiak) Take a shoebox and cut out one of the short ends. Cover this opening with colored plastic wrap. In the opposite short end of the box, cut a peephole. Create your scene inside the box by: painting the sides, bottom, and inside of the lid, pasting different-colored paper inside the box, and gluing figures cut from magazines (or drawn) to cardboard and securing them in the box. When your scene is completed, place the lid on the box and view your scene through the peephole.

- Read *Mama, Do You Love Me?* by Joosse. Discuss how the masks in the book and the objects attached to them represent things that are meaningful to the wearer. Cut out five circles, approximately 3 inches in diameter. On each circle, have the students draw a picture of something that has a special meaning to them. Using paper plates, construction paper, feathers, markers, and the circles, have the students make masks. The students can tell about their masks and why the drawings used are meaningful to them.

- Make a reindeer out of a cardboard toilet paper tube. Around the bottom of the tube (one of the circular openings), cut out four strips (3 inches long by 1 inch wide) spaced an equal distance apart from each other. This makes the reindeer's legs. Paint the tube and cut out eyes and a nose from colored paper to glue on to the tube. You can use a small pom-pom for the nose and buttons for the eyes; or you can draw on the features. Cut out four strips of black paper (1/2 inch long and 1 inch wide) and glue them on the bottom of the legs for hooves. Tie a piece of ribbon or yarn around where the deer's neck would be. Punch holes in either side of the tube and push twigs from a small tree through the holes to serve as antlers.

- Make your own snowperson using paper and scraps of fabric. You will need three different-sized pieces of white paper (approximately 8 1/2 by 11 inches, 7 by 9 inches, and 5 by 7 inches). You can make your snowperson a color other than white, if you want. Fold all three sheets of paper in half lengthwise. Open each sheet up and fold the outer edges of the paper into the center-fold and crease the paper. Then fold the sheet in half lengthwise again and make slits in the paper by cutting from the centerfold to the crease line. The slits should be about 1/2 inch apart. After you have cut the slits, put the uncut edges over each other until they overlap completely. Tape these edges together. With the slit side facing out, bring the ends of the long piece of paper together (wrap it to look like a doughnut) until they overlap slightly. Tape these "rings" together. Then stack your rings on top of each other (largest at the bottom and smallest at the top). Glue or tape the rings in place. Use construction paper to make a hat for your snowperson and to make the eyes, nose, and mouth. You can also wrap a piece of fabric around the neck to serve as a scarf.

- Make your winter a little brighter by making your own candles after a winter snowfall. *Note:* Adult supervision is mandatory to create these candles. This project works best if the snow is good packing snow. You will need: paraffin or beeswax, a stick, waxed paper, a tin can, candle wicking, old crayons, and an oven mitt. Put the paraffin into the tin can and place the can in a pan containing about 2 inches of water. Heat the pan on the stove until the water begins to boil. Then turn down the heat so the water simmers. As the paraffin melts, you can add pieces of old crayons for color, if you like. (Never place paraffin directly in a pan over a burner. It may catch on fire. Always use the double-boiler method.) When the wax is completely melted, turn off the heat. Dip the candle wicking in the melted wax until it becomes quite stiff. Lay the wicking flat on a piece of waxed paper for drying. While you are waiting for the wicking to dry, you can prepare the snow you will need. You need to have a mound of snow that is at least one foot deep. The snow must be able to hold its shape as you poke a hole down through the middle of the mound. Using a stick, poke a hole that is a few inches deep and in the shape that you want your candle to be. (You can experiment with different shaped molds and make more than one candle.) When you are satisfied with your mold, turn the heat back on under your wax and wait for it to melt again. When the wax is ready, put on the oven mitt and carefully carry the can of melted wax and the candle wicking out to your snow mold. Place the wick in the center of the mold. Hold the wick in place as you pour the melted wax around it. Continue to hold the wick in place until the wax cools enough to hold it. Allow the candle to cool for one hour. Carefully dig the candle out of the snow by digging around it with your hands or a small spade. Bring the candle inside and rinse it off under cool water. Trim the wick to approximately 1 inch above the wax and trim off the bottom of the candle so it will stand up straight.

Chapter 4
Tropical Rain Forests

■ Teaching Resources

Books containing experiment(s) relating to the subject matter are marked with a plus sign (+) before and after the title.

P   *Rain Forest Babies,* by Kathy Darling (Walker, 1997)
Photographs and text describe unique young animals of the rain forest such as: frogs, iguanas, macaws, orangutans, and tigers.

P/I *Tropical Forest Mammals,* by Elaine Landau (Children's Press, 1996)
Describes the physical characteristics and habits of rain forest mammals such as: jaguars, tapirs, coatis, sloths, and howler monkeys.

P/I *Tropical Rain Forests,* by Jean Hamilton (Silver Burdett, 1995)
The floor, understory, canopy, and pavilion of the forest are described, with their animals and plant life, through exceptional pictures.

I   *Animals of the Rain Forest,* by Stephen Savage (Raintree Steck-Vaughn, 1997)
Describes the environment of the rain forest and some of the birds, amphibians, mammals, and reptiles that live there.

I   *Antonio's Rain Forest,* by Anna Lewington (Carolrhoda Books, 1999)
A boy describes the Brazilian rain forest and includes information on the discovery, manufacturing, and uses of rubber. Brilliant photos give a perception of life in a Brazilian rain forest.

I   *Flashy, Fantastic Rain Forest Frogs,* by Dorothy Hinshaw Patent (Walker, 1997)
Describes the physical characteristics, behavior, reproduction, and habitat of frogs of the rain forest.

I   *Here Is the Tropical Rain Forest,* by Madeleine Dunphy (Hyperion Books for Children, 1997)
Presents the animals and plants of the rain forest and discusses their relationships with each other and their environment.

I   *Rain Forest Secrets,* by Arthur Dorros (Scholastic, 1999)
Simplistic, color illustrations help describe the characteristics, plant and animal life, and destruction of the world's rain forests.

I   *Save My Rain Forest,* by Monica Zak (Volcano Press, 1992)
True story of an eight-year-old boy who visits southern Mexico's endangered rain forests and expresses his concerns to the president of Mexico. This is an oversized book with watercolor illustrations.

I   *This Place Is Wet,* by Vicki Cobb (Walker, 1993)
Examines the land, ecology, people, and animals of the Brazilian Amazon rain forest.

I   *Tropical Rain Forests Around the World,* by Elaine Landau (Franklin Watts, 1990)
Describes rain forests, environmental conditions, inhabitants, and the dangers of deforestation.

I/U *Discover Rain Forests,* by Lynne Hardie Baptista (Publications International, 1993)
Concise explanation of rain forests and their inhabitants. A good resource with a glossary.

I/U *Green Giants, Rain Forests of the Pacific Northwest,* by Tom Parkin (Owl Communications, 1992)
Describes a rain forest in the United States (which is just as valuable as the ones in the tropics), why it is special, why it is in danger, and what we must do to save it.

I/U *Plants of the Tropics,* by Susan Reading (Facts on File, 1990)
Numerous illustrations and pictures, with helpful text, about plants of the tropical forests of the world and how they adapt to their environmental conditions.

I/U *Rain Forest,* by Barbara Taylor (Barron's Juveniles, 1999)
Close-up photos of the rain forest animals are accompanied by a descriptive text.

U   *+Crafts for Kids Who Are Wild about Rain Forests,+* by Kathy Ross (Millbrook Press, 1997)
Introduces rain forest plants and animals through twenty simple craft projects.

U   *Rain Forests,* by Lois Warburton (Lucent, 1991)
Black-and-white photographs, with an in-depth text, describe native inhabitants, deforestation, and actions that can be taken to preserve the rain forests.

■ Reading Selections

Books marked with an asterisk (*) before and after the title are related to the activities in the activity sections of this chapter.

Anansi the Spider, A Tale from the Ashanti, by Gerald McDermott (Little, Brown, 1997)
    Kwaku Anansi sets out on a long journey fraught with danger. He is saved from a terrible fate by his six sons.

The Ant and the Elephant, by Bill Peet (Houghton Mifflin), 1972
    The elephant helps rescue many of his animal friends, but who will return the favor when the elephant is in trouble?

**The Beginning of the Armadillos,* by Rudyard Kipling (Harcourt Brace Jovanovich, 1985)
    A tortoise and a hedgehog join together and become armadillos to escape a hungry jaguar. (Chapter Book)

Bimwili & the Zimwi, by Verna Aardema (Dial Books for Young Readers, 1992)
    Bimwili sets out with her sisters for the first time to go play by the sea. She ends up having an unusual adventure when she returns to the beach to retrieve the shell she forgot.

The Great Kapok Tree, by Lynne Cherry (Harcourt Brace, 1998)
> The many animals who make their home in a kapok tree try to convince a man not to cut it down.

Jaguar in the Rain Forest, by Joanne Ryder (Morrow Junior Books, 1996)
> Spend a day as a jaguar and experience the life of this rain forest animal.

Josephina Hates Her Name, by Diana Engel (Consortium Books, 1999)
> Josephina hates her name until her grandma tells her about the adventurous great aunt she was named after.

Jumanji, by Chris Van Allsburg (Scholastic, 1995)
> Two bored children find more excitement than they bargained for when they play a mysterious and magical jungle board game.

The King and the Tortoise, by Tololwa M. Mollel (Clarion Books, 1993)
> To all of the animals' surprise, it is the tortoise who is able to prove to the king that he is the cleverest animal in the jungle.

Lyle Finds His Mother, by Bernard Waber (Houghton Mifflin), 1974
> Lyle returns to the jungle in search of his mother, whom he has not seen since he was small.

Once a Mouse . . ., by Marcia Brown (Atheneum), 1972
> Tells the tale of a hermit and his adventures with big and small pets.

One Day in the Tropical Rain Forest, by Jean Craighead George (HarperCollins, 1990)
> A scientist and a young boy search for a rare butterfly in the rain forest of Macaw. Written in diary form.

Papagao, the Mischief Maker, by Gerald McDermott (Harcourt Brace Jovanovich, 1992)
> A noisy parrot helps the night animals save the moon from being eaten.

The Quicksand Book, by Tomie de Paola (Holiday House), 1977
> Presents information on the composition of quicksand and provides rescue procedures, all in enjoyable story form.

Regina's Big Mistake, by Marissa Moss (Houghton Mifflin, 1990)
> Regina has trouble deciding how to draw a jungle in art class. Then, with time running out, she turns a drawing mistake into a creative idea.

17 Kings and 42 Elephants, by Margaret Mahy (Dial Books, 1987)
> A group of kings and elephants encounter a variety of animals as they journey through the jungle.

The Spooky Tail of Prewitt Peacock, by Bill Peet (Houghton Mifflin), 1973
> Prewitt lives in the jungle with the other peacocks. Unlike the other peacocks, his tail is not beautiful but spooky and terrifying. Prewitt is very unhappy until he finds that his tail has an unusual use.

The Tiger's Breakfast, by Jan Mogensen (Crocodile Books, 1991)
> Elephant goes to the Mouse Deer for help after losing a roaring contest to Tiger.

Tigress, by Helen Cowcher (Farrar, Straus & Giroux, 1991)
> Herdsmen must work with a ranger to keep their animals safe from a marauding tigress.

Two Ways to Count to Ten, by Ruby Dee (Henry Holt, 1990)
> A traditional African tale about King Leopard and his search for a successor.

Welcome to the Greenhouse, by Jane Yolen (Putnam, 1997)
>Describes the tropical rain forest, and the life found there, through repetitive phrases and beautiful illustrations.

Where the Forest Meets the Sea, by Jeannie Baker (William Morrow, 1988)
>A young boy on a camping trip with his father thinks about the history of the plants and animals of the Australian rain forest and wonders about their future.

Why Mosquitoes Buzz in People's Ears, by Verna Aardema (Econo-Clad, 1999)
>Retells the folk tale from West Africa of a series of animals trying to discover who killed an owlet, causing Mother Owl great sadness. Because of this, she will not wake the sun.

The Zabajaba Jungle, by William Steig (Farrar, Straus & Giroux, 1987)
>When Leonard visits the Zabajaba Jungle, strange adventures await him.

The following books are out of print, but may be available at the local library.

Amazon Alphabet, by Martin and Tanis Jordan (Kingfisher, 1996)
>Large oil paintings depict rain forest animals for each letter of the alphabet.

Finish the Story, Dad, by Nicola Smee (Simon & Schuster, 1991)
>Ruby is angry that her father has not completed her bedtime story and dreams of a number of jungle animals who transport her on her quest for an ending.

Journey of the Red-Eyed Tree Frog, by Martin and Tanis Jordan (Simon & Schuster, 1992)
>A threatened tree frog journeys to the heart of the Amazon jungle to consult and Oracle Toad for advice on how to stop the destruction.

Jungle Day, by Claire Henley (Dial Books for Young Readers, 1991)
>Relates how a variety of jungle animals spend their days.

Jungle Sounds, by Rebecca Emberly (Little, Brown, 1989)
>Text and illustrations depict sounds associated with the jungle.

Little Polar Bear, by Hans de Beer (North-South Books, 1987)
>A friendly hippopotamus helps a little polar bear return home after he drifts to sea and ends up in the jungle.

A Nice Walk in the Jungle, by Nan Bodsworth (Viking Kestrel, 1990)
>Miss Jellaby takes her class for a walk in the jungle and must confront a hungry boa constrictor to get her class back.

Panther Dream, by Bob and Wendy Weir (Hyperion Books for Children, 1991)
>A young boy learns that man must respect the rain forest and coexist with nature without destroying it. Rain forest animals are illustrated and labeled at the end of the story.

Sister Yessa's Story, by Karen Greenfield (Laura Geringer, 1992)
>Yessa, the storyteller, tells the animals the story of how they were all deposited on the Earth in the areas that they now consider their homes.

A Story, A Story, by Gail Haley (Atheneum, 1970)
>Tells how most African folk tales became known as "Spider Stories."

Tree of Life, The World of the African Baobab, by Barbara Bash (Sierra Club Books, 1989)
>A folk tale describing the baobab tree and how the people and animals use the tree.

■ Science Activities

Layers of Vegetation

The vegetation of the rain forest is often categorized in five layers: the ground layer, the shrub layer, the middle layer, the canopy layer, and the emergent layer. Have the students research these layers, then make a poster that shows plants and animals that inhabit each layer. Drape shredded green tissue paper on the poster to resemble greenery. You can also make a classroom or hallway look like a rain forest by covering several walls with paper on which the layers of the rain forest have been depicted. Add the animal life and then take students on a guided tour through the jungle, explaining interesting facts about the plant and animal life.

Foods of the Forest

Have the students compile a list of foods that come from the tropical forest (coconuts, chocolate, tea, coffee, sweet potatoes, avocados, vanilla, mangoes, papayas, sugarcane, etc.). Locate the tropical forests on a world map. Discuss which food products come from these areas of the world. Have the students prepare (or write a recipe for) trail mix using tropical foods (Brazil nuts, peanuts, banana chips, etc.). Concoct your own (or write a recipe for) tropical drink using citrus juices, sherbet, coconut milk, and so forth.

Ants and More Ants

Besides the larger animals normally associated with the tropical forest, hundreds of kinds of ants (some in colonies of 20 million) inhabit the jungles. Have the students research the different species of ants and compare and contrast several different colonies. As a class, prepare a Venn Diagram and compare the different species. A Venn Diagram consists of two circles that overlap. Any similar characteristics of the objects you are comparing are written in the section where the circles overlap. The parts of the circles that do not overlap are used to record any characteristics that are unique to each object.

What Would You Say?

Have students compile a list of comparison questions pertaining to any aspect of the rain forest, such as:

- Would you rather be a parrot or a monkey?
- Would you like to live in the jungle or in the Arctic?
- Would you rather eat a pineapple or a strawberry?
- Would you rather be an anthropologist or a biologist?

After the list of questions is compiled, have each student answer them. Graph the responses they give. You can also use the answers to work on percentages. What percentage of the total would like to live in the jungle and be a parrot?

Plants and Animals

Divide a piece of poster board or a blackboard into columns. At the top of each column, write the name of a plant or animal indigenous to the tropical forest. Have the students fill in the columns with phrases that describe the plant or animal in question. The age of the students will determine how in-depth you can make this activity. Older students can be given books to scan to find detailed information about the plants and animals being discussed. When your chart is completed, the students can use the facts provided to write a descriptive sentence or paragraph about each subject.

Jungle Animals

Make a chart that lists as many of the animals that make their homes in the jungle as possible. List the names of the animals across the top of the chart and include either a drawing or a photograph with the name. Down the side of the chart, have columns entitled "Appearance," "Sound," "Type of Movement," "Type of Home," "Herbivore/Carnivore/Omnivore." You can include any other categories you want to. Have each student make a chart and fill it in, or you can make one large chart that the students fill in together. (*Why Mosquitoes Buzz in People's Ears* by Aardema; *Jungle Sounds* by Emberly) You could also reinforce language skills by alphabetizing the animals.

Insects Galore

The jungles contain over 20 million different types of insects, many of which are still undiscovered. Have the students do some research and choose one insect to report on. As part of their report, they can make a drawing of the insect, labeling the three body parts (head, thorax, and abdomen). The report should describe the insect's physical characteristics, feeding habits, type of home, means of communication, etc. You could also have the students use their imaginations to create their own insect, pretending it is one of the "undiscovered" species mentioned above.

Animal Adoption

Many zoos have animal adoption programs that allow individuals or groups to "adopt" an animal for a minimal monthly or annual fee. Contact your local zoo to discover if any "tropical" animals are part of their adoption program. Decide which of these "tropical" animals you would like to adopt. You could decide on a money-making project and actually adopt the animal or, if that is not feasible, adopt the animal by learning all you can about it and visiting it at the zoo. Make an appointment to visit the zoo and have the animal's keeper talk to you about what the animal eats, its habits, and the surroundings it lives in at the zoo. Some zoos have programs that they will bring to the school. After returning from the zoo, have the children write a short report on the day's activities, with drawings to go with it.

Products from the Rain Forest

The rain forest serves as a laboratory for science research. Many new plants and animals are being discovered, some of which may have medicinal purposes or provide cures for human ailments. Have students research the different materials that come from the rain forests that are used in the manufacture of products we use in our everyday lives. Make a chart that lists the name of the material, what part of the world we obtain this substance from, the product manufactured from it, and whether the extraction of the original substance causes any ecological problems.

Rain Forest in an Aquarium

Make a class rain forest inside a small aquarium using the following instructions:
- Take cuttings of plants such as spider plants, creeping Charlie, or philodendron. Place the cuttings in water and leave them there until they begin to root. Have students keep a journal detailing the growth.
- Place a layer of gravel in the bottom of the aquarium. Cover the gravel with a layer of charcoal.
- Spread small stones over the charcoal layer to create small hills and valleys. Cover the stones with about an inch of soil.
- Dampen the soil and plant your rooted plant cuttings in it.

- Cover the aquarium with a glass top or plastic wrap. Keep the aquarium in a warm place (but out of direct sunlight) and water the plants as needed.

How's the Weather?

As a class, research the weather in a tropical rain forest. Graph the monthly rainfall. Ask the students: Is there a "rainy" season, or does it rain more or less constantly throughout the year? Is there a little rain almost every day, or does the rain come in occasional downpours? Which would be better for plant growth?

Locate the Rain Forests

Look on a map to find where tropical rain forests exist today. Discuss that most rain forests are near the equator. Look at a globe. Have a student place his or her finger on the equator and spin the globe slowly. Discuss how often her or she touches land, and how often he or she touches water. How does this information emphasize the need to protect the rain forests?

Strange but True!

Because of the warm climate, combined with the heavy rainfall, plants and animals of the jungles grow all year long and, therefore, grow very large in size. For example, there are rodents that weight over 100 pounds, and daisies that are as big as apple trees! Have the students research some of the other enormous species that exist in the rain forests. State some of the advantages and disadvantages of this climate.

Beautiful and Dangerous

Rather than having a camouflaged appearance as many woodland animals do, the arrow poison frogs, which live in the rain forests, are brightly colored, possibly to warn other animals not to eat them. Discuss this unique animal and locate pictures of the various types. Discover what interesting use the tribal hunters of the jungles have found for its poisonous skin.

Living the High Life

Most rain forest animals live in the canopy (the top layer of foliage) because that is where most of the food is located. Many of the animals have curious features that help them adapt to their environment. Two examples are the lemurs' ability to use their tails to swing from branch to branch and the sloth's curved claws and strong arms that enable it to hold onto branches for hours at a time. Have the students research other animals that live in the canopy. Make a chart of the animals they research, listing the special adaptations that enable the animals to survive in such an environment.

■ Creative Writing Activities

Following are instructions to give the students for various writing activities.

- Write a story about an animal that journeys to a land very unlike its own home. What does it do there? Does it stay or journey back home? (*Little Polar Bear* by de Beer)

  Make up a tale of an adventurous aunt or uncle whom your parents named you after, or write a biography that describes the life of the person you are named for. If you are not named after anyone in particular, write about someone you particularly admire. (*Josephina Hates Her Name* by Engel)

- Write a story about a jungle animal that lacks a distinctive feature common to the rest of its species (e.g. an elephant, a trunk; a crocodile, a tail or teeth; a monkey, a tail). What feature is lacking? Is there a story behind why the feature doesn't appear on your animal? What happens as a result of this omission? (*The Spooky Tail of Prewitt Peacock* by Peet)

- Write a story about a mistake you made that you were then able to turn to your advantage. (*Regina's Big Mistake* by Moss)

- Pretend that you can choose to be any jungle animal you want to be. Do some research on the lives of the different jungle animals and pick the one you would like to be. Write an essay describing a typical day in your life as this animal. (*Jungle Day* by Henley) As a variation on this theme, ask the children whether, if they were an animal, they would rather live in a jungle or in a zoo. Why?

- People usually associate slowness with lack of intellect and dullness. Why is that? Is that attitude valid? Write a story about a person or animal that moved slowly but proved to be the most intelligent and clever of the group. (*The King and the Tortoise* by Mollel)

- Pick two jungle animals who have traits that, if joined together, would make a viable "new" animal. Which traits from each animal would the new animal retain? Why? Write an outline to serve as a blueprint of your new animal. Make a drawing to go along with your blueprint. (*The Beginning of the Armadillos* by Kipling)

- Make up alliterations based on an animal found in the tropical jungles. For example: Mindy monkey munches on magnificent mangoes. See how many you can come up with. Write each alliteration on a separate page and illustrate it. Bind the pages to make a book.

- Using the jungle animals as subjects of your sentences, write definitive sentences such as "With my mighty horn, I can . . ." (rhinoceros); or "My long, thin tail helps me . . ." (monkey). Have each student come up with one descriptive phrase. Write each description on a separate piece of paper and have the student illustrate it. Bind all of the pages together to make a class book.

- After researching food products from the tropical rain forests (see "Foods of the Forest" in the "Science Activity" section of this chapter), design a restaurant menu based on these foods. Give your restaurant a catchy name.

- Pretend you are a mouse, insect, or other very small animal of the jungle. How does the forest appear from your point of view? Write an adventure story describing your animal journeying through the rain forest.

- Write a Jack and the Beanstalk type story substituting a giant spider web for the beanstalk. What type of land would your spider web take you to? What would you encounter there?

- Write a letter to the head of a company involved in processes that destroy the rain forest or to an influential government official. State the importance of preserving the rain forest and ask for his or her cooperation.

- Pose this question to your students: Would you rather be an entomologist (study insects), an ichthyologist (study fish), or a botanist (study plants)? Have the students choose and then write reports explaining why they chose the careers they did. They might need to do some research into these careers before deciding. After making their choices, have them decide where they would like to carry out their work and why.

- Imagine that you are a scientist working for a large food-producing company. Your company has sent you to study the rain forest to determine its secret for growing such large plants and animals. Your job is to duplicate the conditions of the rain forest so that your company can produce "giant fruits and vegetables" to sell at home. Write a memo to your boss on your findings, giving any suggestions you might have for duplicating the rain forest. Do you think such a project is possible? Back up your conclusions with facts.

■ Art Activities

Following are instructions to give the students for various art activities.

- Create your own colorful jungle bird by using paper quilling:

    Cut several pieces of paper into 1/2-inch-by-12-inch strips or purchase colored, shredded paper that is usually found where wrapping paper and gift bags are sold. (Advanced students could use even thinner strips.)

    Draw an oval on a piece of paper. The oval will be the body of the bird.

    Roll the strips of paper, some tightly, some loosely. Glue or tape the strips onto the surface of the oval until the entire oval is filled with spirals.

    Use scraps of paper to add wings, feet, and a head to your bird.

- Paint a colorful bird or butterfly using marbles or a small rubber ball.

    Place a white piece of paper inside a 9-by-13-inch glass or aluminum pan. Drop dabs of different colors of paint (about the size of a dime) on the paper. Place the dabs of paint about 1 inch apart, with the largest concentration of paint toward the middle of the paper.

    Roll the marbles, or the small ball, around in the paint allowing, them to make a design on the paper. Set aside to dry.

    On a piece of colored construction paper, draw and cut out the figure of the bird or butterfly you want to make. Make sure that you place the figure in the center of the page and that you do not cut through the edge of the paper when cutting the figure out.

    Discard the figure you cut out and retain the piece of construction paper with the shape of the figure cut out, similar to a stencil.

    When your painting is completely dry, glue the piece of construction paper over the top of the painting so that the colors show through the animal-shaped hole.

- Design a poster that shows the wonders of the rain forest. Include a slogan or saying that helps get across the importance of preserving this natural resource.

- Take a walk through a local forest or woods and collect things with as many different textures as you can. Bring your findings home and glue them to a piece of poster board to make a texture collage. (*Where the Forest Meets the Sea* by Baker)

- Using two paper plates, make a puppet of a monkey or other jungle animal. For the monkey, place the two paper plates on top of each other with the top sides facing each other. Staple the plates together around the outside edges (put the staples about 1/4 inch apart) until the plates are stapled shut halfway around. Fold the open end of each plate back over the stapled section. Slip your hand into the pocket created by the two plates stapled together. This is the upper lip of your animal. The bottom folded plate forms the lower lip, and the top folded section will be the head. Decorate your animal by using crayons or markers to draw the eyes and hair. Make ears out of construction paper and glue or tape them in place. Or, decorate your puppet any way you like. It can be a lion, a tiger, a bird, or any jungle animal you choose.

- Draw a picture of a tropical forest using wet paper (a rough-textured, sturdy paper works best) and colored chalk. When the picture is finished and still slightly wet, iron a piece of wax paper on top of the drawing to hold the chalk in place.

- Many animals living in the rain forest have natural camouflage for safety. Draw a large poster of the foliage of a tropical forest. Afterwards, draw various jungle animals on a different piece of paper, emphasizing their natural coloring. Cut out your drawings and place them on the poster in places where the animals' coloring would blend in the best.

- Read *A Story, A Story* by Haley. Using string or yarn, make spider webs to match the two kinds of webs found in this story.

- Cut out pictures of food products that come from the tropical rain forest from magazines and periodicals. Design a collage with the pictures you have collected.

- Read *The Great Kapok Tree* by Cherry. Make a class "kapok tree." Students should create their own animals to place on and around a mural or large cutout of a tree.

- Make a cutout in the shape of a T-shirt from a piece of white paper. On the front and/or back of your shirt, create a design to show support for the preservation of the rain forest.

- Draw several outlines of the arrow poison frog and fill each outline in with a different brightly colored pattern or design. Cut out your frogs and glue them onto a rain forest scene that includes animals that are camouflaged. Do the frogs stand out against this multicolored background?

- Design a headdress, necklace, or mask using brightly colored feathers, beads, and so forth, that represent your impression of a rain forest dweller's decorative accessories. Refer to pictures in magazines or encyclopedias for assistance.

Chapter 5
Grasslands

■ Teaching Resources

Books containing experiment(s) relating to the subject matter are marked with a plus sign (+) before and after the title.

P/I *Meadow,* by Barbara Taylor (Econo-Clad, 1999)
Detailed text and enlarged pictures tell about animals and plants found in meadows.

P/I *The Roadside,* by David Bellamy (Crown, 1999)
Describes the transformation of a wilderness area when a highway is built through it, and its effects on animals living there.

I *Grasslands,* by Alan Collinson (Dillon, 1992)
Includes information on how the grasslands are surviving changes brought about by people and the climate.

I *One Day in the Prairie,* by Jean Craighead George (Harper Trophy, 1996)
Animals on a prairie wildlife refuge react to a tornado. The text nicely describes the plant and animal life of a prairie, in words and illustrations.

■ Reading Selections

Books marked with an asterisk (*) before and after the title are related to activities in the activity sections of this chapter.

Addie Across the Prairie, by Laurie Lawlor (Minstrel Books, 1991)
Addie is reluctant to leave her home and friends to accompany her family to the Dakota Territory, but slowly adjusts to life on the prairie. (Chapter Book)

Addie's Dakota Winter, by Laurie Lawlor (Minstrel Books, 1992)
In her new pioneer home, 10-year-old Addie finds an unlikely friend and, when stranded alone during a blizzard, learns about courage. (Chapter Book)

Beyond the Ridge, by Paul Goble (Aladdin, 1993)
After her death, a Plains Indian woman experiences the afterlife that her people believe in.

Born Free, by Joy Adamson (Schocken Books, 2000)
The tale of Elsa the lioness's two lives, in the wild and in captivity. (Chapter Book)

Bringing the Rain to Kapiti Plain, by Verna Aardema (Dial Books for Young Readers, 1992)
A cumulative rhyme relating how Ki-pat brought rain to the drought-stricken Kapiti Plain.

Carrots and Miggle, by Ardath Mayhar (Atheneum, 1986)
When a scholarly English child moves to a Texas ranch, everyone must make adjustments.

Eli, by Bill Peet (Houghton Mifflin), 1984

> An old lion, living in the grasslands of Africa, learns an important lesson about friendship from some vultures he has always despised.

Hot Hippo, by Mwenye Hadithi (Little, Brown, 1994)

> Tells the story of why the hippo lives in water.

Ida and the Wool Smugglers, by Sue Ann Alderson and Ann Blades (Groundwood Books, 1999)

> Ida proves that she is big enough to outsmart the smugglers who are trying to steal her sheep and, just maybe, big enough to start participating in the annual sheep run.

Incident at Hawk's Hill, by A. W. Eckert (Little, Brown, 1995)

> A shy, lonely six-year-old ends up in the Canadian prairie and is protected by a badger. (Chapter Book)

Just Like My Dad, by Tricia Gardella (Boyds Mills Press, 2000)

> A young child enjoys the activities of a day spent working on a cattle ranch as a cowhand, just like Dad.

Ladybug, Ladybug, by Ruth Brown (Puffin Books, 1992)

> Blown by a breeze, the ladybug flies over meadows and fields in an attempt to return home to her children.

Little House on the Prairie, by Laura Ingalls Wilder (HarperCollins Juvenile, 1997)

> The story of the Ingalls family as they make their home in the prairie country of America. (Chapter Book)

Little Town on the Prairie, by Laura Ingalls Wilder (Harper, 1941)

> As Laura works for her teaching certificate, blackbirds eat the town's corn and oat crops. (Chapter Book) (Other books by Laura Ingalls Wilder on prairie life are also available.)

Look Again! The Second Ultimate Spot-the-Difference Book, by April Wilson (Dial Books for Young Readers, 1992)

> Find different plants and animals that use camouflage to hide in 12 habitats.

Meanwhile Back at the Ranch, by Trinka Noble (Puffin Books, 1992)

> A bored rancher drives to town, not knowing that amazing things are happening back at the ranch.

The Miller, His Son and Their Donkey, by Aesop (North South Books, 1985)

> A father and son set out across the plain to market. On the way, they find out that it is impossible to please everyone.

The Mother's Day Mice, by Eve Bunting (Clarion Books, 1986)

> Three mouse brothers go into the meadow to find a Mother's Day present for their mother. It takes the littlest mouse to come up with a truly wonderful present.

Nightmare Mountain, by Peg Kehret (Puffin Books, 1999)

> Molly's visit to her aunt and uncle's llama ranch is filled with unexpected danger and suspense. (Chapter Book)

Old Yeller, by Fred Gipson (Harper Trophy, 1990)

> The story of a boy and his dog living in Texas in the 1860s. (Chapter Book)

Rain Player, by David Wisniewski (Clarion Books, 1991)

> To save his village from a drought, Pik challenges the Rain God to a game.

The Right Number of Elephants, by Jeff Sheppard (HarperCollins Juvenile, 1992)
>   A counting book about a girl who needs the right number of elephants to do various activities.

Sarah, Plain and Tall, by Patricia MacLachlan (Harper Trophy, 1993)
>   A young woman travels from the East to prairie country to marry a man she has not yet met and take care of his two children. (Chapter Book)

Theo's Vineyard, by Karen Ackerman (East Eagle, 1989)
>   After traveling from job to job all of his life with his family, Noah's dream of settling down with his family in their very own house finally comes true.

The Three Billy Goats Gruff, by Paul Galdone (Houghton Mifflin, 1981)
>   The classic tale of the three billy goats who must get past the troll who lives under the bridge to get to the meadow full of grass and flowers on the other side.

Tigress, by Helen Cowcher (Farrar, Straus & Giroux, 1991)
>   Herdsmen work with a ranger to keep their animals safe from a marauding tigress.

The White Stallion, by Elizabeth Shub (Bantam Books, 1996)
>   A little girl who is carried away from her wagon train in Texas in 1845 is befriended by a white stallion. (Chapter Book)

You Look Ridiculous, by Bernard Waber (Houghton Mifflin), 1979
>   A hippopotamus longs to have the characteristics of other animals. When she realizes how ridiculous that would look, she finally can appreciate her own uniqueness.

Zella Zack and Zodiac, by Bill Peet (Houghton Mifflin, 1986)
>   A zebra helps a young ostrich when he is still helpless, and the ostrich returns the favor after he has grown up.

The following books are out of print, but may be available at the local library.

All Wet! All Wet!, by James Skofield (Harper & Row, 1984)
>   A small boy experiences, along with the animals of the meadow and forest, the sights, smells, and sounds of a rainy summer day.

Baby Baboon, by Mwenye Hadithi (Little, Brown, 1993)
>   A lazy leopard decides to settle for Baby Baboon for dinner when a rabbit is too hard to catch.

Come to the Meadow, by Anna Grossnickle Hines (Clarion Books, 1984)
>   It takes a picnic to make a family stop their work and go to enjoy the wonders of the meadow.

Freedom for a Cheetah, by Arthur Catherall (Lothrop, Lee & Shepard, 1971)
>   After being set free from a life in captivity, a cheetah is not prepared for life in the wild. (Chapter Book)

How the Rhinoceros Got His Skin, by Rudyard Kipling (Rabbit Ear Books, 1988)
>   A tall tale relating how the rhinoceros got his skin.

Lazy Lion, by Mwenye Hadithi (Little, Brown, 1990)
>   A demanding lion orders his subjects to build him a house before the Big Rain comes.

One Good Horse: A Cowpuncher's Counting Book, by Ann Herbert Scott (Greenwillow Books, 1990)
>   A cowboy and his son count the things they see as they check on the cattle.

Over in the Meadow, by John Langstaff (Harcourt Brace Jovanovich, 1957)
> A counting book that takes place "over in the meadow."

Patulous, the Prairie Rattlesnake, by Jonathan Kahn (Landmark Editions, 1991)
> As a hungry rattlesnake searches for prey, he must also escape the claws and fangs of his own enemies.

A Prairie Boy's Winter, by William Kurelek (Houghton Mifflin, 1973)
> This story depicts the hardships and pleasures of life on the prairie during the challenging 1930s.

Rainflowers, by Ann Turner (HarperCollins, 1992)
> The animals of a meadow scurry for cover as a thunderstorm passes through.

Tricky Tortoise, by Mwenye Hadithi (Little, Brown, 1988)
> Elephant is outsmarted by Tortoise who proves that he can jump over Elephant's head.

Watching Foxes, by Jim Arnosky (Lothrop, Lee & Shepard, 1985)
> While their mother is away, little foxes play and romp in the meadow by their den.

When the Rain Stops, by Sheila Cole (Lothrop, Lee & Shepard, 1991)
> A little girl and her father encounter a variety of wildlife creatures as they walk through the meadow to pick blackberries.

■ Science Activities

The Grass is Always Greener

Have the students hypothesize why grass never runs out in the grassland area even with so many animals grazing non-stop. The following experiment can help explain this phenomenon.

- Fill three small flowerpots with potting soil. Plant grass seed in one pot and chive seeds in the other two. Water each pot well. Water every other day.
- Clip the tops off the grass and off the chives in one pot when they reach 2 inches (5 centimeters). Don't cut the chives in the other pot.
- Trim the same plants' tops one week later.
- Trim all the plants after another week has passed. These plants will have been trimmed like the grass that grows in the grasslands. Animals continually eat the tops of the grass when they graze.
- After two weeks, check the three plants. Which plant has grown the most? (The grass: It grows from its roots, unlike the chives.)

Survival

Many types of animals inhabit the grassland regions. How do each of the following groups survive in their habitat?

- Large herbivores—American bison, guanaco, saiga (by running faster than their pursuers and grazing in herds)
- Medium-sized carnivores—wolves, coyotes (by preying on herbivores and depending on speed to catch their prey)
- Small, burrowing animals—moles, gophers, prairie dogs, souslik (by hiding from predators by burrowing underground. Some find food underground, but most must come to the surface to eat.)

- Small carnivores—pampas cats, snakes, ferrets (by relying on stalking and surprising their prey or using their long, thin bodies to follow prey into their burrows)

Have the students make a poster that is divided into four sections to correspond with the categories listed above. In each section, students list an animal that fits into the category. Next to the animal's name, list a characteristic it has that helps it survive in the grasslands.

Features of the Grasslands

Have the students choose an activity from the following list and share their findings with the class.

- Trees and shrubs often "invade" from nearby forests, but few live long enough to transform the grasslands into forests. Why is this?
- How would the animals of the grasslands be affected if the trees did survive and transformed the grasslands into forests? Imagine being a large hippo or an elephant trying to maneuver in a forest.
- List several grassland animals and compile a list of problems they might face living in a forest.
- What natural adaptations do grasses possess that allows them to survive where trees and shrubs do not?
- Research the grass plant. How is grass more capable of surviving fire than other plants? Does new growth on grass plants come from the tips, similar to trees, or from the base of the plant (base)? How can this feature help grasses survive? Are the root systems of grass plants shallow or deep (deep)? Why is this important?
- Draw an illustration of a grass plant and one of a tree sapling. Label your drawings to show the differences in the two types of plants.
- Discuss the effects of fire on a habitat. Can fire actually be helpful to some habitats? Consider what was learned in the two activities above. Fire can actually serve to "prune" grass plants.

Cereal

The world's cereal supply is grown mostly in grassland regions. As a class, research where several different grains are grown (e.g., corn, oats, barley, wheat, rye). Make a bar graph depicting the continents and how much of each grain they grow (in tons). Assign each grain a different color. Have the students find out how much of each crop is grown on each continent. Fill in the bar graph to show the amount grown by continent. Discuss which continents grow the most grains. Considering the populations of the countries on these continents, which continents do the students believe export the most cereal?

Straw

When some crops, such as wheat and hay, are harvested, the dried stalks of the plants are also harvested and baled as straw. Have the students research some of the original uses of straw (bedding for animals, brooms, mattress stuffing, etc.) and uses that are made of straw today.

Grassland Collage

The grains grown in the grasslands produce many food products we eat. For example, did you know we need corn to make cola? (Corn syrup is used in the manufacture of cola.) Have the students research other foods that require corn products (margarine, pancake syrup, corn bread, tortillas). Cut out pictures of these foods and make a class collage of foods from the grasslands.

Compare and Contrast

Of all the areas of the United States, it seems that we are least familiar with the lifestyle of people who live on the prairies. Discuss which sections of the United States are considered "prairie" states. Have students do a report in which they compare and contrast two U.S. cities, one located on the prairie and one located in a completely different region (e.g., a coastal city, an industrial city, a densely populated metropolis). Some facts to include in the report are:

the geographical location of each city

population per square mile

main occupations

weather

recreational pastimes

Students can include graphs and/or Venn Diagrams to demonstrate how prairie cities compare with other cities that are better known to them.

Experimental Baking

Most grains can be ground into flour and baked as bread. Students can experiment by making breads made out of different flours such as oatmeal, whole wheat, corn, and rye, or purchase these breads from a bakery. Sample the different breads and discuss their similarities and differences in taste, texture, coloring, and so forth. Make a chart on a piece of poster board with a column for each type of bread, possibly with a picture or drawing of the bread at the top of the column. Discuss the properties of each type of bread and list them in the proper column. At the bottom of the piece of poster board, make a graph showing the students' reactions to the taste of the breads. Experiment by substituting a different type of flour in a recipe for muffins or biscuits. Ask the students if they observed any other differences besides the change in taste.

Volume and Density

Use rice to demonstrate volume and density. Measure 1 cup of uncooked rice and weigh it. Prepare the rice according to the package. Measure the rice again. Ask the students how many cups of rice do you have? What does all the rice weigh? What does just one cup of cooked rice weigh? Which is denser, cooked rice or uncooked rice? Why?

And Away We Go

Have the students research some of the animals that live in the grasslands. Students should investigate: Do most live in herds, or do they travel independently? Which types of animals live in herds? (Herbivores graze in herds for protection.) Which animals travel in very small groups, or independently (predators)? Discuss the benefits to each animal of traveling as it does.

All Around the World

The grassland areas have different names in different parts of the world. Discuss where students would find prairies, savannas, steppes, and pampas. Consult a world map and find where these areas are located. Students can also draw their own world maps and show these areas in different colors.

■ Creative Writing Activities

Following are instructions to give the students for various writing activities.

- Write a story about baby animals playing in their natural habitats. (*Watching Foxes* by Arnosky)

- Do you ever feel that you are old enough to do something that your mom or dad won't let you do yet? Write to your parents stating what it is you feel you should be allowed to do and present reasons to back up your request. When you finish, schedule a time to sit down and discuss what you've written. Maybe they will grant your request. At the very least, you will have a better understanding of why they don't feel they can grant your request (*Ida and the Wool Smugglers* by Alderson and Blades). Can you think of things you could do to show your parents you are old enough or to prepare yourself for when you are old enough?

- Write a humorous tale about a grassland animal that finds itself living in a dense forest. What problems does it face? What is the outcome?

- You are planning a surprise picnic in the meadow for your family. What will you pack in your basket? Don't forget items such as a blanket, dishes, and utensils. What activities would you plan to pass the day? (*Come to the Meadow* by Hines)

- You have the opportunity to go on an African safari to hunt wild game. Do you go? Write a letter to the head of the expedition accepting or declining the offer. Be sure to give specific reasons for your decision.

- Choose a favorite grassland animal. Write a story about an adventure it had when traveling to another habitat quite different from its home. How did this journey come about? Does your animal enjoy this new experience or wish that it had stayed put? Why?

- Write a counting book that takes place in another habitat, such as the desert or tropical forest. What animals and sights would you include in your counting book? (*Over in the Meadow* by Langstaff)

- Sometimes lasting friendships are formed between the most unlikely people. Write down the qualities that you feel are most important in a friend and the activities you most enjoy. Think about your closest friend. Write down the qualities he or she possesses and his or her favorite activities. How do the lists of qualities and activities compare? Are you and your friend an "odd couple?" (*Eli* by Peet)

- Write your own version of the classic tale, *The Three Billy Goats Gruff* by Galdone. Who or what will you choose as your lead characters? What type of setting will your story take place in? How will you portray the villain of your tale? Is the ending the same?

- Pretend you are a circus elephant who is being released into the wild. What obstacles do you face? Write a story about your adventures. (*Freedom for a Cheetah* by Catherall)

- Read A *Prairie Boy's Winter* by Kurelek. Talk with family members about life in the 1930s. What were your family members' lives like during that time? Were they affected by the Great Depression? Write an article for a school newspaper relating the information you gathered.

- Imagine you are spending the summer on a real ranch out west. Write a letter home to your best friend describing how your days are spent. Is the life as romantic as it is depicted in the movies? Is it hard work? How do you feel about your choice of vacation spots? (*Just Like My Dad* by Gardella)

■ Art Activities

Following are instructions to give the students for various art activities.

- Using paper, cloth, paints, and other materials around the house, design what you envision as your own "dream house." (*Theo's Vineyard* by Ackerman)

- Find a picture of a grassland scene in a magazine or brochure. Cut the picture into 1 1\2-by-2-inch vertical strips. Distribute the strips to the students, dividing the strips evenly among them. Take a large sheet of drawing paper and cut it into the same number of vertical strips as the grassland scene. Distribute these strips in the same way. Have each student copy the strip from the picture onto the strip of drawing paper. When they are finished, put the drawing-paper strips together to re-create the scene. The strips will not match exactly, but the results will be striking.

- Create a scene on a piece of white poster board using cutouts made of construction paper. Cut out rows of grass in several different shades of greens and browns. Make the rows about 3 or 4 inches high and fringe the top 2 to 2 1/2 inches to make it look like real grass. Glue the rows of grass on top of one another to create a 3-dimensional effect. Do the same thing with flowers, drawing three or four petals in a circular pattern on each different color of paper. Glue the different-colored layers on top of one another and then make a small circle to glue on as the middle of the flower. You can repeat this process with leaves to make a dramatic, beautiful picture. (*Rain Player* by Wisniewski)

- Design an animal by drawing your own creation and using parts of many different animals. Younger students can cut out animal parts from magazines and glue them together to create their own unique animals. Think up a name for your creation. (*You Look Ridiculous* by Waber)

- Find pictures of several grassland animals or draw your own. Glue these pictures onto a large sheet of poster board or bulletin board paper. Have the students draw in the surrounding scenery.

- Color rice by adding a few drops of food coloring to a bowl of uncooked rice and stirring until the rice is colored. Make several different colors of rice and use them to make a wildlife picture on a piece of poster board, a pencil holder out of a juice can, or a coaster on a circular piece of cork.

- Design a gift for someone you know. Purchase a straw wreath from a craft store. Wrap a colorful ribbon around and around the wreath and tie it into a pretty bow. Glue on objects that would mean something to the recipient of your gift. For example, a wreath for a teacher could have crayons, small scissors, erasers, small rulers, and fake apples on it. A wreath for someone who enjoys cooking could include cinnamon sticks, a small wooden spoon, colored sugar cubes, small plastic salt and pepper shakers, and so forth. The more personal the collection of items, the better.

- Make a letter holder that looks like your favorite grasslands animal using the following instructions:

  Take an empty cereal box and tape the open end flap shut. Lay the box on one side. Using scissors or a box cutter, cut about 3 inches off the other side of the box. This cut will remove one side panel and 3 inches of the top and bottom panels of the box. Remind students to handle sharp items carefully.

  On a piece of poster board (or on the inside of another empty cereal box), draw the head and neck of your favorite grasslands animal. Cut out the drawing. Paint the drawing and the cereal box to resemble the animal you have chosen. You can also cover the box with colored paper and then decorate it to look like your animal.

Staple the head of your animal to the back of the letter box so that the head sticks up above the box. You now have an animal box that will hold your family's mail.

- Find a picture or painting of a grassland scene. Imagine that you are standing in that scene. Look beyond the scene in front of you and draw a new scene showing what you see in the distance.

- Read *All Wet! All Wet!* by Skofield. Make a sight-and-touch book that re-creates what you saw in the story. You can add your own ideas to the book as well. For example, glue a piece of sandpaper on one page to represent rough tree bark or a sandy beach, use actual grass and flowers on another page, or use a scrap of rough cloth for an animal's hide. Cut the materials you use to the proper shape and draw in the rest of the scene you are imagining.

Chapter 6
Woodlands and Ponds

■ Teaching Resources

Books containing experiment(s) relating to the subject matter are marked with a plus sign (+) before and after the title.

P   *Pond Life,* by Rena K. Kirkpatrick (Steck-Vaughn, 1985)
Simplistic text and illustrations examine animal and plant life in a pond.

P   *The River,* by Gallimard Jeunesse and Laura Bour (Scholastic, 1993)
Handheld size, with overlapping pages, nice illustrations, and brief text. Explores river animals and plant life.

P   *Signs Along the River,* by Kayo Robertson (Roberts Rinehart, 1986)
Very simple text, with pencil illustrations, describing how to sense the presence of plants and animals in the world around us.

P   *Spoonbill Swamp,* by Brenda Z. Guiberson (Henry Holt, 1994)
Describes a swamp and its inhabitants, focusing on spoonbills and alligators. Animal sounds words are used for a good primary read-aloud.

P/I *Pond Life,* by Barbara Taylor (DK Publishing, 1998)
Examines pond life with enlarged photographs and informative text. (Also: *River Life,* 1992, and *Forest Life,* 1993.)

P/I *Swamp Life,* by Theresa Greenaway (DK Publishing, 2000)
Enlarged photographs and informative text examine the plants and animals inhabiting swamps.

P/I *Wonders of the Forest,* by Francene Sabin (Troll, 1989)
Describes plants and animals interacting throughout the seasons.

I   *Groundwater, Our Endangered Planet,* by Mary Hoff and Mary M. Rodgers (Lerner, 1991)
Describes groundwater locations and properties, the uses and abuses of it worldwide, and ways to preserve this valuable resource through helpful, easy-to-read text and photographs.

I   *How the Forest Grew,* by William Jaspersohn (Mulberry Books, 1992)
Simplistic text, with pencil illustrations, explains the transformation of a cleared farm field into a dense forest.

I/U *Forests, a Fact Filled Coloring Book,* by Bettina Dudley (Running Press, 1990)
Text describes how forests began, what keeps them growing, and forests throughout the world and what their futures hold.

I/U *Save Our Wetlands,* by Ron Hirschi (Delacorte Press, 1994)
Frogs, tule, elk, beaver, and more help explore freshwater swamps, bogs, and lakes, through engaging text and excellent photography.

■ Reading Selections

Books marked with an asterisk (*) before and after the title are related to activities in the activity sections of this chapter.

Animals, Animals, by Eric Carle (Philomel, 1989)
    A collection of poems describing domestic and wild animals.

Annie and the Wild Animals, by Jan Brett (Houghton Mifflin, 1989)
    When Annie can't find her pet cat, she wanders into the woods to find a new friend.

Arthur Goes to Camp, by Marc Brown (Econo-Clad, 1999)
    Arthur runs away into the woods when strange things start happening at the summer camp his parents send him to.

Aurora Means Dawn, by Scott Russell Sanders (Aladdin, 1998)
    A family leaves Connecticut and travels across the forests and prairies to start a settlement in Aurora, Indiana.

Badger's Parting Gifts, by Susan Varley (Lothrop, Lee & Shepard, 1984)
    When their good friend, Badger, dies, the animals find that remembering the good times and what they've learned from him helps make them all feel better.

Birches, by Robert Frost (Henry Holt, 1990)
    A poem that gives the author's impression of what a birch tree says to him.

Come Out Muskrats, by Jim Arnosky (Econo-Clad, 1999)
    In late afternoon, the muskrats come out of the woods to swim and eat in the cove.

A Dark, Dark Tale, by Ruth Brown (Puffin Books, 1992)
    Takes the reader on a cat's dark journey into a spooky old house.

Deep in the Forest, by Brinton Turkle (E. P. Dutton, 1976)
    A little bear discovers a cabin in the forest, with unexpected results. (This is a wordless twist on *Goldilocks and the Three Bears.*)

Gentle Ben, by Walt Morey (Puffin Books, 1992)
    Recounts the friendship between a boy and a bear in the Alaskan wilderness. (Chapter Book)

The Gnats of Knotty Pine, by Bill Peet (Houghton Mifflin, 1984)
    A swarm of gnats help save the animals of Knotty Pine Forest from hunters' guns.

Goldilocks and the Three Bears, by Jan Brett (Dodd, Mead, 1992)
    A tired and hungry young girl helps herself to food and rest when she happens upon a small house in the woods.

The Goodnight Circle, by Carolyn Lesser (Harcourt Brace Jovanovich, 1984)
>   Describes various animals' activities from sunup to sundown.

Grandfather Twilight, by Barbara Berger (Paper Star, 1996)
>   Every evening, Grandfather Twilight walks through the forest to bring night to the world.

Hansel and Gretel, by James Marshall (Puffin Books, 1994)
>   Hansel and Gretel are captured by a wicked witch when they become lost in the forest.

The Incredible Journey, by Sheila Burnford (Yearling Books, 1996)
>   A Siamese cat, a bull terrier, and a Labrador retriever travel together through the Canadian wilderness to find their family. (Chapter Book—also available as the movie *Homeward Bound*)

The Last Wolf of Ireland, by Elona Malterre (Clarion Books, 1990)
>   A young boy and girl try to save a wolf's den they find in the forest from greedy hunters and superstitious townspeople. (Chapter Book)

The Legend of Johnny Appleseed, by Reeve Lindbergh (Little, Brown, 1993)
>   The life of John Chapman (Johhny Appleseed) is told through rhymed text.

The Light in the Forest, by Conrad Richter (Juniper, 1995)
>   The story of a young boy who is taken from his parents at the age of four by Delaware Indians, raised in the forest for 11 years, then returned to his family by a military expedition. (Chapter Book)

Little Fur Family, by Margaret Wise Brown (HarperCollins Juvenile, 1991)
>   Tells of the wonderful day that the fur child spends in the woods around his home.

Little House in the Big Woods, by Laura Ingalls Wilder (Harper Trophy, 1971)
>   A year in the life of two young girls growing up on the Wisconsin frontier. (Chapter Book)

Look Again! The Second Ultimate Spot-the-Difference Book, by April Wilson (Dial Books for Young Readers, 1992)
>   Find different plants and animals that use camouflage to hide in 12 habitats.

The Man in the Woods, by Rosemary Wells (Dial, 2000)
>   Fourteen-year-old Helen investigates what she feels is the false arrest of a classmate and has some terrifying experiences. (Chapter Book)

Merle the High Flying Squirrel, by Bill Peet (Houghton Mifflin, 1983)
>   A squirrel flies west to find the peace and quiet in the forests that is missing in the big city.

The Mitten, by Alvin Tresselt (Lothrop, Lee & Shepard, 1964)
>   The animals of the forest try to find warmth by squeezing into a lost mitten.

Night Tree, by Eve Bunting (Voyager Picture Books, 1994)
>   A family makes its annual pilgrimage to decorate an evergreen tree with food for the forest animals at Christmastime.

The Rabbits' Wedding, by Garth Williams (HarperCollins Juvenile, 1982)
>   A little black rabbit is saddened by the thought of being parted from a little white bunny, until a solution is found.

Rascal, by Sterling North (Puffin Books, 1990)
>   The tale of a mischievous raccoon and the mishaps that befall him. (Chapter Book)

The Sign of the Beaver, by Elizabeth George Speare (Yearling Books, 1994)
> A young boy left alone to guard his family's wilderness home has trouble surviving until he is aided by local Indians. (Chapter Book)

Sleep Out, by Carol Carrick (Houghton Mifflin, 1982)
> Christopher sleeps out in the woods alone for the first time to try out his new camping equipment.

Sleepy Bear, by Lydia Dabcovich (Puffin Books, 1985)
> A story of an expressive bear who prepares for a winter's nap and then wakes up at the signs of spring.

The Teddy Bears' Picnic, by Jimmy Kennedy (HarperCollins Juvenile, 1996)
> Recounts the song of the annual picnic the teddy bears hold in the woods.

Wait Till the Moon Is Full, by Margaret Wise Brown (Harper Trophy, 1989)
> Little raccoon has trouble waiting until the moon is full to see what lies out in the woods at night.

The Woodcutter's Mitten, by Loek Koopmans (Interlink, 1995)
> A woodcutter drops his mitten while walking through the woods, and many forest creatures seek shelter in it.

The Witch of Blackbird Pond, by Elizabeth George Speare (Laurel Leaf, 1978)
> A teenage girl rebels against the narrow-minded ways of the townspeople and befriends a woman who is later accused of being a witch. (Chapter Book)

The Yearling, by Marjorie K. Rawlings (Aladdin, 1988)
> A boy from the backwoods of Florida must decide the fate of a fawn he has raised as a pet. (Chapter Book)

The following books are out of print, but may be available at the local library.

The Grizzly Sisters, by Cathy Bellows (Macmillan, 1991)
> The Grizzly sisters live to regret it when they disobey their mother's warning to stay away from tourists.

The Frog Who Drank the Waters of the World, by Patricia Montgomery Newton (Atheneum, 1983)
> An old Indian tale of a frog who, for revenge, decides to drink all of the water that exists in the forest.

The Man Who Could Call Down Owls, by Eve Bunting (Macmillan, 1984)
> A stranger who tries to steal the power to control the owls finds out that he did not understand this power at all.

McCrephy's Field, by Christopher A. Myers and Lynne Born Myers (Houghton Mifflin, 1991)
> After a 50-year absence, Joe McCrephy returns to his farm to find that it has evolved into a forest.

My Father Doesn't Know About the Woods and Me, by Dennis Haseley (Atheneum, 1988)
> A young boy seems to become some of the woodland animals as he walks in the woods with his father.

Need a House? Call Ms. Mouse, by George Mendoza (Grosset & Dunlap, 1981)
> Henrietta Mouse custom-designs homes for her animal friends.

Nicholas Cricket, by Joyce Maxner (Harper & Row, 1989)
> Nicholas Cricket and his band lead the forest creatures in a huge celebration of the night.

Peter and the Wolf, by Selina Hastings (Henry Holt, 1987)
> Retells the fairy tale of how Peter attempts to capture a wolf.

Someday With My Father, by Helen E. Buckley (Harper & Row, 1985)
> A little girl who is very ill dreams of the day when she and her father will actually be able to do all the wonderful things they talk about.

What a Catastrophe!, by Eileen Christelow (Bradbury Press, 1986)
> A young boy tells how he found a frog in the tall grass outside his home and brought it home for breakfast. The reader is asked to pick his or her own ending to the tale.

■ Science Activities

Surface Tension

Some insects can "walk on water" due to the surface tension of the water of a pond or lake. To demonstrate what this means, have the students try the following experiment.

- Students will need a needle, a small piece of paper towel, and a glass of water.
- Students should rub the needle between their fingers to make its surface waxy. Place the dry needle on the paper towel.
- Put the paper towel (with the needle on top) carefully on the surface of the water.
- The paper towel will soak up water and then sink. Notice that the needle will remain on the top, held up by the surface tension.

Deciduous Trees

The life cycle of deciduous trees (those that lose their leaves) plays an important part in supporting the animal life in the forest. Have the students research how the different animals depend on the trees and create an illustration that shows one such relationship. Have them share their findings with other classmates. Some examples are:

- Spring—Birds build nests out of "winter litter" (i.e., broken twigs and dead leaves).
- Summer—Insects live off the sap of oak and chestnut trees; animals also depend on the trees for food, shelter, and protection.
- Fall—The fallen leaves help provide rich soil and homes for burrowing animals and worms. Nuts are eaten by several animals. Squirrels hide their winter food supply in trees. Woodpeckers eat small insects that live in the bark.
- Winter—Lack of leaves provides additional light that other plants, such as holly, need to survive the winter. These plants can provide food to forest animals. Fallen leaves provide a protective covering against the winter weather.

High Altitudes

As the ground increases in elevation in the mountains, the trees change. As the altitude increases, fewer deciduous trees are present and more coniferous trees emerge. After a certain point, coniferous trees cannot grow either, and a treeless habitat is present. Have the students research some of the plants and animals that live at these high altitudes. Discuss what adaptations they have that allow them to survive. Some plants and animals to research are:

the saussurea plant (Saussurea tridactyla)

Alpine soldanella (Soldanella alpina)

the Rocky Mountain goat (Oreamnos americanus)

Alpine chough (Pyrrhocorax graculus)

the jumping spider (Salticus scenicus)

the golden eagle (Aquila chrysaetos)

Food Chain

In every habitat there are herbivores, carnivores, and omnivores. As a class, discuss the animals in the woodlands. Classify each animal into one of the three categories. After looking at the eating patterns of these animals, make a "food chain." Choose a carnivore. Ask the students: What animal does this carnivore eat? What does that animal eat? Where does the next animal or plant get its energy? Make several chains. It will soon become evident that all animals depend on plants eventually, and all plants need sunlight and water to survive.

More Work with Food Chains

Discuss if most humans are herbivores, carnivores, or omnivores. Have the students make a sample lunch menu modeled on one from their favorite restaurant. Divide the foods they have listed into the following categories: meats, fruits, vegetables, and grains. Each student should decide on the items each would like to have for lunch. Make food chains for the lunch, beginning with you (the human being). Are you an herbivore, carnivore, or omnivore?

Nocturnal Animals

Some birds, such as owls, are nocturnal animals. Ask the students: What does it mean to be nocturnal? Why would it be beneficial to be awake at night? Can you name any other woodland animals that are nocturnal? Have the students research some of these animals and write a paper on the benefits and disadvantages of being a nocturnal animal. (Younger students can make a picture of the environment of a nocturnal animal.)

Hibernation

Discuss what it mean to hibernate. Have the students research woodland animals that hibernate. Investigate how these animals prepare for hibernation and how long they hibernate.

Smokey Bear

Share the story of Smokey Bear. Asks the students: Was there really a bear who was named Smokey? What happened to him? How did a bear come to represent fire safety in the forest? How do forest fires affect the plant and animal life of the woodlands? What plants are the first to grow back after a fire? What animals do you suppose would be the first to reappear after a fire?

Travel the National Parks

Have the students choose one of the national parks and plan a vacation there. Encyclopedias often contain a listing of national parks along with a short description. Your local library should have a copy of *The Complete Guide to America's National Parks: The Official Visitor's Guide of the National Park Foundation.* Have the students write to the park of their choice requesting information. Locate the park on a map and map out the trip using appropriate highways and roadways. Determine how long it will take to drive to the park. Plan an itinerary listing the sites to be seen while on a trip and the activities to participate in. Students should be sure that their reports includess historical information about the park and surrounding area.

Trail Markers

Discuss how different trail markers are used to mark paths through the forest. A scouting handbook may be helpful, or invite a scout master to visit the class to demonstrate how trail markers are made. Learn how sticks and rocks can be used to indicate a path. Afterwards, go outside and mark a trail around the schoolyard or in your neighborhood.

■ Creative Writing Activities

Following are instructions to give the students for various writing activities.

- If you were ill and had to stay in bed, what places and activities would you miss the most? Make a list of your answers. Choose one place or activity and write about why you would miss it. (*Someday with My Father* by Buckley)

- "It was a dark and windy night. The trees in the woods were swaying eerily. . . ." Write a story that begins with these lines. Will your tale have a funny or a scary ending?

- Write a story about an exciting or very scary event. Create three or four different endings for your story. When you are finished, read your story to your family, class, or friends. Have them vote on their favorite ending. (*What a Catastrophe!* by Christelow) Rewrite your story in book form and illustrate the pages. Put the ending that received the most votes first, followed by the other endings in order of preference. Illustrate the pages. You can make a cover for your book by decorating cardboard or using scraps of wallpaper. Older students can graph the results of the story-ending vote or use the results to figure percentages.

- Many trees across the United States have been cut down, especially during the early settling of the country and during the Industrial Revolution, so that people could plant crops, mine resources, and build factories and railroads. Write an editorial that supports or opposes deforestation today. What alternatives would you suggest? Would your view be different if you were living 100 years ago? How?

- Write a poem about your favorite woodland animal. Classroom teachers can compile these into a big book. (*Animals, Animals* by Carle)

- Pretend that you are a bear who is preparing to hibernate. What would you do just before you lie down to sleep? How would it feel to hibernate? What would be the first thing you would do when you woke up? (*Sleepy Bear* by Dabcovich)

- Design a pamphlet to hand out to tourists that tells of the dangers they could encounter from the animals that live in the woods (e.g., bears, moose, etc.). Your brochure should include recommendations on what to do and what not to do if the tourist encounters a wild animal while hiking or driving through the woods. (*The Grizzly Sisters* by Bellows) For information on this subject, you can write to The National Wildlife Federation, 1400 16th Street, NW, Washington, D.C. 20036.

- The spotted white owl controversy has caused considerable animosity between conservationists and lumberjacks of the West. Conservationists want to protect the spotted white owl, which is an endangered animal living in the grand forests of Washington, Oregon, and parts of Canada. The lumber industry relies on these same forests for their products, and this industry supports many local employees and their families. After referring to newspaper articles for both sides of the story, write your own article stating your opinion on this issue and stating the reasons for your opinion. (*The Man Who Could Call Down Owls* by Bunting)

- Write a story about a time when you were lost in the woods. What steps did you take to survive? What forest products were helpful to you? What did you eat? How does your story end?

■ Art Activities

Following are instructions to give the students for various art activities.

- Find a picture of a woodland scene in a magazine or brochure. Cut the picture into 1 1\2-by-2-inch vertical strips. Distribute the strips to the students, dividing the strips evenly among them. Take a large sheet of drawing paper and cut it into the same number of vertical strips as the woodland scene. Distribute these strips in the same way. Have each student copy the strip from the picture onto the strip of drawing paper. When the students are finished, put the drawing-paper strips together. The strips will not match exactly, but the results will be striking.

- Draw four posters or large pictures of a forest scene, one for each of the seasons. Add as much detail as you can to depict how the forest changes. What differences can be seen in the plant life? When do different animals bear their young? Which animals molt or change features for the changing seasons? Which animals hibernate?

- Design a house for your favorite woodland animal. You can make a drawing of the house or use supplies from around your home to make the house you design. (*Need a House? Call Ms. Mouse* by Mendoza)

- Make a pine tree out of paper plates. Paint two paper plates green and let them dry. Cut each plate in half. Cut one of the half-plate sections in half again. On a piece of colored construction paper, arrange the pieces of paper plate in the shape of a tree, using the smaller sections as the top. Glue the pieces in place. Cut out a piece of brown paper to make the trunk of the tree. Draw pine cones and woodland creatures on and under your tree.

- Make a woodland decoration out of rocks and a tree limb. Gather some small, round, flat stones. Wash and dry the stones. Paint the stones to resemble woodland creatures such as squirrels, raccoons, or chipmunks. Find a small dead limb of a tree (find one that is unusual in shape). Arrange your rock animals on the tree limb and glue them in place.

- Make your own bear puppet. Cut along one of the folded side seams of a brown grocery bag. Then cut the bottom out of the bag. You will have a long flat piece of brown paper to work with. Fold the paper in half and draw the outline of a bear on one side. Holding the two sides together, cut through both thickness of paper so that you have two identical bear outlines. Lay one outline on top of the other. If one side has printing on it, make sure that side is to the inside when you stack your outlines. Glue or staple the edges of the outlines together, leaving the bottom open so you can put your hand inside the puppet. Draw the features of your bear on one side of the puppet. You can glue buttons on the front for a shirt, make a tie out of construction paper, make a hat to glue on, and so forth.

- Make a leaf print arrangement. You will need white paper, a box of tissues, a plate, poster/tempera paints, a pencil, fresh leaves and flowers, and a 1-inch-wide paintbrush. Arrange your leaves and flowers in a circular design of your choice. Work with the arrangement until you know exactly what you want to re-create on paper. Using the plate, trace around the outer edge on a piece of paper to define your working area. Make a dot at the center top and center bottom of the outline. Brush the appropriate color paint on the back of the leaf or flower that is at the top center of your arrangement. Gently place the leaf or flower, paint side down, at the top center of the circle you drew. Place it carefully, because once you have placed it, you cannot move it without smudging your print. Place a tissue over the leaf or flower and gently rub to make a complete impression on the paper. Let the leaf or flower sit for several seconds. Then remove the tissue and gently peel the leaf or flower off the paper. Repeat this process until your entire arrangement has been transferred to the paper. (Work from the center top down the left side of the circle to the bottom. Then start at the center top and work down the right side.) Be sure to let the design dry completely.

- Make your own gift bags out of brown lunch bags. On whatever color of construction paper you choose, draw the features for the front of your favorite woodland animal (squirrel, bear, chipmunk, raccoon, etc.). Make legs, ears, a face, a body, even a separate nose, if you want. Do the same thing for the features that you would see from the rear (additional legs, a tail, etc.). Take a brown lunch bag and glue the front features to one side of it and the back features to the other side. You can personalize the bag by printing the recipient's name on it. You can make your animal humorous by gluing a bow tie, necklace, earrings, or other "accessories" on it. Put your present inside the bag, and you have a wonderful surprise for a special friend.

- Gather items from the woods (e.g., acorns, pine cones, leaves, branches) and create a model for a still-life picture. Have the students arrange the objects to their liking and re-create what they see on paper. (Students can view the arrangement from any angle to make their drawings unique.)

- Listen to Tchaikovsky's music for *Peter and the Wolf*. Identify the instrument assigned to each character. Assign parts for each of the main characters and act out the story without using words. (*Peter and the Wolf* by Hastings)

- Follow the ideas given in *Night Tree* by Bunting to make "tasty" decorations for a tree in your yard. Make some hot chocolate afterwards and watch the birds and other animals come to munch on the decorations.

- Place a large sheet of paper on the floor along with some green, brown, black, yellow, and red paint. Let each child paint on the sheet of paper in turn until you (or the other children) count to 10. After each person has had a turn at painting, blow on the wet paint and tilt the paper so that the paint runs. This will create an even more interesting design. (The paint may be dry already if you wait for an entire group to paint before blowing on or tilting the paper.) When the paint is dry, cut the paper into sections so that each child gets a piece. If you are teaching only one or two children, give each child several pieces of the cut-up paper and take some for yourself. Take a walk through a nearby woods and try to find something in nature that matches each piece of your painting. When you return to class, draw a picture of what you found for each piece, gluing the piece of the painting in the proper place on your drawing.

Additional Resources

■ *National Geographic* Articles

Sea Life

November 1993—"The Desert Sea," page 60

December 1992—"Gentle Monsters of the Deep—Whale Sharks," page 123

July 1992—"Pillar of Life," page 95

March 1991—"Eye to Eye with the Giant Octopus," page 86

January 1991—"The Sea Beyond the Outback," page 42

Deserts

April 1992—"The Simpson Outback," page 64

January 1992—"Africa's Skeleton Coast," page 54

December 1991—"Ibn Battuta, Prince of Travelers," page 2

June 1991—"Bats—The Cactus Connection," page 131

Polar Regions

November 1993—"Kodiak, Alaska's Island Refuge," page 34

April 1993—"Alone Across the Arctic Crown," page 70

March 1993—"Reclaiming a Lost Antarctic Base," page 110

August 1992—"Denali, Alaska's Wild Heart," page 63

November 1991—"Alaska Highway: Wilderness Escape Route," page 68

July 1991—"Beneath Arctic Ice," page 2

March 1991—"The Hard Way to the North Pole," page 124

Tropical Forests

March 1992—"Bonobos, Chimpazees with a Difference," page 46

December 1991—"Rain Forest Canopy: The High Frontier," page 78

Grasslands

October 1993—"The American Prairie," page 90

April 1991—"Extremadura: Cradle of Conquerors," page 116

■ Organizations and Magazines

National Audubon Society
950 Third Ave.
New York, NY 10022

Sierra Club
730 Polk St.
San Francisco, CA 94109

National Geographic Society
17th and M Sts., NW
Washington, D.C. 20036

Sea Life

The Dolphin Log (bi-monthly magazine)
Cousteau Society
870 Greenbrier Cir., Suite 402
Chesapeake, VA 23320
804-523-9335

Project WILD
Salina Star Route
Boulder, CO 80302
Project WILD-Aquatic

Mystic Marinelife Aquarium
Education Department
55 Coogan Blvd.
Mystic, CT 06355-1997
The Classroom Ocean, Schoolword
newsletter

Sea Grant Marine Advisory Services
Virginia Institute of Marine Science
Gloucester Point, VA 23062
Fishy Activities (K–6)

National Aquarium/Baltimore
Education Department
501 E. Pratt St., Pier 3
Baltimore, MD 21202
*Living in Water: An Aquatic Science
Curriculum* (grades 4–6)

Sea World
1720 South Shores Rd.
Mission Bay, San Diego, CA 92109
curriculum guides, videos, posters, activity packets

National Wildlife Federation
1400 16th St., NW
Washington, D.C. 20036-2266
NatureScope issue: "Diving into Oceans"
(grades K–8)

South Carolina Sea Grant Consortium
221 Fort Johnson Rd.
James Island, Charleston, SC 29412
*Sea Sampler: Aquatic Activities for the Field and
Classroom (Elem./Sec.)*

Office of Marine Affairs
400 Oberlin Rd., Suite 300
Raleigh, NC 27605-1315
saltwater fish posters

The Whale Museum
P.O. Box 945
Friday Harbor, WA 98250
Gentle Giants of the Sea

Deserts

Arizona-Sonora Desert Museum
2021 N. Kinney Rd.
Tucson, AZ 85743

Death Valley Natural History Association
P.O. Box 188
Death Valley, CA 92328

California Native Plant Society
909 12th St., Suite 116
Sacramento, CA 95814

Many Feathers
2626 W. Indian School Rd.
Phoenix, AZ 85017

Southwest Parks and Monuments
Association
221 N. Court Ave.
Tucson, AZ 85701

Tucson Audubon Society
300 E. University Blvd., Suite 120
Tucson, AZ 85705

Polar Regions

The Alaska Geographic Society
P.O. Box 4 EEE
Anchorage, AK 99505

EDC Distribution Center
55 Chapel St.
Newton, MA 02160
films, videos

ALASKA Magazine
P.O. Box 10562
Des Moines, IA 50340

KYUK Video Productions
P.O. Box 468
Bethel, AK 99559
films, videos

Alaska Northwest Publishing Co.
130 Second Ave., South
Edmonds, WA 98020
children's and adult's books, maps,
magazines, catalog

Nunam Kitlutsisi
P.O. Box 2068
Bethel, AK 99559
booklets, videos, catalog, curriculum units

Documentary Educational Resources
24 Dance St.
Somerville, MA 02143
films, videos

Tundra Drums Newspaper
P.O. Box 868
Bethel, AK 99559

Woodlands

American Forest Institute
1619 Massachusetts Ave., NW
Washington, D.C. 20036

Minnesota Forest Industries
208 Phoenix Bldg.
Duluth, MN 55802

American Paper Institute
260 Madison Ave.
New York, NY 10016

National Arbor Day Foundation
100 Arbor Ave.
Nebraska City, NE 68410
Celebrate Arbor Day (poems, ideas for plays, activities)

Carolina Biological Supply Co.
2700 York Rd.
Burlington, NC 27215
posters

National Arbor Day Foundation
100 Arbor Ave.
Nebraska City, NE 68410
Celebrate Arbor Day (poems, ideas for plays, activities)

Industrial Forestry Association
225 S. W. Broadway, Room 400
Portland, OR 97205

Nova Scotia Department of Lands and Forests
Forest Resources Education
P.O. Box 68
Truro, Nova Scotia B2N 5B8

USDA Forest Service
P.O. Box 96090
Washington, D.C. 20009

USDA Forest Service
Woodsy Owl Campaign
P.O. Box 1963
Washington, D.C. 20013
leader's guide, posters, recordings, song
sheets, reproducibles

■ Videos

Ambrose Video Publications
1290 Ave. of the Americas, Suite 2245
New York, NY 10104

National Geographic Society Educational Services
Department 89
Washington, D.C. 20036

Educational Images, Ltd.
P.O. Box 3546
West Side Station
Elmira, NY 14905

Population Reference Bureau
774 14th St., NW
Washington, D.C. 20005

■ Web Sites

The following Web sites reference additional Web sites relating to different habitats. These Web sites are created especially for children. All sites were accessed in February 2001 and were active at that time.

Deserts: http://www.yahooligans.com/science_and_oddities/the_Earth/Ecology/Deserts

Forests: http://www.yahooligans.com/science_and_oddities/the_Earth/Ecology/Forests

Marine life: http://www.yahooligans.com/science_and_nature/Living_Things/Animals/Marine_Life

Oceans, lakes, rivers, and streams: http://www.yahooligans.com/science_and_oddities/Earth_the/
    Ecology/Oceans_Lakes_Rivers_and_Streams/

Rain forests: http://www.yahooligans.com/school_Bell/Social_studies/Geography/Bodies_of_water/

THE HUMAN BODY

- Key Concepts

- Comprehensive Teaching Resources

- Chapter 1: The Five Senses

- Chapter 2: Body Systems and Health

- Chapter 3: Nutrition and Exercise

- Chapter 4: Diseases, Disabilities, and Disorders

- Additional Resources

■ Primary Concepts

Students will be able to:

1. Explain that the eyes are the part of the body that we use for seeing and recognize that light is necessary to be able to see (Chapter 1).

2. Explain that the ears are the part of the body that we use for hearing and match common household sounds to their sources (Chapter 1).

3. Explain that the skin is the part of the body that we use for feeling and identify appropriate objects that could be described as "smooth," "rough," "soft," and "hard" (Chapter 1).

4. Explain that the nose is the part of the body that we use for smelling and match appropriate substances to their related smells (Chapter 1).

5. Explain that the tongue is the part of the body that we use for tasting and match various foods to the labels "sweet," "sour," "salty," and "bitter" (Chapter 1).

6. Differentiate between the muscular and skeletal systems, providing a simple description of the function of each, while understanding that these systems work together (Chapter 2).

7. Separate a variety of foods into categories of healthy and unhealthy foods (Chapter 3).

8. Explain that a variety of foods is essential for a balanced diet (Chapter 3).

9. Explain why eating proper food, combined with rest and exercise, is necessary for good health and will facilitate growth (Chapters 2, 3).

10. Explain that a healthy body can protect itself against harmful germs (Chapter 2).

11. Explain sanitary practices to help protect one's self against germs (Chapter 2).

12. Understand that germs cause disease (Chapters 2, 4).

13. Understand that germs can enter the body through the air we breathe and the water we drink (Chapters 2, 4).

■ Intermediate Concepts

Students will be able to:

1. Identify the cell as the basic building block of the human body (Chapter 2).

2. Distinguish among cells, tissues, organs, and systems (Chapter 2).

3. Name and identify on a model the various organs that make up the digestive system (Chapter 2).

4. Explain the function of each major organ in the digestive system (Chapter 2).

5. Explain and describe the following features of the nervous system (Chapter 2):

   a. The three main divisions of the nervous system and their functions (central nervous system, peripheral nervous system, and autonomic nervous system).

   b. The three types of nerve cells and their functions (cell body, axon, and dendrites).

   c. A reflex.

   d. The three main parts of the brain and their functions (cerebrum, cerebellum, and brain stem).

6. Identify the following parts of the circulatory system and explain the function of each: heart, arteries, veins, blood, capillaries (Chapter 2).

7. Explain the structure of the heart (Chapter 2).

8. Understand that blood is made of red and white blood cells, platelets, and plasma (Chapter 2).

9. Diagram the flow of blood through the body (Chapter 2).

10. Identify the parts of the respiratory system on a diagram (nose, windpipe, trachea, bronchial tubes, lungs) Trace the passage of air through the respiratory system. (Chapter 2).

11. Discuss how the movement of air from the lungs and through the windpipe causes vocal cords to vibrate, making speech (Chapter 2).

12. Explain and describe the following features of the skeletal and muscular systems (Chapters 2–4):

   a. The functions of the skeletal system (hold body erect, protect major organs, manufacture blood cells, allow for precise movement).

   b. The differences among the terms joint, ligament, and tendon.

   c. Three types of muscle tissue (skeletal, smooth, and cardiac).

   d. How muscles cause bones to move.

   e. The differences and similarities between voluntary and involuntary muscles.

   f. The differences among a fracture, sprain, strain, and cramp.

   g. The importance of proper exercise, rest, and nutrition to healthy muscles and bones.

13. Locate and name the following parts of the male anatomy on a model or chart, explaining the function of each: penis, testicles, scrotum, bladder, and urethra (Chapter 2).

14. Locate and name the following parts of the female anatomy on a model or chart, explaining the function of each: ovaries, uterus, fallopian tubes, and vagina (Chapter 2).

15. Define the following terms: puberty, pituitary glands, hormones, sperm cell, egg cell, menstruation, period, egg, ovulation (Chapter 2).

16. Understand the changes that occur in males and females at puberty (Chapter 2):

   Each boy and girl grows at a different rate and reaches puberty at a different time.

   Hormones produced by glands control growth.

   Some temporary changes often occur at puberty, such as acne, increased perspiration, and emotional stress.

17. Explain the physiology of human reproduction using appropriate terms (Chapter 2).

18. Recognize how a healthy digestive system is maintained and why this is important (Chapter 2).

19. Keep a record of food intake for a week, applying it to the food pyramid, and monitor exercise and rest. Afterwards, evaluate it, making necessary recommendations for changes, and note areas of strength (Chapter 3).

20. Explain the relationship between proper eating habits, aerobic exercise, and normal blood pressure (Chapter 3).

21. Understand the damaging effects that alcohol, drugs, and tobacco have on the digestive system (Chapter 4).

22. Understand and be able to explain what Acquired Immune Deficiency Syndrome (AIDS) is and the different ways that it can and cannot be contracted (from a mother before or during birth, through blood transfusions, through sexual contact with someone who is infected, by sharing needles during intravenous drug use) (Chapter 4).

■ Upper Concepts

Students will be able to:

1. Describe the functions of the skeleton (Chapter 2).

2. Diagram the human skeleton, labeling the major bones (Chapter 2).

3. Name the three main parts of a bone and describe the importance of bone marrow (Chapter 2).

4. Define and differentiate among (Chapter 2):

    a ligament

    a joint

    cartilage

5. Differentiate among (Chapter 4):

    a break

    a fracture (simple and compound)

    arthritis

6. Describe the functions of the muscles (Chapter 2).

7. Name and describe the functions of the three main muscle types (skeletal muscles, smooth muscles, and cardiac muscles) (Chapter 2).

8. Diagram the human muscular system (Chapter 2).

9. Identify and differentiate between a flexed and a relaxed skeletal muscle (Chapter 2).

10. Describe how muscles move bones (Chapter 2).

11. Explain the function of a tendon and describe its relationship to the skeletal system (Chapter 2).

12. Describe the following muscular disorders (Chapter 4): cramp, strain, tear, tendinitis, muscular dystrophy.

13. Describe correct methods of warming up prior to exercise, recognizing causes of exercise-related injuries and explaining how to prevent them (Chapter 3).

14. Explain the functions of the glandular system (Chapter 2).

15. Label the following glands on a diagram and explain each gland's function (Chapter 2): pituitary, adrenal, thyroid, parathyroid, liver.

16. Compare and contrast duct and ductless glands (Chapter 2).

17. Describe the purpose of circulation (Chapter 2).

18. Diagram the heart and label its parts (Chapter 2).

19. Contrast an artery to a vein, explaining where each goes and what it carries (Chapter 2).

20. Discuss the functions of arteries, veins, and capillaries (Chapter 2).

21. Describe blood pressure and blood flow (Chapter 2).

22. Draw a diagram of the circulatory system (Chapter 2).

23. Name the three main blood cells (red, white, and platelets) and their functions (Chapter 2).

24. Name the four main blood types (A, B, AB, and O) (Chapter 2).

25. Discuss various circulatory disorders (e.g., anemia, leukemia, hemophilia) (Chapter 4).

26. Discuss the functions of the nervous system (Chapter 2).

27. Draw a diagram of a neuron (include the cell body, axon, dendrites, and nerve membrane) and describe the functions of the three types of nerve cells (sensory, association, motor) (Chapter 2).

28. Draw a diagram of the brain, labeling and listing the functions of each part (Chapter 2).

29. Compare and contrast the voluntary and involuntary nervous systems, listing two actions governed by each (Chapter 2).

30. Describe each of the following central nervous system disorders (Chapter 4): Parkinson's disease, cerebral palsy, epilepsy, stroke, nervous breakdown, polio myelitis.

31. Draw a diagram of the eye and label the main parts (Chapter 2).

32. Differentiate between nearsightedness and farsightedness (Chapter 2).

33. Explain how eyeglasses use different types of lenses to correct sight disorders (Chapter 4).

34. Draw a diagram of the ear, labeling the main parts and listing the function of each (Chapter 2).

35. Describe how the sense of balance and the vestibular organs in the inner ear are related (Chapter 2).

36. Describe various auditory disorders (tinnitus, otitis media, otosclerosis, acoustic neuroma, etc.) (Chapter 4).

37. Draw a diagram of the layers of the skin, labeling each (epidermis, dermis, and subcutaneous tissue) (Chapter 2).

38. Describe how the mechanics of touch are related to the nervous system (Chapter 2).

39. Recognize the sections of the tongue that distinguish (Chapter 2) salt, sour, sweet, and bitter.

40. Describe the smelling process and its relationship to the nasal cavity and the olfactory nerve (Chapter 2).

41. Diagram the digestive system and describe its functions (Chapter 2).

42. Describe the function of each of the following organs (Chapter 2): mouth, esophagus, stomach, duodenum, small intestine, large intestine.

43. Describe enzymes and their importance in the digestive system (Chapter 2).

44. Name the organ of the body in which each of the following food types are broken down (Chapter 2): starches, proteins, fats, and sugars.

45. Discuss the relationship between metabolism and the digestive processes (Chapter 2).

46. After reviewing guidelines for healthy eating habits, which promote proper digestion, and by referring to the nutritional pyramid, choose high-fiber, low-fat foods that demonstrate healthy food choices and include nutrients, vitamins, and minerals (Chapter 3).

47. Discuss symptoms of eating disorders (anorexia, bulimia) and how to access local resources in the community to obtain help for those suffering from these disorders (Chapter 4).

48. Describe the functions of the respiratory system (Chapter 2).

49. Draw a diagram of the respiratory system and label the main organs (nose, trachea/windpipe, two lungs, bronchial tubes) (Chapter 2).

50. Contrast internal and external respiration (Chapter 2).

51. Describe the steps involved in the breathing process (Chapter 2).

52. Describe the relationship between the circulatory system and the respiratory system (Chapter 2).

53. Discuss various respiratory disorders (asthma, pneumonia, black lung, etc.) (Chapter 4).

54. Set realistic fitness goals that can be incorporated into a healthy personal lifestyle (Chapter 3).

Comprehensive Teaching Resources

Listed in the table are books that cover a wide range of topics in the area of the human body. One of these books could serve as your main teaching guide while studying this unit. Each book is listed with a short summary, and the chapters it applies to are noted. The books are listed by degree of difficulty, easiest to most difficult.

BOOK AND SUMMARY	AUTHOR	CHAPTERS			
		1	2	3	4
The Immune System: Your Magic Doctor (Shire Press) This picture book, with brief text, based on a film, introduces the reader to the immune system. Sections include information on fever, pus, vaccines, allergies, colds, cancer, and AIDS. Also contains advice on how to stay healthy.	Helen Garvy, (1992)		X		X
The Pulse of Life, The Circulatory System (Dillon Press) Text details the heart, heart disease, and ways to stay healthy. (This is part of the Body Talk Series, which includes *Breathing, Reproduction, Digestion, Mind and Matter, Movement, Sound and Vision, Smell, Taste, and Touch.*)	Jenny Bryan, (1993)	X	X		X
Eyewitness Books: Human Body (DK Pub) Explicitly illustrates and explains the parts of the body and how they work, including circulation, digestion, the five senses, and movement.	Steve Parker, (1999)	X	X		
The Brain And Nervous System (Raintree/Steck Vaughn). Describes the makeup, functions, and disorders of the nervous system.	Steve Parker, (1997)		X		X

Each chapter in this section lists reference books that focus on the specific area of the human body being addressed. These books can be used to complement and expand upon the basic information provided in the comprehensive resource books listed in the table.

The reference books in each chapter have been classified by age level to help you select those that best fit the needs and interests of the student(s).

Chapter 1
The Five Senses

■ Teaching Resources

Books containing experiment(s) relating to the subject matter are marked with a plus sign (+) before and after the title.

P   *The Five Senses: Touch,* by Maria Rius (Barron's, 1985)
Short, concise description of our sense of touch, accompanied by helpful illustrations. (Also: *Smell,* 1985; *Taste,* 1985; *Hearing,* 1985; and *Sight,* 1985.)

P   *Look at Your Eyes,* by Paul Showers (HarperCollins, 1992)
Describes the parts of the eye and how they work.

P   *My Five Senses,* Aliki (Harper Trophy, 1990)
Bright illustrations, with simple text, depict the five senses from a child's point of view.

P/I *Professor I.Q. Explores the Senses,* by Seymour Simon (Boyds Mills Press, 1993)
Discusses the five senses, with simplistic text and comic-like illustrations.

I   *Ears,* by Douglas Mathers (Troll, 1992)
Describes the ears' functions of hearing, balance, and determining distances.

I   *Eyes,* by Aleksander Jedrosz (Troll, 1992)
Describes the parts of the eye, how they work, and other aspects of seeing, including health.

I/U *+Looking at Senses,+* by David Suzuki (John Wiley & Sons, 1991)
Describes the five senses and also uncommon ones such as ESP, with projects and activities. Author is the host of television's "The Nature of Things."

■ Reading Selections

Books marked with an asterisk (*) before and after the title are related to activities in the activity sections of this chapter.

Arthur's Eyes, by Marc Brown (Little, Brown, 1986)
     Arthur must get glasses and is teased by his friends. Finally, he learns to wear his glasses with pride.

Arthur's Nose, by Marc Brown (Little, Brown, 1986)
     Arthur decides to visit the doctor to get a new nose.

Ben's Trumpet, by Rachel Isadora (Mulberry Books, 1991)
> Ben stops to listen to the musicians at a neighborhood nightclub whenever he can and dreams of playing the trumpet himself.

Brown Bear, Brown Bear, What Do You See?, by Bill Martin, Jr. (Henry Holt, 1996)
> A variety of animals look at each other in a variety of different colors.

The Chocolate Touch, by Patrick Skene Catling (Dell, 1996)
> A young boy gets his wish that everything that touches his lips should turn to chocolate. (Chapter Book)

Cock-a-Doodle Dudley, by Bill Peet (Houghton Mifflin, 1990)
> A spiteful goose questions Dudley's ability to make the sun rise with his crowing.

Each Peach, Pear, Plum, by Janet Ahlberg and Allan Ahlberg (Penguin UK, 1999)
> In rhyming verse, this book takes the reader through fairy-tale land, allowing you to find your favorite characters in the pictures that accompany the verse.

Figment, Your Dog, Speaking, by Laura Hawkins (Houghton Mifflin, 1991)
> Marcella Starbuckle learns to make friends and stop lying with the help of a talking stray dog that she takes in. (Chapter Book)

Flatfoot Fox and the Case of the Missing Eye, by Eth Clifford (Houghton Mifflin, 1990)
> A clever detective solves the mystery of the disappearance of Fat Cat's stolen glass eye. (Chapter Book)

Flatfoot Fox and the Case of the Nosy Otter, by Eth Clifford (Houghton Mifflin, 1992)
> Flatfoot Fox teams up with Secretary Bird to locate the kidnapped Nosy Otter. (Chapter Book)

Glasses, Who Needs 'em?, by Lane Smith (Viking Penguin, 1991)
> A doctor provides an unhappy boy with an imaginative list of well-adjusted eyeglass wearers.

Half a Moon and One Whole Star, by Crescent Dragonwagon (Aladdin, 1990)
> Susan falls asleep listening to all of the wonderful sounds of a summer's night.

I Can Hear the Sun, by Patricia Polacco (Philomel, 1996)
> A girl who cares for animals and listens to the sun believes a childless boy who tells her he has been invited to fly away with a flock of geese.

I See, by Rachel Isadora (William Morrow, 1987)
> A baby reacts to all the things she sees during a day.

I See the Moon, and the Moon Sees Me . . . , by Helen Craig (Puffin Picture Books, 1998)
> A collection of nursery rhymes, most of which involve the use of one of the five senses.

Is It Rough? Is It Smooth? Is It Shiny?, by Tana Hoban (Greenwillow, 1984)
> Color photographs without text introduce objects of many different textures.

Lizard Music, by D. Manus Pinkwater (Bantam Books, 1996)
> After being left to take care of himself, Victor meets a community of intelligent lizards and learns of an invasion from outer space. (Chapter Book)

Look! Book!, by Tana Hoban (Greenwillow, 1997)
> View objects through a cut-out hole and try to determine what the entire object is.

Look! The Ultimate Spot-the-Difference Book, by April Wilson (Dial Books for Young Readers, 1990)
> Presents a pair of pictures that seem to be the same, but the second picture actually contains 12 differences. Can you find them?

Look Again! The Second Ultimate Spot-the-Difference Book, by April Wilson (Dial Books for Young Readers, 1992)
> Find different plants and animals in 12 habitats that use camouflage to protect themselves in their surroundings.

Martha Speaks, by Susan Meddaugh (Houghton Mifflin, 1995)
> Martha, the family dog, eats a bowl of alphabet soup and begins to talk.

Moongame, by Frank Asch (Aladdin, 1987)
> Bear plays hide-and-seek with the Moon only to become very worried when the Moon finds a hiding place that is too good.

My Five Senses, by Aliki (Harper Trophy, 1990)
> An casy-to-rcad presentation of the five senses and how we use them.

My Hands, by Aliki (Econo-Clad, 1999)
> Describes the parts of the hands and the many wonderful things a child can do with them.

My Very First Book of Sounds, by Eric Carle (Thomas Y. Crowell, 1986)
> Pages split to make many different combinations of words and pictures.

Night in the Country, by Cynthia Rylant (Aladdin, 1991)
> Describes the sights and sounds of night as it happens in the country.

Night Noises, by Mem Fox (Harcourt Brace, 1992)
> Old Lily falls asleep to the night sounds outside and awakens to an unexpected surprise.

Nobody Listens to Andrew, by Elizabeth Guilfoile (Modern Curriculum Press, 1980)
> Andrew tries to warn his family about an emergency in his house, but everyone is too busy to listen.

Not So Fast Songololo, by Niki Daly (Aladdin, 1996)
> While everyone rushes and fills the house with noise in the morning, Malusi prefers to take things slow and enjoy his day.

Only the Cat Saw, by Ashley Wolff (Walker, 1996)
> As the family settles down for the night, Amy's cat gets ready to explore and see many things.

Opt: An Illusionary Tale, by Arline Baum and Joseph Baum (Puffin Picture Books, 1989)
> A tale of optical illusions in which images change shapes and appear and disappear.

Peace at Last, by Jill Murphy (Dial Books for Young Readers, 1992)
> Mr. Bear has a very hard time getting to sleep because of the noise going on in his home at night.

Peek-a-Boo!, by Janet Ahlberg and Allan Ahlberg (Viking Children's Press, 1997)
> Describes what a baby sees as he goes through the activities of his busy day.

Polar Bear, Polar Bear, What Do You Hear?, by Bill Martin, Jr. (Henry Holt, 1997)
> Children imitate the different sounds that animals make, from polar bears to walruses.

The Princess and the Pea, by Janet Stevens (Holiday House, 1989)
> The Queen, discouraged about not finding a suitable princess for the Prince, gives one more princess a test.

Salt Hands, by Jane Chelsea Aragon (Econo-Clad, 1999)
> When a young girl discovers a deer in her yard in the middle of the night, she fills her hands with salt and goes out to try to make friends.

Song and Dance Man, by Karen Ackerman (Alfred A. Knopf, 1992)
> Grandpa and his grandchildren spend the day enjoying the songs, dances, and jokes that Grandpa remembers from his days as a vaudeville performer.

Storm in the Night, by Mary Stolz (Harper Trophy, 1990)
> While sitting through a thunderstorm that has put all the lights out, Thomas listens to Grandfather tell about a time when he feared thunderstorms.

Tasty Poems, by Jill Bennett (Oxford Press, 1988)
> Illustrated collection of poems about food from English and American authors.

Thunder Cake, by Patricia Polacco (Paper Star, 1997)
> When a storm approaches her grandmother's farm, a little girl learns not to be afraid of the thunder by helping her grandmother make her famous Thunder Cake.

Watch Out, Ronald Morgan!, by Patricia Reilly Giff (Econo-Clad, 1999)
> Ronald finds that he doesn't have nearly as many mishaps after he gets a pair of eyeglasses.

We Hide, You Seek, by Jose Aruego and Ariane Dewey (Greenwillow, 1979)
> Readers must find animals that are hidden in their natural habitats.

Wheels on the Bus, by Raffi Songs to Read (Crown, 1998)
> The passengers collected by a little bus in a small town make a variety of sounds, and so does the bus.

When the Woods Hum, by Joanne Ryder (Morrow Junior Books, 1991)
> A little girl listens in awe to the sound of the cicadas, then returns 17 years later with her son to hear them again.

Where's Our Mama?, by Diane Goode (Puffin Books, 1995)
> Two little children lose their mother in a Paris train station. Their description of what mama looks like makes it difficult for the gendarme to track her down.

Wood-Hoopoe Willie, by Virginia Kroll (Charlesbridge, 1995)
> Willie finds many ways to create noises and rhythms using everyday items.

The following books are out of print, but may be available at the local library.

Do Not Touch, by Lark Carrier (Picture Book Studio, 1988)
> Follows a child through her day with special pictures and words within words.

Jack and Jake, by Aliki (Greenwillow Books, 1986)
> Provides visual and audio clues to help the reader tell the differences between twin brothers, Jack and Jake.

The Magnificent Moo, by Victoria Forrester (Atheneum, 1983)
> When a cow is scared by the loud mooing sound she makes, a cat agrees to switch sounds with her.

Mara in the Morning, by C. B. Christiansen (Atheneum, 1991)
>   When Mara wakes up before the rest of the family, she moves around quietly, listening to all of the sounds of the morning.

Places I Like to Be,, by Evelyn M. Andre (Abingdon Press, 1980)
>   Explores some of the favorite places and things that children like to go and do.

The Quiet Farmer, by Marni McGee (Atheneum, 1991)
>   A quiet farmer hears many different sounds as he goes through his daily tasks.

Rain Talk, by Mary Serfozo (Margaret K. McElderry, 1990)
>   A child enjoys a day of listening to the various sounds that rain makes as it falls from the sky.

Stop That Noise!, by Paul Geraghty (Crown Publishers, 1992)
>   A small mouse is no longer annoyed by the noises of the forest after he experiences the sounds of a machine that has come to tear down the forest.

Under the Moon,, by Joanne Ryder (Random House, 1989)
>   Little mouse learns how to find his way home by remembering its special smells, sounds, and textures.

What's So Funny, Ketu?,, by Verna Aardema (Dial Press, 1982)
>   Ketu is rewarded for saving the life of a snake by being allowed to hear what animals think. This wondrous gift ends up getting Ketu in quite a bit of trouble.

■ Science Activities

Sensing Your Way

Have the students describe how to get to their houses from another location (school, church, the shopping mall, a friend's house) without depending on the sense of sight. Ask them to consider: What sounds would you hear? What bumps and vibrations would you encounter? How long would it take? Students can write a set of directions from the location they chose to their homes. Be sure that the directions do not require any visual assistance. Students could also make a map of their route by making drawings to designate the sounds, smells, and other sensations that help them reach their destination.

What's That Smell?

Check to see how keen your students' sense of smell is. The day before doing this activity, prepare samples for the students to smell. These samples should be things with a distinctive odor (an orange slice, apple cider, vanilla, onion, almond extract, cinnamon, garlic, etc.). Place the samples in individual small paper cups. Number the cups and record what item is in each. Let the samples sit in the cup overnight. Then remove the samples so that only the scent remains in the cup (or leave the samples in, but cover them with cotton balls so they can be smelled but not seen). Pass the cups around and have the students sniff each cup, then write down what scent they detected. Check their answers against the list of correct answers.

Sensations

- Touch is one of the five senses, but how many different sensations can we detect by using touch? Give the students different objects to feel and list the words they use to describe these objects (sticky, mushy, rough, smooth, hard, soft, scratchy). Can they think of other sensations we can detect through touch (hot, cold, pressure, pain, etc.)?

- Words we use to describe what our senses detect are usually adjectives. Introduce, or review, adjectives with the students. Have them think of a specific object. Then have them describe the object by listing as many adjectives as they can think of to describe it. See if others can guess what the object is by reading the list of adjectives associated with it.

- Another variation to the previous activity would be to place an object inside a brown bag. Have the students touch the object inside the bag and describe it to the class or family using descriptive words and phrases. See if the class or family can guess what the object is.

Hearing

Sound Out

Ask the students if there are sounds around them that they "block out." Have the students close their eyes for a few minutes and listen to all the different sounds they can hear. Discuss some of the sounds they hear. Discuss why they weren't aware of them before. Which sense do most of us depend on the most?

What's That You Hear?

Our ears and sense of hearing allow us to detect a sound, such as a bell ringing. However, even a simple sound, such as a bell, can have many different sounds. Gather as many different bells as you can and, as a class, compare the sounds. Ask the students: How are they different? What makes the various pitches different? What controls the loudness? Do some rings last longer than others? Our sense of hearing is very specialized to detect all of these differences.

Demonstrate pitch to the class. Gather five glasses about the same size and shape (or use test tubes). Pour water into the glasses, filling the first glass up to 1/2 inch from the rim. Fill each subsequent glass 1/2 inch less than the one before it so that each glass contains a different amount of water. Lightly strike the glasses, one at a time, with a spoon, and listen to the sound they make. Discuss if the sounds are the same or different? Why? (Water slows down the vibration of sound waves, making the pitch lower.) If using test tubes, blow into the test tubes which will create a sound. How do these sounds compare to the different levels of water? (They will be the opposite of before.) Older students can do this activity individually and investigate sound waves and patterns. How can the waves represent differences in pitch? In loudness?

Shoe Box Symphony

Have the students take a shoe box, without the lid, and place rubber bands of different lengths and thicknesses around it, widthwise. Have them pluck the different rubber bands. Discuss how the pitches compare. Which have a higher pitch: the shorter bands or the longer ones? The tight bands or the loose ones? The thin bands or the thick ones? Why?

Discuss whether an object must vibrate to create sound. Ask the students: Can a rubber band make a sound when it is not vibrating? Place your hand on your throat and hum. What do you feel? Must your voice box vibrate to create sound?

Sound Absorption

Knock on a table or floor with your fist. Repeat the activity, but this time place something soft, such as a pillow, on the surface. Ask the students: How did the sound change? Why? What objects in your home (or school) absorb sound (e.g., carpet, draperies, soft furniture)? What objects bounce sound off (e.g., walls, hardwood floors, wood furniture)?

What Does It Sound Like?

Make an audiotape of different sounds around your house, school, or neighborhood. Play the tape for the class and see if they can guess what the sounds are.

Silent TV

Have the students watch a designated television program with the sound off. Have each student write down what he or she thought the story was about. (The teacher should watch the program with the sound on.) The next day, discuss what the program was about. Compare that to the written stories.

Good Vibrations

"See" a vibration. Have the students lay one end of a ruler or knitting needle on the end of a table, letting the other end (most of the ruler/needle) hang out in mid-air. They should hold the end that is resting on the table with one hand and snap the end that is hanging out with their other hand. They will be able to see the object vibrate.

I See That Sound!

Have the students stretch a piece of clear plastic over the top of a jar tightly. They should use a rubber band to hold it in place. Then have the students sprinkle a small amount of salt or sugar over the plastic and spread it out evenly. The teacher can hold a metal tray or the tip of a cookie tin close to the jar and bang it somewhat loudly with a spoon. As the teacher moves around the room, notice how the grains "dance" over the plastic as he or she hits the tray. That is caused by the sound vibrations moving through the air.

Be a Sound Wave

To duplicate the process of sound producing movement in your ear:

- Write the parts of the ear on individual cards. Tie a separate piece of string through the upper corners of each card to make nine individual necklaces. The cards you will need are Outer Ear, Ear Canal, Ear Drum, Malleus, Incus, Stapes, Oval Window, Cochlea, and Hearing Nerve.
- Have nine children wear the necklaces and stand next to each other in the order listed above, holding hands.
- A "leader" will squeeze a "message" into the first child's hand (one long squeeze, then one short squeeze, or whatever the leader chooses).
- Each child should then in turn transfer the message to the next person in line. (See if the correct message makes it all the way through the line of children.)
- This is the same process your ear goes through every time it hears a sound.

Make a String Telephone

Have the students make a string telephone. Each pair of students will need two empty plastic cups and some strong, thin string (about 8–12 feet). Have the students make a small hole in the bottom of each cup and thread an end of the string through each hole. Then have them tie a knot on the inside end of the string to keep it in place. Be sure that they keep the string stretched tightly as they talk. The cup acts as both the mouthpiece and earpiece. Discuss how the voice of the person at one end gets to the person at the other end.

Sight

Build an Eye

Using hardening clay and a diagram from a textbook, have the students make a model of the human eye. After the clay has hardened, paint each section of the eye and label it. Discuss how the human eye compares to the eyes of different animals. Have the students look at the eyes of cats, insects, sharks, and so forth, and record their observations. Compare this information to what they have learned about the human eye.

Eye Contractions

Have a student stand in a bright spot in the room for one or two minutes. When the time is up, have the student look in a mirror at his or her eyes. Ask the students: What is the size of the pupils? Move the student to a dark spot (inside a closet or bathroom with no window is ideal) and have him or her stay there for another one or two minutes, then look into the mirror again. Discuss: Did the size of the pupils change from before? Why? Why is it important that the iris and pupil be able to contract?

Ask the students: Does the color of our eyes have any bearing on our ability to see? Test out the classes' predictions. Write different letters of the alphabet on separate 3-by-5-inch note cards. Have the class line up in front of the room. Show one of the cards to each of the students in turn. Ask the student to read the letter. If the student identifies the letter correctly, move on to the next student and the next letter. If the student cannot correctly identify the letter, have that student sit down. Keep repeating this process, moving a few steps farther away from the students each time you start over at the beginning of the line.

When only five or six students are left in line, check to see the color of each student's eyes. (There should be a mixture of eye colors left standing—assuming you began with a representative mixture of colors—because eye color has nothing to do with how well we see.)

Vision

Even a person with excellent vision cannot see the details of many of the things around us. Have the students look at a leaf, a piece of yarn, and other objects under a magnifying glass (or better yet, a microscope). Ask the students: What details about the object can you see under a magnifying glass that you cannot see with the naked eye? Would it be advantageous for us to be able to see everything in such minute detail?

Eye Talk

Light is reflected differently through different lenses, which is why eyeglasses are custom made for each individual person. Ask the class to find what the difference is between an optometrist, optician, and an ophthalmologist. What duties does each perform?

Have the students look at different pairs of eyeglasses. Have them note if the lenses are convex or concave. (If the lenses are concave, objects will appear smaller. The glasses are correcting nearsightedness. Convex lenses correct farsightedness and magnify objects.) Discuss what bifocals are and their purpose.

Optical Illusions

Sometimes what our eyes see is not necessarily what's actually there. Obtain an experiment book on optical illusions (i.e., *Experiments in Optical Illusions* by Beeler and Branley) and look at some examples of optical illusions. Ask the students: What are optical illusions? How are they deceiving? Are there other times when our eyes can deceive us? For example, what causes mirages? Why do we see less clearly in the dark? If possible, demonstrate some magic tricks in which "what you see is not really what's there."

Examine drawings in which a 3-dimensisonal picture is hidden behind a graphic design. It takes time for your eyes to adjust and see the 3-D object that is hidden. (Many people never see the hidden object.)

Bring in a variety of pictures and find out who in your class is the champion at seeing the hidden object the fastest. (There are calendars available that offer a good sampling of these pictures, and some newspapers print "hidden pictures.")

Looking at the World Through Rose-Colored Glasses

Here's a trick that causes someone to see blue by looking at red. You will need one sheet of red paper and one sheet of white paper for each student. Have the students stare at the piece of red paper for about one minute. Immediately after, stare at the white paper. The white paper will appear to be a blue-green color instead of white. This phenomenon is known as "after-image." (You eyes became tired after staring at the red paper for so long. White reflects all the colors in the spectrum. When you switched to the white paper, your eyes could no longer see red, so they switched to the other end of the spectrum and saw blue-green.) Have the students try this experiment using the other basic colors to determine if any other colors have after-images. Record your findings.

It's Me Again, and Again, and Again . . . !

Lean two large mirrors against opposite walls (in a hallway) so that each mirror's reflection shows into the other mirror and they are a few feet apart. Have the students sit down between the two mirrors and observe how many of them are there. Before you actually perform this experiment, have the participants predict how many images will appear. The light that reflects your image to your eyes is also bouncing back and forth between the mirrors. Each bounce makes you appear smaller and smaller until poof! you've disappeared!

Taste Test

How many different types of tastes can we detect? Prepare some food samples for tasting (e.g., onions, pickles, apples, salt, sugar, lemon slices/juice, orange slices/juice, instant coffee crystals, unsweetened chocolate, milk chocolate). Have each student hold his or her nose and close his or her eyes and taste each sample. The student should record whether the sample is sweet, salty, sour, or bitter. Could all of the samples be recorded in one of these categories? Older students should make diagrams showing where on the tongue each taste (sweet, sour, salty, bitter) is detected. (Sweet is on the front of the tongue; bitter in the back center; salty on the front sides; and sour on the back sides.) Ask the students: If you had to choose to have only the sense of smell or the sense of taste, which one would you choose? Why?

■ Creative Writing Activities

Following are instructions to give the students for various writing activities.

- Write a story about a time when you offered an animal food in hopes of making friends with it. (*Salt Hands* by Aragon)
- Would you like to be able to hear what other people are thinking? Decide whether this would be a good skill to have and write a paper explaining your point of view. (*What's So Funny, Ketu?* by Aardema)
- Compare the sights and sounds of night in the country with the sights and sounds of night in the city. Depending on your location, you may need to interview others who have experience to draw on or find additional books to provide you with information. (*Night in the Country* by Rylant)
- Often a scent can trigger a memory. The smell of pine brings thoughts of cutting down a Christmas tree; the smell of chocolate chip cookies baking may bring memories of a special time. Write a story about some pleasurable experience you had that involved the scent of something. Be sure to detail why that event is special to you.

- You were fast asleep one Saturday morning, when, all of a sudden, you heard the most peculiar noise! Where was it coming from? What was causing it? Write a diary entry for that Saturday that tells "Dear Diary" what happened.

- Pretend that you work for an ear, nose, and throat doctor. The doctor has asked you to help him prepare a pamphlet to give to his patients informing them of how they should take care of their ears. Research the proper method of caring for and protecting human ears. Design a pamphlet that will communicate this information to the doctor's patients.

- Imagine that you have just regained your hearing after an accident that left you temporarily deaf. What sound do you think would be the most beautiful to you? Would there be any sounds that annoy you? Write a story telling about this event in your life. Do you think this experience would change the way you live in any way?

- Write about a time when you had to "eat your words." What would you do differently the next time you get in a similar situation?

- Create a restaurant menu. Instead of using the usual categories to list your foods (appetizers, entrees, salads, soups, desserts, etc.), categorize your food offerings under the titles "Sweet," "Sour," "Salty," and "Bitter."

- You have always wanted to have a twin brother or sister. Pretend you have the ability to design a twin to your exact specifications. How would your twin resemble you? In what ways would he or she be different? Would you like your twin to be the same gender as you? Why or why not? (*Jack and Jake* by Aliki)

- Write a humorous story about two animals who decide to exchange sounds with each other (e.g., a cow that now "quacks" and a duck that now "moos"). (*The Magnificent Moo* by Forrester)

- Write a poem about someone or something that is very special to you. Your poem should include descriptions of things about this person or object that affect at least three of your five senses (e.g., "A faint smell of lilacs enters the room just before she does."). This can also be a good practice exercise for the use of similes and metaphors (e.g., "His hair is short and curly like a piece of steel wool.).

- A new pill has been invented that will fulfill all of your dietary needs. Would you rather sit down to eat a meal the "old-fashioned way," or simply take a pill and be able to continue with your daily activities uninterrupted? Write a letter to the company that is producing this pill to give them your opinion of the merits or shortcomings of their invention.

■ Art Activities

Following are instructions to give the students for various art activities.

- Read *Do Not Touch* by Carrier. Get four or five sheets of legal-sized white paper. Fold the bottom one-third of the paper up to make a flap that can open and close. Close the flap, turn the paper lengthwise, and write your own short sentence ending with a word-within-a-word as the book does. Open the flap and write the word contained in the longer word and illustrate the sentence (e.g., I just saw an elephant!—ant). Staple the pages together to make your own book. You can design a cover for your book.

- Draw a map of how you get to your favorite place. Draw in pictures of landmarks you pass on the way. (*Places I Like to Be* by Andre)

- Make your own eye chart using pictures rather than letters. The top picture should be the largest, and each subsequent row of pictures should be a little smaller than the one before it. You can give your eye chart a theme (using similar pictures) or use any pictures that strike your eye.

Depending on the age of your students, you can use your eye chart in a game where the child must tell what letter the object depicted in each picture begins with or how the name of the picture is spelled.

- Design your own pair of eyeglasses. Make sure they fit your particular personality. Would your glasses be wild, funny, glamorous, or studious? (*Spectacles* by Raskin) Cut out pictures of your favorite personalities from magazines. Draw glasses on the ones who don't have them, or decorate the glasses of personalities who already wear them. Try to make the glasses outlandish or amusing.

- Look at different types of musical instruments. Try to determine what is vibrating in each instrument to allow it to make sounds. Look up the information about the instruments in the encyclopedia or a library book to see if you are correct. See if you can group similar instruments together into "sections" (e.g., vibrating strings, reeds, bars, surfaces, or air columns).

- Draw a "noisy-looking" picture. Turn the paper over and draw a "quiet" picture on the back. Which one do you like the best?

- Have the students design a musical instrument. It could be something that shakes (maraca-style), something that is plucked (guitar-style), something that is banged on (drum-style), or something that vibrates to make its sounds (comb with waxed paper over it that you use like a harmonica). This is a great activity to do to emphasize using "recyclables" that are found around the house. Create as many different sounds as you can. Go wild!

- Make a "split" book of sounds. Cut 8 1/2-by-11-inch paper into quarters (4 1/4 by 5 1/2 inches). On several sheets of paper, draw a picture of an object or animal that makes a sound. On the other sheets, write the words that depict the sound. Along the left side, staple all of the pictures together, then staple the words together. Take a full-sized piece of 8 1/2-by-11-inch paper and fold it in half to make a cover. Insert the booklets of pictures and words and staple the cover so that the booklets are held in place in the cover. Students can then flip the words or pictures and make humorous situations. *(My Very First Book of Sounds* by Carle)

- Make noisemakers out of empty soda cans. Wash out and dry an empty soft drink can. Place 10 to 20 pennies, beans, and popcorn seeds inside the can. Cover the opening of the can with a piece of scotch tape. Cover the can with aluminum foil and decorate it with stickers.

- Place an object (figurine, vase, toy, etc.) inside a brown paper bag. Let each student reach inside the bag and run his or her hands over the object for about 30 seconds. Then have them recreate on paper what the object felt like to them. Compare the students' pictures with the actual object.

- Listen to a piece of classical music, preferably one that is very quiet and flowing (e.g., "Spanish Rhapsody"). On paper, "record" your feelings about the piece in the form of a picture. Then play something quick and moving (e.g., "Sabre Dance"). Again, record your feelings on paper. How do your pictures compare? Look at various pieces of art by artists such as Van Gogh, Monet, and Rembrandt. What type of music would you think of to go with each piece of artwork? For fun, choose a specific song to go with each painting you view.

Chapter 2
Body Systems and Health

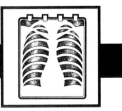

■ Teaching Resources

Books containing experiment(s) relating to the subject matter are marked with a plus sign (+) before and after the title.

P   *A Book about Your Skeleton,* by Ruth Belov Gross (Cartwheel Books, 1994)
Collage illustrations, with concise text, describe the vital things bones do for us.

P   *Here Are My Hands,* by Bill Martin and John Archambault (Henry Holt, 1987)
Children of various ethnic backgrounds are shown key body parts through chalk illustrations. It concludes with a child in a bathtub whose skin "bundles me in."

P   *How Many Teeth?,* by Paul Showers (HarperCollins, 1991)
Cute verse, with nice ink and water color illustrations, describes how many teeth we have, their loss, and their replacement.

P   *I Am Growing,* by Mandy Suhr (Carolrhoda Books, 1992)
Simple, brief text, with appealing illustrations, explains our need for food, sleep, and exercise to grow.

P   *I Can Move,* by Mandy Suhr (Carolrhoda Books, 1992)
Simplistic text describes how our bones and muscles help our body move.

P   *I Wonder Why I Blink and Other Questions about My Body,* by Brigid Avison (Kingfisher Books, 1997)
Question-and-answer format describes things such as why we have bones, why we need food, how our bodies grow, why teeth fall out, and why we blink.

P   *Look Inside Your Body,* by Gina Ingoglia (Grosset & Dunlap, 1998)
Shows what happens to the food we eat, why we have bones and muscles, the difference between the sexes, and how all organs work together.

P   *My Dentist,* by Harlow Rockwell (William Morrow, 1987)
Simple text and illustrations describe a visit to the dentist.

P   *My Hands,* by Aliki (HarperCollins Juvenile, 1992)
Brief, simple text and bright illustrations describe the functions of the hand.

P   *What Happens to a Hamburger?*, by Paul Showers (Econo-Clad, 1999)
Concise, simple explanation of the digestive system.

P   *Your Insides,* by Joanna Cole (Paper Star, 1998)
Describes the different body parts and how they work, including the muscles, digestive system, and lungs. The brief text and enjoyable illustrations include four see-through pages.

P   *Your Skin and Mine,* by Paul Showers (HarperCollins, 1991)
Describes the skin's properties, how it protects the body, and how the color can vary.

P/I   *The Magic School Bus Inside the Human Body,* by Joanna Cole (Scholastic, 1989)
Basic information about the major body systems is entertainingly presented.

P/I   *The Skeleton Inside You,* by Philip Balestrino (HarperCollins, 1989)
Appealing illustrations identify the main parts of our skeleton and their purpose.

I   *Body Battles,* by Rita Golden Gelman (Scholastic, 1992)
Engaging text and illustrations describe our natural defensive systems, such as mucus, cilia, earwax, skin, stomach acid, the immune system, and the brain.

I/U   *Dr. Ruth Talks to Kids,* by Dr. Ruth Westheimer (Aladdin, 1998)
Explicit book discusses the physical and psychological changes that occur when a child grows up.

I/U   *Human Body* (Time-Life Student Library, v.5, 2000)
A question-and-answer format with information on the human body's anatomy and functions, including reproduction.

U   *Body Atlas,* by Steve Parker (Dorling Kindersley, 1993)
A "Pictorial Guide to the Human Body," in large-size format, thoroughly describes the body parts, systems, musculature, and functions, with realistic illustrations.

U   *The Body and How It Works,* by Steve Parker (Reader's Digest Books, 1999)
Looks at the systems and parts of the body and how they work, including blood, bones, skin, the heart, and lungs.

U   *The Body Book,* by Sara Stein (Workman, 1992)
Comprehensive text about body systems, including information on vaccines, tears, tans, dandruff, and other relevant topics.

■ Reading Selections

Books marked with an asterisk (*) before and after the title are related to activities in the activity sections of this chapter.

Abby, by Jeannette Caines (Harper Trophy), 1984
> Explores the relationship between Kevin and his adopted sister, Abby.

Alpha and the Dirty Baby, by Brock Cole (Sunburst, 1995)
> Alpha uses soap and water to deal with a devil's imp, his wife, and their baby.

The Amazing Bone, by William Steig (Sunburst, 1993)
    A little pig's life is saved when she befriends a talking bone.

Anancy and Mr. Dry-Bone, by Fiona French (Little, Brown, 1999)
    Anancy and Mr. Dry-Bone both wish to marry Miss Louise. Who will win her hand?

Anastasia Krupnik, by Lois Lowry (Bantam Books, 1998)
    Although Anastasia is enjoying most of her tenth year of life, she is very unhappy about the prospects of a new baby brother entering the household. (Chapter Book)

Angelina's Baby Sister, by Katharine Holabird (Pleasant, 2000)
    Angelina becomes jealous of her new baby sister when the baby becomes the center of attention.

Arthur Meets the President, by Marc Brown (Little, Brown, 1991)
    Arthur is very nervous when he must read his contest-winning essay to the president at the White House.

Arthur's Baby, by Marc Brown (Joy Street Books, 1990)
    Arthur isn't sure he likes having a new baby around the house until his sister needs his help.

Badger's Parting Gifts, by Susan Varley (Mulberry Books, 1992)
    When their good friend, Badger, dies, the animals find that remembering the good times and what they've learned from him helps make them all feel better.

Because She's My Friend, by Harriet Sirof (Atheneum, 2000)
    Two girls meet in a hospital; one is a volunteer and the other has lost the use of her leg. Antagonistic at first, they become friends and help each other face their problems. (Chapter Book)

To Bed . . . Or Else!, by Ewa Lipniacka (Kane/Miller, 1996)
    Hannah and Asha imagine all kinds of horrible things when Hannah's mother tells them "To bed . . . or else!"

The Berenstain Bears Get Stage Fright, by Stan Berenstain and Jan Berenstain (Random House, 1986)
    Sister Bear is nervous about her part in the school play, while Brother Bear has no fear. The results are not what the family expected.

Big Old Bones, by Carol Carrick (Clarion Books, 1992)
    Professor Potts finds some old bones and puts them together in a very peculiar way to construct a dinosaur that he believes once ruled the Earth.

Birthday Presents, by Cynthia Rylant (Econo-Clad, 1999)
    A mother and father describe her previous birthdays to a five-year-old girl.

Can't Catch Me, I'm the Gingerbread Man, by Jamie Gilson (Beech Tree Books, 1997)
    When the family health food store burns down, 12-year-old Mitch is even more determined to win first prize in a bake-a-thon with his special gingerbread recipe. (Chapter Book)

Clean Enough, by Kevin Henkes (Greenwillow, 1982)
    A little boy finds lots to enjoy in the bathtub besides getting clean.

Clyde Monster, by Robert L. Crowe (E. P. Dutton, 1993)
    Clyde refuses to go to sleep in his cave because he is afraid of the dark.

Cowardly Clyde, by Bill Peet (Econo-Clad, 1999)
> Clyde, a big war horse, is a hopeless coward. In the end, Clyde learns that he can be brave when he must.

Crutches, by Peter Hartling (Lothrop, Lee & Shepard, 1988)
> A 12-year-old boy searches for his mother in Austria at the end of World War II. He becomes friends with a one-legged man called Crutches. (Chapter Book)

Curious George Goes to the Hospital, by Margret Rey and H. A. Rey (Houghton Mifflin, 1966)
> George causes quite a ruckus when he is taken to the hospital after swallowing a piece of a jigsaw puzzle.

Everett Anderson's Nine Month Long, by Lucille Clifton (Henry Holt, 1987)
> Nine months is a long time for Everett and his family to wait for a new family member.

The Growing-up Feet, by Beverly Cleary (Mulberry Books, 1997)
> Twins who are in a hurry to grow up choose new red boots that will stretch as their feet grow.

Harriet's Recital, by Nancy Carolson (First Avenue Editions, 1997)
> Harriet is nervous and unhappy as her ballet recital approaches.

Here Are My Hands, by Bill Martin Jr. and John Archambault (Henry Holt, 1987)
> Children of different ethnic backgrounds identify key parts of the human body.

How Many Kisses Good Night, by Jean Monrad (Random House, 1997)
> A mother helps her little girl get ready for bed while she counts her toes, eyes, ears, and nose.

I Want to Be, by Thylias Moss (Puffin Picture Books, 1998)
> A young girl describes in poetic form the kind of person she wants to grow up to be.

Izzy, Willy-Nilly, by Cynthia Voigt (Aladdin, 1995)
> A 15-year-old loses her leg after a drunk driving accident. She faces a changed body and feelings along with those of her family and friends. (Chapter Book)

Jafta, by Hugh Lewin (Carolrhoda Books, 1989)
> Jafta discusses his feelings by comparing them to the sounds and actions of familiar animals.

Julius the Baby of the World, by Kevin Henkes (Mulberry Books, 1995)
> It takes someone outside of her family to convince Lilly that her new brother Julius is really special.

The Knight Who Was Afraid of the Dark, by Barbara Shook Hazen (Penguin Books, 1992)
> The castle bully tries to use Sir Fred's fear of the dark to stir up some trouble.

Mama, Daddy, Baby and Me, by Lisa Gewing (Spirit Press, 1989)
> The preparation for and arrival of a new baby are described from a small child's point of view.

Max's Bath, by Rosemary Wells (Dial Books for Young Readers, 1998)
> Even though Max gets two baths, he ends up dirtier than ever.

Max's Daddy Goes to the Hospital, by Danielle Steel (Delacorte Press, 1989)
> Max's father, a firefighter, is injured while responding to a fire. Max is very worried about him until he finally can visit him in the hospital.

Middle School Blues, by Lou Kassem (Avon Books, 1998)
> A 12-year-old girl is apprehensive about starting seventh grade but finds that she fits in and makes new friends. (Chapter Book)

Nana Upstairs & Nana Downstairs, by Tomie de Paola (Puffin Books, 2000)
> A little boy learns to deal with the death of his great-grandmother and, later, his grandmother.

Now One Foot, Now the Other, by Tomie de Paola (Econo-Clad, 1999)
> After his grandfather has a stroke, Bobby helps him learn to walk, just like Grandfather helped Bobby when he was small.

Our Teacher's Having a Baby, by Eve Bunting (Clarion Books, 1992)
> A first-grade teacher's class writes letters to her unborn baby and designs a baby room on the class bulletin board.

Rachel Fister's Blister, by Amy MacDonald (Houghton Mifflin, 1990)
> The entire community comes to Rachel's aid with remedies for her blister.

Randy's Dandy Lions, by Bill Peet (Econo-Clad, 1999)
> Randy's lions have a terrible case of cage fright and become very shy every time they have to perform. What will Randy do?

She Come Bringing Me That Little Baby Girl, by Eloise Greenfield (Harper Trophy, 1993)
> A small boy loses his jealousy over a new baby sister when he discovers the importance of his role as big brother.

A Summer to Die, by Lois Lowry (Laurel Leaf, 1984)
> Meg, who has always envied her sister's beauty and popularity, finds it hard to deal with Molly's illness and subsequent death. (Chapter Book)

Taking Care of Carruthers, by James Marshall (Houghton Mifflin, 2000)
> Carruthers has a terrible cold, so his friends, Eugene and Emily, try to cheer him up with tales of an adventure they shared on the river.

There's a Monster under My Bed, by James Howe (Atheneum, 1986)
> Alex is sure that monsters live under his bed at night, because he can hear them breathing.

Tree of Cranes, by Allen Say (Houghton Mifflin, 1991)
> A mother folds origami silver cranes in preparation for Christmas as a young boy recovers from a bad chill.

Tucking Mommy In, by Morag Loh (Orchard, 1991)
> A young mother, who is tired after a day's activities, is tucked in by her two daughters.

Twice Mice, by Wendy Smith (Carolrhoda Books, 1989)
> Thelonius is very happy being an only mouse, but soon learns to love his new twin sisters.

Waiting for Baby, by Tom Birdseye (Henry Holt, 1998)
> The new baby that comes home with Mom is very different than Big Brother imagined.

What's Claude Doing?, by Dick Gackenbach (Houghton Mifflin, 1986)

Claude refuses all his friends' offers to come out to play in order to stay home with his sick master.

What's under My Bed?, by James Stevenson (Greenwillow, 1987)

Mary Ann and Louie are afraid to go to bed when they are staying with Grandpa. So Grandpa tells one of his famous stories about when he was in a similar situation.

When I'm Sleepy, by Jane R. Howard (E. P. Dutton, 1996)

A little girl is very sleepy; she thinks about all of the different places she could lie down. She finally ends up choosing her own, warm bed.

When Sheep Cannot Sleep, the Counting Book, by Satoshi Kitamura (Farrar, Straus & Giroux, 1988)

When Woolly cannot sleep, he takes a walk and observes other animals in their nightly activities.

Who's Sick Today?, by Lynne Cherry (Voyager Picture Books, 1998)

Rhyming text introduces the reader to a variety of animals with a variety of ailments.

The following books are out of print, but may be available at the local library.

Air Mail to the Moon, by Tom Birdseye (Holiday House, 1988)

Ora Mae's tooth disappears before she can leave it for the tooth fairy, so she sets out to find the culprit.

Aren't You Lucky!, by Catherine Anholt (Little, Brown, 1991)

An older sister doesn't always feel so lucky when a new baby arrives in the house. This book chronicles the nine months of waiting, the trip to the hospital, and the baby's arrival at home.

Ben's Baby, by Michael Foreman (Harper & Row, 1987)

Ben asks for a baby for his birthday and ends up having a baby brother by the time his birthday arrives.

Dirty Kurt, by Mary Serfozo (Margaret K. McElderry, 1992)

Describes Kurt's great fondness for dirt.

Eugene the Brave, by Ellen Conford (Little, Brown, 1978)

Because he is afraid of the dark, Eugene, the possum, decides to sleep all night rather than to go out and look for food.

How Do I Feel?, by Norma Simon (Albert Whitman, 1970)

Tells of the many feelings a young boy deals with as he goes through a typical day.

In My Bathroom, by Carol Thompson (Delacorte Press, 1997)

A young pig tells how he cleans himself when getting ready for bed.

Jonathan Mouse and the Baby Bird, by Ingrid Ostheeren (North-South Books, 1991)

Jonathan asks all of the farm animals to help him when he decides to care for a lost baby bird and teach it to fly.

Katie Morag and the Tiresome Ted, by Mairi Hedderwick (Little, Brown, 1986)

Katie becomes so angry when her baby sister is born that she throws her teddy bear into the sea. The teddy bear is returned, and so are Katie's good spirits.

Martin and the Tooth Fairy, by Bernice Chardiet (Scholastic, 1991)
> Martin decides to buy his friends' teeth to put under his pillow when he finds out that he received more for his teeth than his friends did.

Mr. Jordan in the Park, by Laura Jane Coats (Macmillan, 1989)
> Shows the changes that take place in Mr. Jordan's physical appearance as he grows from childhood to an old man.

My Feet, by Aliki (HarperCollins, 1990)
> Provides a close look at the structure of the foot and tells of the many things our feet allow us to do.

New Big Sister, by Debi Fliori (Bradbury Press, 1991)
> Describes the pregnancy of a young girl's mother from the moment she is pronounced pregnant to the birth of twins.

Sick in Bed, by Anne Rockwell and Harlow Rockwell (Macmillan, 1982)
> A little boy who is sick with a sore throat describes how he feels and the experiences he has while staying in bed.

The Tooth Witch, by Nurit Karlin (J. B. Lippincott, 1985)
> An apprentice witch is turned into the new Tooth Fairy.

When Francie was Sick, by Holly Keller (Greenwillow Books, 1985)
> Francie must stay home from school when she wakes with a scratchy throat and a stomachache.

The Wild Washerwomen, by John Yeoman (Greenwillow Books, 1979)
> After escaping from an overbearing boss, seven strong washerwomen travel wildly around the area, only to find that the challenge of seven dirty woodcutters gives them reason to settle down.

■ Science Activities

The Amazing Machine

The human body is an amazing, living machine composed of many types of cells. Have the students make a booklet that describes some of the different body cells we have (e.g., skin, nerve, red blood, white blood, muscle, bone). If possible, look at these cells under a microscope. (You may be able to borrow one from a high school.) If not, find pictures of these different cells. Students should draw pictures of these cells to include in their booklets.

Diffusion and Osmosis

The cells of the body depend on diffusion and osmosis, as certain substances pass through cell membranes while others are blocked. Demonstrate diffusion by placing a tea bag into a glass of warm water. Discuss why the water changes color. Why don't the entire contents of the tea bag diffuse out? The tea bag serves a similar function to a cell membrane, allowing some substances to seep out and blocking others.

Tissue

A tissue is a group of cells that work together to perform a function in the body. Examples of tissues include muscular tissue, supporting and connective tissue (bones, tendons, cartilage, ligaments), nervous tissue, vascular tissue (composes most blood components), and epithelial tissue (forms coverings and linings of the body).

Have the students examine a raw chicken leg and the different tissues. The skin is epithelial tissue. The leg meat is muscular tissue. The bone is supporting tissue. The tendon is a type of connective tissue. The clear material covering the meat (gelatin and fat) is also tissue. Be sure that students wash their hands after handling the raw meat.

Lymph System

The circulatory system is responsible for carrying food and oxygen to the capillaries. As a class, discuss the function of the lymph system. What does lymph do? Have the students find where in the body the lymph nodes and vessels are. Discuss why the prognosis is usually grim when cancer is found in many lymph nodes.

Heart and Circulation

Heart and Circulatory System

The heart and circulatory system adjust to meet the needs of our bodies. Have the students take their pulses for one minute and record their pulse rates. Then have the students jump up and down, or run in place, for a minute or two. Have them take their pulses again. Continue to monitor the pulse rates until they return to their pre-exercise rates. Ask the students: How long did it take? How many times a day does the heart beat? Use the resting rate for your calculation.

The Heart as a Pump

The heart has valves that open and close to make sure that blood goes in only one direction as it is pumped throughout the body. To demonstrate this, you will need an empty squeeze bottle (like one used for dishwashing detergent) that has a cap that opens and closes and a tub of water.

- At the lower end of one side of the bottle, cut out a small hole. (You should be able to cover it completely with your finger.)
- Hold the bottle under water until it fills with water. Replace the cap on the bottle and leave it in the open position.
- Place your finger over the hole you made in the bottle and lift the top part of the bottle out of the water. (The bottom portion of the bottle will still be underwater.) Squeeze the bottle as much as you can.
- With the bottle still squeezed, close the cap and remove your finger from the hole. The bottle will refill with water.
- After the bottle has refilled, you can repeat the steps above. This demonstration shows how the heart gets bigger and smaller as it sucks in blood and then pushes it out.

Blood Types

Humans have four basic blood types: A, B, AB, and O. Ask the students: Why is it important to know your blood type? Blood type AB is considered the universal acceptor, while type O is considered the universal donor. Why? What would happen if someone received the wrong type of blood in a transfusion?

(Two serums can be present in blood that can cause red blood cells to clump: serums A and B. Blood types A and AB can withstand serum A and not clump. Blood types B and AB can withstand serum B. Blood type O cannot tolerate either serum.) What is the Rh factor? How could you find out if you are Rh+ or Rh-? What would that mean?

More with the Heart

The human body is composed of a large variety of cells. Each cell needs oxygen, glucose (or another source of energy), and essential amino acids. Each cell must also dispose of carbon dioxide and wastes. The circulatory system is responsible for meeting the needs of these cells 24 hours a day. Have the students draw an outline of the human body and then draw the heart and lungs inside, along with the major arteries. (This is fun to do with life-sized drawings on bulletin board paper.) Follow the path of the circulatory system by beginning at the heart and using numbers to show the path that the blood cells follow. Have students label the major arteries. Where does the pulmonary artery go? Why? (It goes to the lungs so that the blood cells can pick up oxygen and release carbon dioxide.) Where does the blood go after it leaves the lungs? (It goes back to the heart, ready to be pumped out to the body.) Students can also use modeling clay to create a model of an open heart showing each of the chambers inside.

Efficient Transportation

Our body depends on our blood to transport food and oxygen to all of our body cells. Our blood also transports antibodies to fight disease and hormones that send chemical messages to our bodies. Discuss how one fluid can do so much. Have the students research what types of particles are present in blood (red blood cells, erthrocytes; white blood cells, leukocytes; platelets; and plasma). Make a chart with four columns. Title the columns "Erthrocytes," "Leukocytes," "Platelets," and "Plasma." In each column, write facts about each blood component. Information could include how long the cells live, where the cells are produced, and what function(s) the cells serve.

Nervous System

Nerves

Most living things are able to respond to stimuli through movement of their bodies. The nerve cells, along with the brain, spinal cord, and parts of other organs, make up the nervous system. Have the class give specific examples of responses their bodies make to certain stimuli. (Answers will vary, but could include: pulling your hand away when you touch something hot, turning around when someone taps you on the shoulder, shivering when cold.)

Brain Teaser

This activity might be best as an "at home" activity where each student can select the temperatures of the waters. Give the students the following instructions: Did you know that you can confuse your brain (on purpose)? You need three bowls that are big enough for you to submerge your hand in. Fill one of the bowls with cold water (include several cubes of ice), fill the second bowl with very warm water (but not hot enough to burn yourself), and fill the third bowl with water that is room temperature. Place the bowls in a line with the one containing the room temperature water in the middle. Submerge one hand in the ice water and the other hand in the hot water. Leave your hands in the water until they become accustomed to it (at least two minutes). Then take both hands out of the water they have been in and put them in the middle bowl. Flex the fingers of your right hand and try to determine the temperature of the water with that hand. Flex your left hand and try to determine the temperature of the water with that hand. Does the water feel the same or different with the two different hands? (To the hand that was in the ice water, the water will seem hot. To the hand that came out of the warm water, the water in the middle bowl will seem cold.)

Digestive System

Food is needed by our bodies to provide energy to our cells, but cells cannot use food in the form that it exists in when we eat it. The digestive system converts the food we eat into a form cells can use. As a class, trace the digestive system from beginning to end. Point out that at several stages of the digestive system, juices are added to aid in breaking down food (e.g., in the mouth, in the stomach).

To demonstrate how these juices help food digestion, have the students add a few drops of vinegar to some baking soda. The vinegar is very acidic, just as the juices in the stomach are. Watch as the vinegar "digests" the baking soda.

That's Long!

- Cut off a 32-foot length of yarn or adding machine tape. This represents the length of a person's digestive system. Wrap the yarn into a ball, or roll up the adding machine tape, and place it in your pocket. As you are pulling out the yarn/tape, ask the students to guess how long the digestive system is.

- Mark on the yarn/tape with a magic marker whenever someone guesses. This exercise is a great way to introduce the digestive system. If you use the adding machine tape, you could cut the tape into segments and have each student write the organs of the digestive system on a piece.

Pardon Me!

- In some parts of the world, if you burp after a meal, you have complimented the cook! What causes someone to burp? The pressure of the gases in your stomach is higher than the air pressure outside, and a burp quickly releases excess pressure. Ask the students if they can find two ways that air and gases would get into your stomach and cause you to burp.

  Swallowing air: This can be done while you are eating, when you swallow air with your food. Carbonated beverages contain gas in the bubbles, which you swallow.

  Chemical reactions: Remember the vinegar and baking soda in the activity listed above? The juices in the stomach can react with foods and produce gas. Are there any foods that can promote gas production in the stomach?

- The average person burps about 15 times a day. The next time you burp, try to determine what might have caused it.

The Mouth

- The first step in digestion takes place in the mouth. Have the students look in a mirror at the different types of teeth they have. Research the names of these teeth. Ask the students: How do these different teeth aid in the process of digestion? What do the incisors do? What are molars used for? Why is it important to chew your food thoroughly before swallowing?

- Considering the different types of teeth, have the students determine the best method for cleaning their teeth. Discuss: Which direction should one brush for each type of tooth? What purpose does mouthwash serve? Why do we floss our teeth? Have the students design a poster for his or her bathroom that outlines proper dental care.

- Scientists can often tell what animals eat by the type of teeth they have. Ask the students: What type of teeth would meat eaters have? What type of teeth would be present in plant eaters? Have the students investigate the teeth of several different animals and make a prediction about what type of teeth they think the animal will have. Then have students research to see if the predictions were correct.

- Besides your teeth, your mouth uses its tongue and saliva to help digest food. Ask the students: What function does the tongue serve? (Moves the food around in your mouth.) What is saliva used for? (It begins breaking down foods, such as changing starches to sugars.) To demonstrate this, give each student a cracker (preferably unsalted). Have the students chew the crackers for one full minute before swallowing. Discuss how the cracker tasted initially. Did the taste change as saliva was mixed with the crackers? What other changes did were noticeable?

Esophagus and Stomach

When food leaves the mouth, it travels down the esophagus to the stomach. Have the students hypothesize what would happen if you try to eat upside-down? Recruit a few volunteers to try to eat something while standing on their heads or while hanging upside-down from a bar on a piece of playground equipment. Could they swallow the food? Why? (The esophagus is made of muscles that push the food along.)

Health and Exercise

A Healthy You

Brainstorm with the students about what is necessary to be healthy. Will eating the right foods make you healthy? Will regular exercise alone make you healthy? What happens if you don't get enough rest? After the discussion, four major ideas should emerge: proper nutrition, proper exercise, rest, and cleanliness. Instruct each student to divide a piece of paper (or poster board) into four sections. Label each section for one of the four major health ideas. Look through magazines to find pictures that demonstrate each concept and glue them in the proper section on the poster. If the picture accompanies an interesting article, have the student bring in the article and share it with the class.

Defense Mechanisms

What are defense mechanisms? Discuss the ways in which the body defends itself against sickness, accidents, or other causes of bodily harm (blood clotting, skin, blood, perspiration, muscles used to flee from danger, good eyesight, good hearing, white blood cells to fight infection, tears). Have the students divide a sheet of paper into two columns. Title one column "Similarities" and the other column "Differences." In the first column, list how human defense mechanisms are similar to those of other animals. In the second column, list how they differ. Give examples of animals that have heightened senses or special abilities that are used for defense purposes.

Working up a Sweat

Discuss that when we exercise vigorously or are subjected to hot weather, we sweat. Have the students discuss how, when, and why we perspire. How does that help us cool off? As a class, make a list of some rules to follow during hot weather or when you engage in strenuous exercise. Be sure to include "drink lots of fluids."

Cleanliness and Health

Why is it so important to wash our hands before eating? This activity will help students to "see" the answer to this question.

- Before class, sterilize two jars with lids by boiling the jars (lids off) and lids in water for 20 minutes. Have a student peel a potato without washing his or her hands first. Place the potato in one jar and screw on the lid.

- Have a student wash his or her hands thoroughly and peel a potato. Place the second potato in the other sterile jar and put on the lid. Place the jars where they can be observed for several days. Which potato shows mold growth first?
- Check with a nearby high school to see if you can borrow two petri dishes and some agar media. Prepare the agar as directed and pour it into petri dishes. Cover one of the dishes to serve as the control. Have everyone touch the contents of the second dish before covering it.
- Let both dishes sit for 48 hours and then compare the contents. The different colored and shaped "blobs" represent colonies of different types of bacteria. Do not let students open the petri dishes or touch the bacteria.

Get Your Rest

Most students require eight to ten hours of sleep per day, along with rest periods or quiet time during the day. Have the students keep a journal for one week, recording how many hours of sleep they had each night. Also, they should record, during the week, periods in which they felt tired: after lunch, after a hot bath or shower, when they got up in the morning. Have the students see if they can determine any correlation between their tired times and their sleeping patterns. This activity correlates well with the journal activity monitoring exercise.

Simon Says, "Touch Your Femur"

To reinforce the names of bones or muscles, play a game of "Simon Says." Students enjoy the chance to get up and move around and will quickly learn the names so they won't be "out." Another good game is the "Hokey Pokey": "Put your ulna in, put your ulna out," etc.

What is Half?

- Read the story *The Half-Birthday Party* by Pomerantz and discuss how we grow and change. Then use the idea of a half-birthday to introduce the math concept of one-half.
- Discuss other appropriate (or funny) "half" presents.
- Use math manipulatives in differing amounts and have students take away "half."
- Have children color "half" of pictures that you give them (copied sheets from coloring books, etc.).
- Give out math sheets and have children do "half" of the problems.

The possibilities are endless.

Male and Female

Does every animal species consist of males and females? As a class, look at different pictures of male and female animals (lions, horses, bears, birds). In some species, the male and female members have visible differences. Discuss what the visible differences are and why they exist. This activity could also lead to a discussion of how male and female humans differ and the proper terms for male and female organs.

Reproduction

Most humans have just one child at a time when they reproduce, whereas other animals may have two, four, or even ten. As a class, look up several different animals whose offspring occur from live births (sheep, dogs, mice, pigs, whales, etc.). Determine how many offspring are usually born per birth. Have the students make a pictograph showing what they have learned. On the left side of a chart, students draw a picture of the adult animal. Next to the mother, they draw pictures of the offspring (show the same number of offspring as is normal for a birth). You could also discuss why offspring born in the same litter do not all look alike.

And Then There is Fat

- Besides all of our muscles, bones, organs, and body fluids, there is one more body tissue that we all have: fat! Even though too much fat can be unhealthy, we all need some fat. Have the students research why our bodies need fat and what purpose it serves. What percentage of our body should be fat?

- There are many books and charts available that show how much fat is contained in one serving of different kinds of foods. Have the students make a list of favorite foods (meats, vegetables, dairy products, desserts, etc.). Check the nutritional labels of these foods and see how much fat one serving of each contains. Discuss whether their favorite foods are good for them. You can also have students bring in a snack that has the nutritional label on it. Create a chart with the columns "Fat," "Protein," "Carbohydrates," and "Sodium." Have them complete the information from their particular snack. As a class, discuss which snacks are the most nutritious.

- Have the students write down, on a piece of paper, everything they eat during a day's time. Check this listing against a book or chart showing how much fat they consumed on that day. Using the same book or chart, have the students compile a day's worth of food (meals and snacks) that contains an acceptable amount of fat. Discuss if you can eat any of the foods you love. Would a low-fat diet be hard to stick to?

- Discuss some of the consequences of being overweight. What are the medical ramifications of being too heavy? What are some of the emotional consequences?

Cholesterol

Some cholesterol is essential for good health, but our bloodstream cannot dissolve excessive amounts of this type of fat. Have the students fill a small jar half full with water. Tint the water red to simulate blood. Slowly add three to four drops of mineral oil (or vegetable oil) into the colored water. (The mineral oil represents cholesterol.) Screw the lid on tightly and allow a child to shake the jar. Repeat this process, but add two to three tablespoons of mineral/vegetable oil to the second jar of tinted water. Let both jars sit for a few minutes and then have the class observe both jars. Did the "cholesterol" in either jar dissolve into the "blood?" What differences do you see in the contents of the two jars?

Body Movement

Your muscles work to move the body by contracting (or getting shorter) and releasing. Muscles can work in only one direction: They pull in. Have the students follow these instructions to build a model of an arm joint:

- Roll up one full page of newspaper to make a tight tube. Tape the tube so it holds its shape. Repeat this process three times to make three tubes.

- Stack the three newspaper tubes on top of one another and push a straight pin through all three of the tubes at one end. Take the middle tube and bend it out. Tape the two remaining tubes together at the loose ends.

- Take two long balloons. Place one balloon on top of the newspaper tubes and the other balloon underneath the tubes. Secure the tops of the two balloons to the newspaper tubes that have been taped together (about 2 inches from the end of the tubes) by wrapping a rubber band around the tops of the balloons and the two tubes that are taped together. Secure the other ends of the balloons to the single newspaper tube (about 2 inches from the loose end) by wrapping another rubber band around the bottoms of the balloons and the newspaper tube.

- By opening and closing the "arm joint" you have constructed, you can see that muscles work only by pulling; they do not push.

Teeth as Manipulatives

- When studying the body with younger students, you can use parts of the body (such as teeth, hands or fingers, feet or toes) as manipulatives to reinforce math or language arts skills. Cut teeth shapes out of a piece of poster board. Cut each tooth in half. On the left-hand side of each tooth, write the number you want to add or subtract (e.g., 2 +, 5 -). On the right-hand side of the tooth, write a number from 1 through 10, followed by an equals symbol. Have the students match up two sides of a tooth and solve the equation. Although primary students will find that some of the subtraction problems will not be solvable (e.g., 5 - 7 =), it is good practice to present these problems so that young students realize that you cannot subtract a higher number from a lower one.

- Study compound words by writing one word (such as "tooth") on one half of a tooth and another word (such as "brush") on the other half. See if the students can match up the halves to make compound words.

- Write different words on a number of teeth and then ask students to name rhyming words, opposites, or words with similar vowel sounds.

- Write the names of animals on different teeth. Ask the students to determine if the animals written down have teeth of their own. (Animals that do not have teeth include birds, frogs, whales, turtles, and insects).

- You can also poll the students to determine which toothpaste they use and then have the class graph the results. You could also graph what color of toothbrush the students use, how many times a day they brush, and how many baby teeth they have lost.

■ Creative Writing Activities

Following are instructions to give the students for various writing activities.

- Write a story in which you take responsibility for caring for a baby brother or sister for the day. Which responsibilities do you enjoy performing? Which ones aren't so enjoyable? Think of a new skill that you can try to teach your ward. How does it turn out? (*Jonathan Mouse and the Baby Bird* by Ostheeren)

- Write a diary entry about a time when you were really nervous. What was happening to make you so nervous? How did the situation turn out? How did you feel after the experience was over? (*Harriet's Recital* by Carolson; *The Berenstain Bears Get Stage Fright* by Berenstain and Berenstain)

- Write a "top 10" list of reasons why you would like or would not like to have a new baby in your family. (*Aren't You Lucky!* by Anholt; *Arthur's Baby* by Brown; *Ben's Baby* by Foreman)

- Write a story about a time when you reacted hastily to a situation, out of anger, and did something you regretted later. (*Katie Morag and the Tiresome Ted* by Hedderwick)

- You have just discovered some strange-looking bones in your backyard. Write a news article detailing the find, speculating on what type of animal the bones belong to and how they got in your backyard and explaining how you will go about finding out the truth about the bones.

- One of your neighbors has a mysterious scar on his or her body. Write an adventure story explaining the details of how the neighbor obtained the unusual scar.

- Pretend that you have the opportunity to become microscopic in size and to enter another person's body to perform scientific research. What organs of this body would you visit? Why? How would you travel through the body? Keep a journal of your travels detailing how you react to your journey and what valuable information you obtain.

- Adults often tell children that "brain is better than brawn," but children are seldom convinced of this fact. Before assigning this exercise, consider dividing the students into two "camps" and having a small debate about this saying. After the students have been exposed to many different ideas of their peers on this subject, have them write a story about a time when "brains" won out over "muscles."

- How does your body react when you are nervous? Some people sweat, some visibly shake, some have nervous twitches, and some have a compulsion to eat. Write a suspense story in which you become tense and nervous. Be sure to describe exactly how your body manifests these feelings.

- The heart is a universal symbol for love and is closely associated with the celebration of St. Valentine's Day. Research the origin of St. Valentine's Day. Was there a person named Valentine? How did the custom of sending cards to loved ones evolve? In which countries is St. Valentine's Day celebrated? Write an essay based on the information you uncover about this special day.

- You must stay at home in bed for several days because you are sick. Keep a mini-diary of your activities during the day along with medical notations on how you are feeling (e.g., What is wrong with you? Do you have schoolwork to do? Do you watch television? What do you wish you were doing?) (*Sick in Bed* by Rockwell and Rockwell; *When Francie Was Sick* by Keller)

- Have you ever had a cold and had all your friends suggest remedies that you should try? Come up with your own, surefire remedy for the common cold. Describe what the patient must do and explain why and how the remedy works.

- Make up a new, just-discovered illness. What are the symptoms of this malady? How do you catch it? What is the cure? Be creative!

- Make a book of rules for good dental care. Cut out pages for your book in the shape of a tooth. On each page, write a good rule to follow for taking care of your teeth. Rules can include visiting the dentist regularly, flossing every day, brushing after meals, drinking milk, using fluoride toothpaste, and eating healthy food.

- Write a story in which the Tooth Fairy is the hero of the day. What did the Tooth Fairy do that was so helpful? Did it involve all those teeth that she collects? What does your Tooth Fairy look like? (*Martin and the Tooth Fairy* by Chardiet; *Air Mail to the Moon* by Birdseye; *The Tooth Witch* by Karlin)

- Write a story about an animal that has a deep-rooted fear that has a major effect on its life (e.g., a hippopotamus that is afraid of water, a monkey that is afraid of heights, a bat that is afraid of the dark). (*Eugene the Brave* by Conford)

- Write a story in which the main character experiences many different emotions (surprise, happiness, anger, fear, relief, etc.) as the plot unfolds. (*How Do I Feel?* by Simon; *Jafta* by Lewin)

- Write a poem in which you explain what type of a person you would like to be when you grow up. You can include physical traits, career goals, and/or character traits you hope to possess. (*I Want to Be* by Moss)

■ Art Activities

Following are instructions to give the students for various art activities.

- Make an album of pictures and explanations that depict your past birthdays. Notice how you have grown and changed from year to year. Talk to your parents about how you celebrated your past birthdays. Be sure to find out about any special family traditions. Look for photographs of past birthday celebrations or draw pictures that depict the activities that your parents told you about for each birthday. Write a caption under each picture to explain its significance.

Make a cover for your album out of construction paper, white paper, or wallpaper and decorate it as you want. (*Birthday Presents* by Rylant)

- Make art forms out of handprints. Trace your hands on colored construction paper. Draw other shapes and attach your handprints to complete your object. You can use your handprints as wings on an angel or a bird, antlers on a reindeer, the tail feathers for a turkey or a peacock, and so forth. See how creative you can be with your hands!

- It is often said, "You are what you eat." Draw a picture of yourself using your favorite foods as body parts. You can draw the foods yourself or cut out foods from magazines and glue them together on a piece of paper.

- Draw a portrait of yourself (head and shoulders). Imagine that it is 20 years from now, and you are having your picture taken. Draw a portrait of yourself as you think you will look in 20 years. How have you changed? (*Mr. Jordan in the Park* by Coats)

- Cut out hearts of varying sizes. (Cut out one very large heart, one or two large ones, three or four medium ones, four small ones, and four very small hearts.) Using only these hearts, see how many different animals you can make. Once you find your favorite configuration, glue the cutouts on a piece of paper. Color a background to depict your animal's home (jungle, forest, or domestic surroundings).

- Draw the outline of a shirt or pants on a white piece of paper. Splatter the clothes with "dirt" by using an old toothbrush and some paint (several different colors, if you want). Dip the toothbrush in the paint and then rub back and forth over the toothbrush with a pencil or a table knife (be sure the toothbrush is angled so, as the paint splatters, it lands on the drawing and not on your clothes). The splatters will create the look of "soiled" clothes. (*The Wild Washerwomen* by Yeoman)

- Look at a picture of someone with an injury (such as a broken leg). Draw a picture of what you think happened to cause this injury. Because most injuries are a result of accidents, draw another picture showing how this accident could have been averted.

- Make a collage that represents special events in your life. First, write down events from your life (your birth, a special Halloween, your first day of school, special outings, etc.) that you want to have represented in your collage. Cut 3-inch squares out of white paper (one for each event) and draw a picture that depicts one of the events you wrote down. When all of your pictures are complete, glue them on a piece of colored poster board. Write a short description under each picture that includes the age that you were when the event took place.

- Draw a picture of an arm or a leg that has a cast on it. Make the cast the focal point of the picture. Decorate the cast the way you think it would look if your friends and family signed it for you.

- Pretend that you have won a contest by designing an AIDS awareness poster. Part of your prize is the opportunity to have lunch with the president of the United States, who will present you with a merit medal. Design the poster. Draw a picture that shows you having lunch with the president.

- Draw a picture of the outline of a human body. Instead of drawing the actual organs of the body inside the outline, depict some of the humorous sayings you have heard about the body, such as "butterflies in the stomach" and "frog in the throat."

Chapter 3
Nutrition and Exercise

■ Teaching Resources

Books containing experiment(s) relating to the subject matter are marked with a plus sign (+) before and after the title.

P   *Dinosaurs Alive and Well! A Guide to Good Health,* by Laurie Krasny Brown and Marc Brown (Little, Brown, 1992)
Simple text and appealing illustrations give suggestions for good nutrition, exercise, family and friend relationships, and ways of dealing with stress.

P/I +*Fats,*+ by Rhoda Nottridge (Carolrhoda Books, 1993)
An introduction to the different types of fats, which explains why they can be both useful and harmful to our bodies and how we can cut down on fat by eating correctly and exercising. (Part of a series that includes *Additives, Proteins, Sugars, Fiber,* and *Vitamins.*)

U   *Exercise,* by Don Nardo (Chelsea House, 1992)
Discusses exercise and how it benefits the body. Also discusses physical fitness.

■ Reading Selections

Books marked with an asterisk (*) before and after the title are related to activities in the activity sections of this chapter.

Apples and Pumpkins, by Anne Rockwell (Econo-Clad, 1999)
> A family visits a local farm to pick apples and pumpkins in preparation for Halloween.

The Big Snow, by Berta Hader and Elmer Hader (Aladdin, 1993)
> As winter approaches, the woodland creatures gather food and find warm, dry places to live.

Bread and Jam for Frances, by Russell Hoban (HarperCollins Juvenile, 1993)
> Frances finds that, although she likes bread and jam above all things, maybe she doesn't want to eat it at every meal.

The Cake That Mack Ate, by Rose Robart (Little, Brown, 1991)
> A book of cumulative verse about the many steps that it took to make the cake that Mack ended up eating.

Chicken Sunday, by Patricia Polacco (Philomel, 1992)
> Several children wish to thank Eula for the wonderful chicken dinners she cooks them each Sunday. They decide to raise money and buy Eula a new Easter hat.

The Chocolate Touch, by Patrick Skene Catling (Dell, 1996)
> A young boy gets his wish that everything that touches his lips should turn to chocolate. (Chapter Book)

Cloudy with a Chance of Meatballs, by Judi Barrett (Atheneum, 1978)
> Life is delicious in the town of Chewandswallow, where it rains soup and juice, snows mashed potatoes, and blows storms of hamburgers—until the weather takes a turn for the worse.

Curious George Plays Baseball, by Margret Rey and Alan J. Shalleck (Houghton Mifflin, 1986)
> George becomes the hero of the day when he makes a catch and a rescue that none of the other baseball players can make.

Daddy Makes the Best Spaghetti, by Anna Grossnickle Hines (Houghton Mifflin, 1999)
> Daddy can do anything: act like a barking dog, dress up like a superhero, and make the best spaghetti.

The Doorbell Rang, by Pat Hutchins (Greenwillow, 1986)
> Every time the doorbell rings, the kids know there will be more people to share their cookies with.

Everybody Cooks Rice, by Norah Dooley (Carolrhoda Books, 1991)
> When a child goes to find a younger brother at dinnertime, the child discovers that people can cook the same food in many different ways.

Feast for 10, by Cathryn Falwell (Clarion Books, 1993)
> A number book that relates how a family shops and works together to prepare their meal.

Five Little Monkeys Jumping on the Bed, by Eileen Christelow (Houghton Mifflin, 1998)
> A counting book that also demonstrates that, even though it is obviously dangerous, sometimes even mom can't resist jumping on the bed.

Frog Goes to Dinner, by Mercer Mayer (Dial Books for Young Readers, 1992)
> A wordless story that tells of the many mishaps that take place when a little boy takes his frog out to dinner with him.

Green Eggs and Ham, by Dr. Seuss (Random House, 1960)
> Sam-I-Am tries to convince another Seuss creature to try the delicious green eggs and ham that he loves so much.

Gregory, the Terrible Eater, by Mitchell Sharmat (Scholastic, 1989)
> Gregory and his parents must learn to compromise when Gregory, a goat, wants to eat fruits, vegetables, and orange juice rather than tin cans and shoes.

Growing Vegetable Soup, by Lois Ehlert (Harcourt Brace Jovanovich, 1987)
> A child and father grow vegetables in their garden and use them to make vegetable soup.

Hansel and Gretel, by James Marshall (Puffin Books, 1994)
> Two children who have been left in the woods by their parents find a witch's house made of cookies, candy, and cake.

Harriet and the Garden, by Nancy Carlson (Carolrhoda Books, 1999)
> During a game of baseball, Harriet ruins a neighbor's prize flower. Does Harriet confess?

How My Parents Learned to Eat, by Ina R. Friedman (Houghton Mifflin, 1984)
> An American and a Japanese who are courting try, in secret, to learn each other's eating customs.

How Pizza Came to Queens, by Dayal Kaur Khalsa (Potter, 1989)
> Some girls help an Italian visitor to Queens, New York, make the pizza she so misses.

I Need a Lunch Box, by Pat Cummings (Harper Trophy, 1993)
> A little boy wishes for a new lunch box even though he hasn't started school yet.

If You Give a Mouse a Cookie, by Laura Joffe Numeroff (Harper & Row, 1985)
> Tells the tale of all the things that can result from the harmless offer of a cookie to a hungry mouse.

Lily Takes a Walk, by Satoshi Kitamura (Sunburst, 1998)
> While Lily enjoys her walk, her dog is fending off many unseen dangers.

Mama Don't Allow, by Thacher Hurd (Harper Trophy, 1985)
> Miles and the Swampland Band learn to play songs, other than loud ones, to keep themselves from becoming dinner after their performance.

Max, by Rachel Isadora (Aladdin, 1984)
> Max starts warming up for his Saturday baseball games by joining in his sister's ballet class.

One Hungry Monster, by Susan Heyboer O'Keefe (Little, Brown, 1992)
> Monsters demanding food increase in number from just one to ten, until a young boy finally must banish them from his bedroom.

The Outside Inn, by George Ella Lyon (Orchard, 1997)
> This book of rhyming verse presents all kinds of appetizing meals that can be eaten outdoors.

Pancakes for Breakfast, by Tomie de Paola (Harcourt Brace, 1990)
> A little old lady has to find a creative way to get pancakes for breakfast after her initial attempts are unsuccessful. This is a wordless book.

Pancakes, Pancakes, by Eric Carle (Aladdin, 1998)
> Jack helps make his breakfast pancakes by gathering all the necessary ingredients from their original sources.

The Popcorn Book, by Tomie de Paola (Holiday House, 1989)
> Presents a variety of facts about popcorn and includes two recipes.

A Rose for Abby, by Donna Guthrie (Abingdon Press, 1998)
> After seeing a homeless woman on her street, Abby decides to prepare a dinner for the homeless people of her neighborhood.

Sam's Sandwich, by David Pelham (Dutton Children's Books, 1991)
> When Sam's sister asks for a sandwich with "everything" on it, Sam decides to slip in some little surprises.

Stone Soup, by Tony Ross (Puffin Books, 1992)
> The Big Bad Wolf intends to eat Mother Hen, but she outwits him with the help of her grandmother's favorite soup.

This Is the Bread I Baked for Ned, by Crescent Dragonwagon (Econo-Clad, 1999)
> Tells the story, in cumulative verse, of the meal that Glenda prepares for Ned.

The Wolf's Chicken Stew, by Keiko Kasza (Paper Star, 1996)
> A hungry wolf doesn't get the results he expects as he tries to fatten up a chicken for his dinner.

The following books are out of print, but may be available at the local library.

Alligators Arrive with Apples, by Crescent Dragonwagon (Macmillan, 1987)
Numerous animals and their special foods celebrate Thanksgiving together.

Gino Badino, by Diana Engel (Morrow Junior Books, 1991)
Gino would rather sculpt mice out of dough than sweep the floor in his family's pasta factory, but when the factory falls upon hard times, Gino's mice save the day.

Grandpa's Too-Good Garden, by James Stevenson (Greenwillow Books, 1989)
Grandpa tells Louie and Mary Ann about the garden he grew when he was a boy.

The Legend of Johnny Appleseed, by Reeve Lindbergh (Little, Brown, 1990)
The life of John Chapman (Appleseed) is told through rhyming text.

Marathon and Steve, by Mary Rayner (E. P. Dutton, 1989)
Marathon has never been excited about his daily run with his master. Then an injury introduces an alternative form of exercise.

Pizza for Breakfast, by Maryann Kovalski (Morrow Junior Books, 1991)
Frank and Zelda regret wishing for more customers at their pizza restaurant.

Who Stole the Apples, by Sigrid Heuck (Alfred A. Knopf, 1986)
A horse and bear try to find out who stole all the apples from a tree that grows in the forest.

The Wonderful Feast, by Esphyr Slobodkina (Greenwillow Books, 1993)
After Farmer Jones feeds his horse, several other animals feast on the leftovers.

■ Science Activities

Raisin Races

For this activity students will each need club soda or seltzer water, 3-4 raisins, and an 8-ounce clear plastic cup.

- Fill the plastic cup about three-quarters full of club soda or seltzer water. Drop three or four raisins into each cup and watch what happens. After observing for a minute or more, each of the raisins should have floated to the top of the soda. Have the students count how many times each raisin rises to the top.
- Have the students remove the raisin that floated up and down the greatest number of times. As a class, look at the raisin. What qualities does it have that would make it float up and down better than the other raisins? (Hint: Bubbles forming on the raisins brought them up to the surface. What made the bubbles form? What made the raisins sink again?)
- To find the champion raisin, pour fresh club soda or seltzer water into another cup. On the count of three, have two students place their champion raisins in the new soda. Keep track. The raisin that floats up and down the greatest number of times in two minutes is the winner. Repeat with the other raisins and continue the tournament until a champion raisin is declared. (You can have several races going on simultaneously.)

Breads and Carbohydrates

- As a class, look at wheat, rice, and other grains. Discuss: How are they made into bread? What are other foods in the "bread" category? Have the students trace a bread food such as rice. How is it planted? Where is it grown? How is it harvested? How is it made into flour? What part of the plant provides the grain?

- Discuss why parents and teachers are always urging children to eat many different kinds of foods. Ask the students if it would be nutritious to eat just one food as the mainstay of one's diet. Have the students choose a food they think would be very nutritious and research its nutritional composition. What vitamins and minerals are present? What nutrients are missing? What other foods would need to be added to one's diet to make it well balanced? (*Bread and Jam for Frances* by Hoban)

- Bring in a variety of breads (such as whole wheat, white, pita, and cornbread) and have students sample each one. Discuss what gives each type of bread its unique flavor. Look at the labels and nutritional information for each type of bread. Discuss: What nutrients are present in each type of bread? How many grams of fat, protein, and carbohydrates does each include? How many calories are present? Compare the nutritional information for each type of bread on a bar graph. Have the class decide which type of bread is the best nutritional choice.

- For a teacher demonstration, make a recipe of pancakes. Divide the batter into four bowls. In one bowl, add 1/4 cup milk. To the second bowl, add 1/4 cup flour. To the third bowl, add one egg. To the fourth bowl, add nothing. Have the students predict how a pancake made with each of the four batters would differ from the others. Cook four pancakes, one from the batter of each of the four bowls. Record the characteristics of each pancake and any other observations students have while it cooks. How do the actual results compare with the students' predictions?

- Discuss whether pancakes would be considered bread. Examine the ingredients of pancake batter and compare them to the ingredients of bread. Upper-level students can study the ingredients and determine what nutrients are present in pancakes. What is the calorie count? What are the functions of some of the ingredients?

- A favorite "carbohydrate" snack is popcorn. Ask students what they know about this popular food. Have them estimate the number of unpopped kernels present in 1/4 cup of popcorn. Then count the actual number of kernels and find out how close the students' estimates were. Have the students predict how many of the kernels will actually pop when cooked; how many cups of popped popcorn will result from cooking the 1/4 cup of popcorn kernels; and what the weight of the popped corn will be. Pop the corn and compare the results to the predictions. Have the students research the history of popcorn. Where did it originate? Why does popcorn "pop?" Cut a seed in half and try to pop it. Why won't it pop? Ask the students to predict what will happen if they plant a popcorn seed. What if you planted colored popcorn seeds? Plant different types of popcorn and record the results. Did the results match your predictions?

- Examine different types of flour. When flour is mixed with water, a rubbery substance is formed. This complex is called "gluten." The amount of gluten formed varies by flour's protein content. The more gluten present, the denser the bread will be. As a class, prepare a favorite muffin recipe. After hand-mixing for just 25 strokes, divide the batter in half. Place half of the batter into oiled muffin tins. Take the rest of the batter and beat it for another 75 strokes before placing it into oiled muffin tins. Bake as the recipe directs. Discuss how the muffins mixed for different lengths of time compare in appearance, volume, taste, and texture. Why is it important not to overbeat muffin batter or excessively knead biscuit or pastry dough? Repeat the steps using a different type of flour. Are the results the same?

Fruits and Vegetables

- As a class, discuss where vegetables come from. What part of each plant is eaten? Have the students divide a paper into four columns. Have them list as many vegetables as they can that are roots in one column. List vegetables that are stems in another column. List vegetables that are actually the leaves of the plant. The list vegetables that are the "fruit" of the plant.

- Gather seeds from a number of different fruits and vegetables. Have students study the different seeds and try to predict which fruit or vegetable would grow from each seed.

- Discuss what important vitamins we can get from fruits and vegetables. List the vitamins and minerals recommended for daily consumption (vitamins A, C, D, and E; folic acid; niacin; riboflavin; thiamin; vitamins B6 and B12; calcium; phosphorus; iodine; iron; magnesium; and zinc). Have the students find three sources for each of these vitamins and minerals. Ask the students: Are there any particular foods that have all the recommended daily allowances? Why is it important to eat a variety of fruits and vegetables each day?

- Have the students list as many fruits and vegetables as they can. Practice alphabetizing skills by rearranging the fruits and vegetables in alphabetical order. You can have the students do all fruits and vegetables together; make a list with just fruits; or make a list with just vegetables.

- As a class, make dried fruits like the pioneers used to do. Cut fruit into very thin slices, place on a cookie sheet, and bake the slices at 200–250 degrees Fahrenheit for four to six hours.

- With a marker, write a word such as "Delicious," "Cortland," or "Georgetown" on an apple cutout or draw several outlines of apples on a sheet of paper and write the words inside the apples. Some of the words should be varieties of apples and some should be "fakes." Have the students guess which words are really types of apples and which words are the "fakes." Then have the students research apples and verify which words are actual types of apples. Different fruits and vegetables can be substituted for apples. As an extra challenge, have students write down one fact about each type of apple they find.

- Take a survey of the class's favorite fruit. Graph the results to see what fruit is most popular. Then have the students research that fruit. Where is the favorite grown? Does it grow locally or is it imported? Is this fruit difficult to grow? Students can find out which fruits are grown in their state.

- Bring in some fruits that may not be familiar to your students (mango, papaya, star fruit, kiwi, etc.). Have the students compare the tastes of these fruits. Have them vote for their favorite of these "new" fruits. Make a fruit salad out of the fruits for a snack.

- Discuss whether a banana has seeds. Peel a banana and break the fruit in half. Ask if they can see that the fruit has three sections. Have the students break one half of the banana into the three sections. Then have them rub away the shiny white fibers of the banana with their fingers. The tiny, dark specks they see are the seeds.

- Many fruits undergo a browning process when exposed to air. This is caused when the oxygen in the air reacts with the enzymes in the fruit. Divide the class into groups. Give each group six slices of apple and 12 banana slices each 1/2-inch thick. Students will have six test groups, with one apple slice and two banana slices in each group. They should place each test group on a paper plate and number the test groups 1 through 6. Dip each test group into the following solutions that corresponds with the number assigned to it for five seconds:

  1. Lemon juice
  2. Pineapple juice
  3. A commercial fruit preservative (ascorbic acid)
  4. A solution of 1/2 teaspoon salt in 1/4 cup water

5. A solution of 3 tablespoons sugar in 1/4 cup water
6. No treatment

Label each fruit group after it has been treated and let it sit for one hour. While you are waiting, have the children predict which solutions they think will retard the browning process. After one hour, check each fruit group and record the results. Which solutions slowed the browning process? Discuss why a particular solution helped prevent browning. (Lemon juice and commercial preservatives are acidic and act as anti-oxidants. Pineapple juice contains sulfhydryl groups that retard oxidation.) Let the fruits sit out overnight and check the results again the following morning.

Challenge question: Why don't canned fruits brown? (Heat treatment kills the enzymes.) Compare some canned fruits with fresh fruits. How do they differ?

Meat and Protein

- Have the students make a chart to compare some of the different sources of proteins we consume. In the first column, list sources such as ground beef, chicken breasts, pork chops, ground turkey, eggs, bacon, fish (be specific, e.g., salmon or cod), peanut butter, cheese, and beans or lentils. In the following columns, chart additional information (based on a 4-ounce serving) for each source of protein:
  1. Calories
  2. Grams of fat
  3. Grams of protein
  4. Grams of salt

  Have the students debate which meats appear to be the healthiest protein sources. Discuss which meats we should consume more sparingly.

- Become a wise shopper! When purchasing ground beef, it is more economical to buy the most meat and least fat for your money. Purchase 4 ounces each of ground beef, ground round, ground chuck, meat labeled as "lean" ground beef, and any other variations you want. As a class, weigh each sample as precisely as possible. Make one or two patties out of each sample and broil the meat or fry in an electric skillet until it is well done. Place on a paper towel to absorb excess fat. Weigh the cooked patties and calculate how much fat was lost and how much meat is left to eat. Have students calculate how much of each type of raw meat they would have to buy to have one pound of cooked meat. Use the following equation to make your calculation:

$$x = \frac{16 \ (weight \ of \ uncooked \ meat)}{weight \ of \ cooked \ meat}$$

  X = The amount of uncooked meat you must purchase to get a pound of cooked meat. Multiply the answer by the cost per pound of the meat, and you will have determined your cost for one pound of cooked meat. Which meat is actually the best buy?

- As a class, look at which meats are eaten in different areas of the world. Why do the Japanese eat so much fish? Why would the Eskimos eat primarily seal and blubber? Have the students pick a culture and research the diets of its people. Where does their food supply come from?

- Have the students research the different cuts of beef and pork. Some cuts are considered lean cuts, some are considered tougher cuts, and others are considered tender cuts. (If you cannot find information on this, consult a local grocer or butcher.) Discuss where on the animal these different cuts of meat come from. Why does a butcher recommend that different cuts of meat be cooked in different ways? Give each student the name of a different cut of beef or pork. Have them research the best method to cook it and write a recipe that reflects this method.

Use two identical cubes of chuck roast approximately 2 inches wide. As a class, weigh both cubes and record their weight. Place one cube in a roasting pan and bake at 325 degrees Fahrenheit. Place the other cube in a roasting pan with 1/2 cup water and cover it with a lid. Cook both cubes until done. (To be more exact, cook until the internal temperature is 160 degrees Fahrenheit.)

Weigh both cubes again. Which cube has the most weight loss? Which cube is tenderer to eat? Why?

Divide one flank steak into two pieces (or use chuck cubes). Place each piece of meat in a separate baking dish and cover with 1/4 cup barbecue sauce. Cook one piece of meat at 275 degrees Fahrenheit for two hours or in a crock-pot overnight. Cook the other piece of meat at 400 degrees for one hour. How does the baking temperature affect the tenderness, juiciness, and flavor of the meat?

Water, Milk, and Dairy

- Have the students guess which six nutrients the human body needs (carbohydrates, fat, protein, vitamins, minerals, and water). We often forget that water is one of the nutrients that is important to our body for many reasons. Discuss some of the reasons that our bodies need water. It is recommended that adults consume a total of eight cups of water every day. (Besides actually drinking water, the foods we eat contain water.) Have the students track how much water they drink in one day and record the foods they eat. Ask them: When did they find that they were thirstiest? Together, brainstorm five activities that make you thirsty and list five foods that make you thirsty. Discuss why these activities and foods make you thirsty.

- Some of the water our bodies need is gained through milk consumption. What other nutrients that our bodies need are present in milk? Have the students examine the nutritional information on a carton of whole milk and make a chart that represents the amount of each nutrient that is present in the milk. Repeat this procedure for 2 percent, 1 percent, 1/2 percent, skim, and buttermilk. Ask the students: How do the nutrients vary? Which type of milk would seem to be the best for a child of your age to drink? Why?

- To demonstrate that milk and cream contain fat, make butter. Buy 1 cup (1/2 pint) of heavy whipping cream (30–35 percent fat). Whip the cream until the butterfat separates from the liquid (curds and whey). Whip 1 cup of coffee cream (half milk and half cream). Does it make butter? Compare the amount obtained to that made with the heavy whipping cream. Whip 1 cup of whole milk. Will it make butter? Why or why not? ("Commercial milk" is homogenized, which makes it very difficult to separate out the cream.) If possible, repeat this procedure using fresh milk from a dairy or farm. Can you produce butter now?

- It is said that in France you could eat a different kind of cheese every day of the year. Brainstorm how many different cheeses the class can name. Have the students bring in samples of different cheeses. Good examples are brie, bleu, Muenster, Swiss, cheddar, parmesan, mozzarella, cream, cottage, Neufchatel, Roquefort, gouda, romano, and Edam. Compare and contrast the different types of cheeses.

Cheeses are often classified in two ways: degree of moisture and if they are ripened/unripened. Chart which cheeses are unripened (not aged) and which are ripened (aged). (*Unripened*: cream cheese, cottage cheese, Neufchatel, mozzarella; *Ripened*: brie, bleu, Roquefort, cheddar, Edam, Muenster, Swiss, gouda, parmesan, romano.) Ask the students how the tastes of unripened cheeses compares to ripened cheeses. (Unripened cheeses have a milder flavor.)

Chart these cheeses by degree of moisture (soft, semi-soft, and hard, sometimes referred to as semi-hard). (*Soft*: cream cheese, brie, cottage cheese, Neufchatel, Roquefort; *Semi-soft*: bleu, muenster; *Semi-hard*: mozzarella, cheddar, Swiss, Edam, gouda; *Hard*: parmesan, romano.)

Discuss what other ways we could categorize the cheese samples.

Junk Food versus Healthy Food

- Discuss food categories. (The four basic food groups have now been replaced with the food pyramid.) Create a food pyramid and discuss the recommended servings for each group. Have students cut out pictures of the different foods or bring in boxes that foods come in and add them to the related section of the food pyramid.

- Have the students create restaurant menus using the six categories of the food pyramid (fats, milk, meat, vegetables, fruit, and bread) as headings of sections on the menu. Under each heading, students list examples and give a price that the food will sell for at his or her restaurant. Students design the covers and name their restaurants. Now they are ready to play "restaurant." Divide the class into small groups. Select one person to be the waiter. Each patron should select foods that make a healthy meal. Other members of the group will decide whether the person's choices constitute a "healthy" meal. For additional math practice, the waiter can add up the cost of each meal.

- Before class, prepare a list of foods with prices (e.g., one package of 8 hot dogs at $1.75; one package of 10 hot dog buns at $.95; one package of frozen corn (6 servings) at $1.35). Using the foods on the list, have each student or a small group of students plan a dinner or lunch menu, keeping in mind the guidelines for healthy eating. Have the students pretend that they are planning a meal for 12 people. How many packages of each food did they need to buy? What was the cost for each meal? Which dinner was the cheapest? Which dinner was the most nutritious? Which dinner appealed to the most students? Repeat this process with several different lists of foods.

- Place a variety of groceries in a grocery bag or use the empty containers from various foods. Tell the class that you will be pulling out one product at a time and placing it either on the right-hand side of the table or on the left-hand side to create two categories of food. The students must guess what two categories you are dividing the foods into (healthy versus junk foods). Stop periodically to let students hypothesize. After they have guessed what categories you were thinking of, have a discussion about the wisdom of eating healthy foods versus junk foods. You could use this same exercise to compare and contrast fruits and vegetables, look at foods low in fat versus those high in fat, or introduce two or more groups of food.

- A favorite snack food is chocolate. Plan a chocolate day!

  Have the students research what plants chocolate is obtained from. Where do these plants grow? Where is most of the chocolate we eat imported from? Research how chocolate is processed. Why must it be processed before we eat it? (The original form of chocolate is very bitter.)

  Find Hershey, Pennsylvania on a map. As a class, write to the Chamber of Commerce and ask for information on the chocolate plant in Hershey and the processes that are performed there. You can obtain a set of maps and have the students plan a car trip to Hershey. How many miles away is it? How long would it take to get there from your school or house? What activities would you take part in once you got to Hershey?

Read *The Doorbell Rang* by Hutchins. Prepare math problems for the students using chocolate chips and chocolate chip cookies. For example: If you had 20 chocolate chip cookies to divide among four children, how many cookies would each child get? Bring in a jar filled with chocolate chips and have the students estimate how many chips are in the jar. The winner could get to keep the container. For younger students, round circles can be decorated to look like chocolate chip cookies. Older students should be given more difficult problems to solve.

Bring in different types of chocolate, such as white chocolate, milk chocolate, and dark chocolate, to taste and compare. Make a graph showing the students' favorites. Next, have the students taste several different brand names of the same kind of chocolate chips, such as milk chocolate chips. Discuss the results and whether students could tell the difference. Discuss whether the most expensive chips taste the best.

Make hot chocolate for a snack. Older students can make different types of hot chocolate using water and different milk products and compare them. Read *The Chocolate Touch* by Catling while students enjoy their snack.

- Plan a pizza day.

    Have the students list the different ingredients used to make pizza. Discuss what food groups or categories the ingredients belong to. How many different ingredients can they think of?

    Study fractions while making pizzas. This can be done using real food or paper cutouts to represent the different foods, although this activity is much more exciting when the students can eat their work! Give specific instructions such as: Prepare your pizzas in the following manner:

    > one-half with sausage and one-half with pepperoni
    >
    > one-third with mozzarella cheese and two-thirds with Swiss cheese
    >
    > one-quarter with onion, one-quarter with mushrooms, and one-half with green peppers

    Older students can design their pizzas themselves. Have them make "blueprints" of their plan before actually making their pizza.

    Discuss if pizza would be a good breakfast food. Why or why not? As a class, create your own breakfast pizzas. Line the bottom of a 9-by-13-inch pan with crescent rolls (use two cans containing eight rolls each). Add a layer of hash brown potatoes, thawed and uncooked. Add your favorite pizza toppings: bacon, sausage, ham, mushrooms, onions, green peppers, and so forth. Top with shredded cheddar cheese (8 ounces). Pour six beaten eggs over the pizza and bake for 35–45 minutes at 350 degrees Fahrenheit. (*Pizza for Breakfast* by Kovalski) If you can't actually bake the pizza, discuss the ingredients and give the children the recipe to try at home. Also, discuss what substitutions could be made in the recipe to make it healthier.

- Bring in empty boxes, cans, and foods created in the art activity section of this chapter and make your own grocery store. Be sure every food has a price. Younger students can give fictitious prices such as $.05 and $.10; older students can look at grocery ads and try to determine realistic prices for the foods. Have the students simulate a shopping trip while they practice math skills. Ask the students: How much did you spend on food for one day's meals? What would you spend to feed just yourself for one week? How many meals could you make with only $10 to spend? How much would it cost to feed a family of four for one day? One week?

- Cereal can be an excellent breakfast food, unless it is full of sugar. There are many forms of sugar found in cereal, such as dextrose, fructose, glucose, sucrose, lactose, maltose, corn syrup, honey, molasses, sorbitol, maltitol, xylitol, and mannitol. Have students bring in different boxes of cereal or bring in the nutritional and ingredient information from boxes of cereal. Students should compare nutritional information and discuss: Which cereals have no added sugar? Which form of sugar is present in some of the students' favorite cereals? How does your favorite cereal measure up to one with no sugar added?

Is It Healthy?

- Besides discussing basic nutrition (the food pyramid), look at other factors that influence how healthy a food is. Have the students investigate what pesticides and herbicides are used today. Discuss why it is important to carefully wash fruits and vegetables before eating them. What foods are "enriched"? Enriched with what? What foods are high in sugar? High in fat? High in cholesterol?
- Have each student create a notebook and choose 20 processed foods. For each food, have the student attach the part of the label identifying the nutritional information to a page in the notebook. Under this label, the student should include comments on how healthy he or she thinks the food is. Share the information in the notebooks with the class.

Natural Foods

Ask the students: What are "natural" foods? What does it mean if a food is unprocessed or unrefined? Bring in several "natural" foods such as special peanut butter, corn chips, or carob cookies. As a class, compare these "natural" foods with the foods they usually consume. How do they compare in taste? How do they compare in nutritional value? How do the costs of the two items compare?

Cookie Power

- Prepare a favorite cookie recipe with the students. Use the different measurements in the recipe to teach math facts. As the cookies are placed on a cookie sheet to bake, have students predict how many cookies the recipe will produce.
- As the cookies are baking, add or multiply to determine how many fit on each tray, have been completed, are in the oven, and so forth. When all the baking is done, check the actual yield against the students' predictions. (*The Doorbell Rang* by Hutchins)
- The same results can be achieved without doing any baking. Have students bring a copy of their favorite recipe to class. Draw as many cookies as you can on a sheet of paper and photocopy the number of copies you will need. Use the measurements in the recipe to teach math facts and then do all the other activities listed above, substituting paper cookies for the real ones. You can still do predictions by piling up all of the paper cookies you will be using and having the children estimate how many there are in total.

Holidays and Food

Ask the students: How are different foods associated with different holidays? Which foods do you associate with Thanksgiving? Christmas? Chanukah? Easter? Birthdays? Have them research a holiday (possibly one that their family does not celebrate) and look at the foods associated with it. Another option would be to research foods associated with Christmas as it is celebrated in another country. Prepare one or two of the dishes the students studied that would be new to them. Emphasize that everyone enjoys traditions, and there is no right or wrong way to celebrate.

In the Kitchen

While discussing different foods, research different cooking methods and kitchen terms and tools.

- Have a "treasure hunt" of vocabulary words. Bring in several cookbooks (with glossaries). Give the students a list of terms. They get one point for every definition they write down and one point if they can find the term in a recipe. Suggested terms are *bake, beat, boil, chill, chop, dice, mince, grate, cream, whip, dilute, reduce, dissolve, drain, strain, flour, fry, roast, broil, parboil, grease, sauté, sift,* and *simmer.*

- Look at kitchen gadgets. Collect as many different gadgets as possible. Number each gadget and let the students write down how they think the utensil is used. Discuss the utensils and some of the guesses students wrote down. Then explain the actual use of the tool. This is also a good time to discuss kitchen safety. Discuss some basic safety rules for the kitchen and have students design their own safety posters.

- Volume and weight can also be studied in the kitchen:

    Compare customary measuring units and equivalents: 1 quart = 2 pints, 3 teaspoons = 1 tablespoon, 4 cups = 1 quart, 4 tablespoons = 1/4 cup, 16 ounces = 1 pound, and so forth.

    Compare customary and metric measuring units: 1 teaspoon = 4.9 milliliters, 1 cup = 237 milliliters, 1 ounce = 28.4 grams, 1 pound = 454 grams, and so forth.

    Compare volume and weight. What is the difference? Weigh 1 cup of butter or margarine (two sticks) and then weigh 1 cup of flour. How do they compare in weight, although they have equivalent volumes?

Preservation and Storage

How are foods preserved and stored? Discuss the problems of food production, distribution, and consumption. How can food be transported long distances without spoiling? Have the students compare and contrast different food preservation methods such as canning, drying, freezing, salting, smoking, and pasteurizing and irradiating milk. Which methods retard bacterial growth by removing the liquid (salting, drying, smoking)? Which methods kill bacteria by using heat (canning, pasteurizing, and irradiating)?

Physical Fitness

What is physical fitness? Ask the students to describe what characteristics they think are important to be physically fit. Once they determine the five parts of physical fitness (muscular strength, muscular endurance, flexibility, heart fitness, low amount of body fat), have each student design their own fitness program for one week. Be sure the personalized program includes activities students enjoy and that work on all five areas of physical fitness.

Exercise

- Discuss proper exercise. Which is better for your body: to run as fast as you can for 5 minutes or to walk briskly for 30 minutes? Why? Why is it important to warm up and cool down before and after exercising?

- Have students plan a personal exercise program that properly exercises their muscles (including the heart) and their lungs. Be sure to make the exercise program fit their lifestyles and their interests.

- Have the students record their activities for a two-week period. Did they actually put their program into action? How easy or difficult was it to do? Do they feel healthier?

Eating Habits

Besides watching *what* we eat, it is also important to watch *how* we eat. Discuss what problems can arise from: not chewing food thoroughly, eating too fast, participating in strenuous exercise or sports directly after eating, periodic fasting, or not taking fluids with meals? Have the students write a list of good rules to follow when eating.

The Olympics

- The most famous athletic event in the world is the Olympics. Have the students research the history of the Olympics. How did they come into being? What events make up the Summer Games? The Winter Games? When were women first allowed to compete? What does the Olympic symbol (the five interlocking colored rings) represent? Older students can research how world politics has affected the Olympic Games. Were the games ever cancelled? What effect did politics have on the 1972, 1980, and 1984 games?

- Have the students research some athletes who showed personal strength or triumphed over tragedy. Some examples are Jesse Owens, Wilma Rudolph, Jim Thorpe, Dan Jansen, Nancy Kerrigan, and Jackie Joyner-Kersey.

- Some Olympic events have unusual names. Have the students speculate what the following events are: javelin, pentathlon, luge, steeplechase, biathlon, and equestrian.

- The Olympic Games have several symbols: the Olympic flag, the Olympic motto, the Olympic flame, the Olympic oath, and the Olympic medals. Have the students find the meanings behind these special symbols and then design their own versions of these symbols.

- Have your own Olympics with unusual events such as shoe tying, hopping races, and longest time standing on one foot. You could also have an academic Olympics with relay races to solve math problems on the blackboard or jumbled spelling words to correct.

Food over the Years

- How have the foods we eat changed over the years? Have the students pretend they are preparing a meal of beef stew 100 years ago. Where would they obtain the beef? How would they get the herbs and vegetables for the stew? What about the spices they need? What methods would they use to prepare and cook the stew?

- Compare the process discussed above with opening a can of prepared beef stew and heating it in the microwave oven or on the stovetop. Discuss how the nutritional contents of the two types of stew might compare. What about the amount of fat in the stews? Has the canned stew been enriched with any vitamins and minerals? Discuss which type of stew the students think they would prefer; the one made 100 years ago or today's version?

The Heart as a Muscle

The heart is the most important muscle in the body. It must be exercised regularly. The heart is responsible for pumping blood to all areas of the body. As a class, list what types of activities exercise the heart. Have the students track their activities for one week and keep a diary of everything they do. Discuss which activities they participated in that helped strengthen the heart?

■ Creative Writing Activities

Following are instructions to give the students for various writing acitivities.

- Write a "tall" tale describing the first time corn was popped. (*The Popcorn Book* by de Paola)

- Write a descriptive story describing how it might feel to be a kernel of popcorn in the process of being popped. In what ways can people act in a similar manner?

- Write an ABC book similar to *Alligators Arrive with Apples* by Dragonwagon. Make a separate page for each letter of the alphabet, and choose an animal to bring food to you. For example, the "B" page could say: "Birds bring bananas." Illustrate each page. Make your own cover and then laminate the book for a wonderful keepsake.

- Write a short biography of Johnny Appleseed (John Chapman). Read several versions of Johnny Appleseed's life (*The Legend of Johnny Appleseed* by Lindbergh) before you start. Combine the information you learned to make your own biography.

- Write a note to your parents or teacher giving five reasons why it would be a good idea to plant an apple tree in your yard or the schoolyard. (*Who Stole the Apples* by Heuck)

- Fold a sheet of paper in half. On the outside, write a description of your favorite fruit or vegetable. On the inside, draw a picture of your selected fruit or vegetable and write its name beneath the picture. Pass these puzzles around to classmates or family members and see how many can guess the correct fruit or vegetable from the description.

- Write a weather forecast for next week for the town of Chewandswallow, where the weather is based on foods. Be as creative as you can. (*Cloudy with a Chance of Meatballs* by Barrett)

- Do you know someone who is a very picky eater? Prepare questions to ask that person in an interview aimed at determining why he or she is so particular about food. What type of information would you obtain from this picky eater? Write down the questions you would ask and then conduct the interview.

- Write the results of your interview as a news story on the 6:00 P.M. news' health segment. Include facts you have learned that compare this picky eater's diet to a healthy diet. (*Gregory the Terrible Eater* by Sharmat)

- Write a letter to your mother in which you attempt to convince her that pizza would be an excellent food to serve for breakfast. (*Pizza for Breakfast* by Kovalski)

- Create a personalized recipe book. Choose five of your favorite foods and describe how to prepare them. Design a cover for your cookbook. (A great Mother's Day gift.)

- Describe what you would consider as the ideal snack food. For example, design your own candy bar or type of cake. Give the product a name, design the wrapper or box it would come in, and write an advertisement to introduce your product to the rest of your class or neighborhood.

- Write a letter to a friend giving him or her your special recipe for making pancakes. Include instructions on how to cook the pancakes. (*Pancakes, Pancakes* by Carle)

- Write a recipe for the perfect sandwich. Tell what the ingredients are and how to put it together. Name the sandwich after yourself. (*Sam's Sandwich* by Pelham)

- You are an aspiring Olympic athlete. Write an outline of your daily routine (including the foods you eat, your practice and workout times, and when you fit in school work and relaxation). Reading articles about actual Olympians may prove helpful.

- Create a personalized exercise program for yourself. Make sure the exercises you choose are well suited to your lifestyle and interests. Make an exercise chart to list the exercises and the number of repetitions you do each day. (*Marathon and Steve* by Rayner)

- Record, on a tape recorder, a story that a grandparent or elderly friend has told you about "old times." Or have the grandparent or friend record the story for you so that it will be preserved in the teller's own voice. (*The Midnight Eaters* by Hest)
- Have the students pick a food that they eat often at home (chicken, fish, rice, noodles, etc.). Have them copy and bring to class several different recipes that are used to prepare this staple. Then have them make up their own recipe that tells a way in which they think this food could be prepared that would make it taste its very best. (*Everybody Cooks Rice* by Dooley)

■ Art Activities

Following are instructions to give the students for various art activities.

- Read *The Wonderful Feast* by Slobodkina. Draw a farm scene using the same technique as the author by drawing the individual parts of the scene inside different-colored rectangles.
- Using breadcrumbs, construction paper, poster board, and glue, draw a woodland scene and then create a path to the gingerbread house. (*Hansel and Gretel* by Marshall)
- Wash and then dry seeds you have collected from sunflowers, watermelons, apples, oranges, and so forth. Cut a circle (about 3 inches in diameter) out of a lightweight piece of cardboard. Glue a row of the seeds around the outer edge of the circle with the pointed end of the seed to the inside of the circle. Glue two to three more rows of seeds overlapping the first row (moving in toward the middle of the circle). When you reach the center of the circle, glue a row of different-colored seeds (like popcorn seeds) for the center of the flower. Make leaves out of green construction paper or felt and glue them to the back of the flower. Glue on a safety pin, and you have made your own flower pin. (This same idea can be used in any design you want to make.)
- On a colored piece of poster board, draw the outline of any bird you would like to make. Inside the outline, glue seeds to represent the feathers of your bird (white and black bean seeds, apple seeds, colored popcorn seeds, etc.). Use a different-colored seed for the bird's beak and for its eyes. When your seeds have dried in place, you can create a scene around your bird, use scraps of ribbon or wallpaper to make a frame around your picture, and make a loop out of yarn to hang your picture.
- Use Popsicle or ice cream sticks to make a teepee, log cabin, boat, or object of your choice. Make a sketch of the object you want to make as your blueprint. Then arrange your sticks in the proper shape and glue them together to make your project. You may want to use construction paper or white paper that you have drawn designs on for the roof of your house, cover for your teepee, or sail for your boat. What other food-related "recyclables" could you save for art projects?
- Draw a picture of yourself participating in your favorite form of exercise (roller skating, basketball, soccer, aerobics, etc.).
- Cut pieces of old wallpaper into 9-by-12-inch rectangles to make your own placemats. If you are using prepasted wallpaper, wet the back of the wallpaper with warm water and paste it onto a piece of 10-by-13-inch colored poster board. This will leave a 1/2-inch edge of the poster board as a border around your wallpaper. If you are using plain wallpaper, spread some rubber cement on the back and paste it onto the poster board. Make a border around the edge of the wallpaper by gluing rick rack or ribbon around it. Punch holes 1 inch apart around the edge of the wallpaper, weave a piece of ribbon or yarn through the holes, and tie a bow at one corner of the placemat, or place stickers around the edge of the wallpaper. You can laminate your placemat as well.

- You can also make placemats by cutting out pictures of healthy foods and gluing them onto a piece of construction paper. Decorate the rest of the placemat however you want and laminate it. Students can create a placemat for each member of their family (or for a special friend) and try to use each person's favorite foods as the decorations. They can also write the person's name on the placemat for a personalized gift.

- Wash a small pumpkin or gourd with warm, soapy water, and dry it thoroughly. When the pumpkin or gourd is dry, polish the outside skin with a soft cloth. With acrylic paints, paint the image of an appropriate animal (one that matches the shape of the pumpkin or gourd you have chosen) on the fruit's skin. If your fruit does not stand up on its own, glue it to a small piece of wood to make a stand for it.

- Create your own birthday cake. Find three rectangular boxes of different sizes to make the three layers of the cake. You can use boxes from cereals, cake mixes, brownie mixes, bread mixes, rice, and so forth. Cover the boxes by gluing paper, the color you want your icing to be, to the top and sides of each box. Stack the boxes on top of each other, largest on the bottom and smallest on the top, and glue the boxes in place. For younger students, decorating a one-layer cake may be challenging enough. Decorate the cake with small pieces of candy, designs cut out of construction paper, or pasta shells. The pasta shells can be made different colors by mixing one tablespoon of poster paint with one tablespoon of water in a plastic bag that can be tightly sealed. Drop in as many pasta shells as you want to color and shake them around in the paint mixture. Remove the shells and place them on an old newspaper to dry. Touch up any of the shells that need it with a paintbrush.

- Make a class book showing your favorite lunches. Give each student a brown paper lunch bag. On the outside of the bag, the student should glue pictures of foods that represent his or her favorite lunch. Stack all the paper bags on top of each other, punch two holes in the top of each bag, and add rings in the holes to bind your book.

- Make an animal napkin holder using the following instructions:

  Cut a 1-inch-long section off the end of a cardboard tube from a roll of toilet paper or paper towels. Cover the roll with construction paper that is the color of the animal you wish to make. Draw the head, paws, and tail (if needed) of the animal on the same color of construction paper that you used to cover the 1-inch roll.

  Glue the eyes and other necessary features on the face using colored construction paper. Glue the paws on one side of the tube and the head on the opposite side of the tube. If you have a tail, glue it under the paws so that it sticks out at the back of your animal. Roll up a napkin and place it through the tube. Stand your napkin holder up on its paws.

- Make a bouquet of seed flowers in your own flowerpot. For each flower that you make, cut a 1-inch circle out of cardboard. Poke two holes (about 1/4 inch apart) in the center of each circle. Feed a green pipe cleaner through the holes to make the stem of the flower and twist the end fed through the flower around the stem directly under the circle. Glue large seeds around the edges, pointed end of seed toward the center. Leaves for the flowers can be made by twisting additional green pipe cleaners into the desired shape and twisting them onto the stem. Make a flowerpot to hold your flowers by using a small, round can (a peanut or mixed nut can is a good size). Decorate the outside of the can with fabric, wallpaper scraps, paint, or ribbon. Put green clay or a piece of green Styrofoam inside the can and insert your flowers into it.

- Make apple prints. Cut an apple in half from top to bottom. Try cutting in half crosswise, too, to find the "star." Place the cut edge of the apple into paint of a color you have chosen (pour the paint into a small plate or bowl for easy use). Press the apple with the paint on it onto a piece of paper or fabric to make your apple design. This works best if you do not use too much paint at one time. "Stamp" once on some scrap paper before stamping onto your good paper.

- Make a wreath out of apple slices and cinnamon sticks. Cut through the entire apple to make thin, full-sided slices. Let these slices dry in the oven, at 200 degrees Fahrenheit, for four to six hours. Glue the dried slices to a grapevine or cardboard wreath, then add cinnamon sticks and red bows to make a scented kitchen decoration.

- Design an advertisement for your favorite food. Be sure to use colors that show the food at its best. Arrange your poster so that it presents your food in its very best light. Try to make the people who see your poster feel hungry.

- Make a poster advertising a class or competition involving your favorite form of exercise (swimming, skiing, walking, bike riding, etc.). Give details of the class or competition and create drawings that will enhance the viewers' understanding of what the poster is advertising.

- Use recyclables, or bread dough, to create your favorite foods. Examples would be: a nylon stocking stuffed to look like a potato or a walnut painted to look like a strawberry. Bread dough can be shaped and painted to resemble anything from a blueberry pie to corn on the cob.

Bread Dough
_____

1 cup salt
2 cups flour
1 cup water

Mix, shape, then bake at 200 degrees F for 2–4 hours, depending on the amount of dough. The item should be very hard and not indent when pressed.

- Gather various sports or exercise equipment (e.g., tennis ball, baseball glove, weights, football, jump rope, roller skates) and have the students arrange the items into a model for a "still life" drawing or painting. Each student should re-create the model on paper using markers, crayons, pencils, and so forth.

- Make a chart on a piece of poster board that has the names of different types of pasta (spaghetti, macaroni, lasagna, ravioli, etc.) listed in columns across the top of the chart. Have each student draw a picture of his or her favorite type of pasta (or students can cut a picture out of a magazine). Glue the drawings on the chart in the appropriate column, creating a pictograph. Then create a bar graph of the results or use the results to study ratios and percentages (e.g., what percentage of all the people responding chose lasagna). Use the pastas to create a decorative picture. Glue the different shapes (e.g., shells, bow-ties, macaroni) onto a paper plate in a design of your choice. Spray paint the finished product with gold paint and display.

- Prepare for the animals that inhabit your backyard during the winter as follows (*The Big Snow* by Hader and Hader):

  Take a pine cone and wrap a thin wire or pipe cleaner around the bottom of it. Bend the wire/pipe cleaner into the shape of a hook. Spread the cone with peanut butter. Roll the pine cone in bird seed or sunflower seeds and hang it on the limb of a tree in your yard for the birds to eat from. Get a length of strong string or fishing line. Thread the string through a needle, then string cranberries or popcorn onto the length of string. Drape these food garlands on a bush as food for the animals.

  Make a bird feeder out of a plastic milk container or a 2 liter bottle. Cut a rectangle (about 5 inches long by 3 inches wide) out of one side of your bottle. You can make a perch by snipping down an additional 1/2 inch on each side of the bottom of the rectangle and folding this strip of plastic out. Fill the bottom of the bottle with birdseed, breadcrumbs, or cut-up pieces of fruit. Set the bird feeder on a windowsill or tie a string around the cap of the bottle and hang your bird feeder in a tree.

Use cookie cutters to cut out different shapes in pieces of bread. Hang these cutouts on a tree.

Cut an orange in half and remove the fruit. Make a small hole on two sides of the orange rind and tie a string to the rind to serve as a handle. Fill the bowl-shaped rind with birdseed and hang it on a branch outside.

Chapter 4

Diseases, Disabilities, and Disorders

■ Teaching Resources

Books containing experiment(s) relating to the subject matter are marked with a plus sign (+) before and after the title.

P   *Chris Gets Ear Tubes,* by Betty Pace (Kendall Green, 1987)
Simple text and illustrations describe a young child, with chronic ear infections, who is helped with ear tubes.

P   *Even Little Kids Get Diabetes,* by Connie White Pirner (Whitman, 1994)
Appealing illustrations and simple text describe a girl who has had diabetes since she was two years old and how she has adjusted to her disease.

P   *Germs Make Me Sick,* by Melvin Berger (HarperCollins Juvenile, 1995)
Bright illustrations help explain why we get sick, how doctors help us, and how our bodies try to heal. Bacteria and viruses are discussed in simple terms. (Also *Why I Cough, Sneeze, Shiver, Hiccup, and Yawn.*)

P   *Someone Special, Just Like You,* by Tricia Brown (Owlet, 1995)
Easy-to-read text, with black-and-white photographs, shows preschoolers with disabilities, emphasizing the pleasures they share with others.

P   *We Can Do It!,* by Laura Dwight (Star Bright Books, 1998)
Five special needs children show what they can do, with brief text and numerous photos.

P/I *Mom's Best Friend,* by Sally Hobart Alexander (Macmillan, 1992)
A child describes her family's grief when her mom's guide dog dies. It follows her mom at Seeing Eye in Morristown, New Jersey, where she goes to train a new dog.

P/I *Our Brother Has Down's Syndrome,* by Shelley Cairo, Jasmine Cairo, and Tara Cairo (Annick Press, 1985)
Brief text, with accompanying photographs, explains a family's acceptance of a Down's syndrome child. Includes a brief explanation of what causes the condition.

P/I *Our Teacher's in a Wheelchair,* by Mary Ellen Powers (Whitman, 1987)
Brian Hanson shows how he can lead an active existence as a nursery school teacher, despite partial paralysis.

P/I/U *Living with Arthritis,* by Dr. John Shenkman (Franklin Watts, 1990)
Easy-to-understand and numerous illustrations and photos describe types of rheumatic disease, their causes, symptoms, and treatments.

I *Epidemic,* by Christopher Lampton (Millbrook Press, 1994)
The major communicable diseases that have caused epidemics are described in graphic detail. This book may appeal to children who are curious about medicine or to reluctant readers.

I *Focus on Drugs and the Brain,* by David Friedman (Twenty-First Century Books, 1991)
Thorough text, with helpful illustrations, describes the use and misuse of drugs and their effects on the human brain.

I *Focus on Medicines,* by Susan DeStefano (Twenty-First Century Books, 1990)
Describes the different kinds of drugs, their history, and their uses.

I *I'm the Big Sister Now,* by Michelle Emmert (Concept Books, 1989)
The nine-year-old author explains the good and bad times involved with living with a sister who is severely disabled with cerebral palsy.

I/U *On the Wings of a Butterfly, a Story about Life and Death,* by Marilyn Maple, Ph.D. (Parenting Press, 1992)
A gentle, touching, beautifully illustrated story about Lisa, a young child with cancer. Her life is compared to a caterpillar and the changes they both go through. Encourages discussions about the process of dying and life cycles.

I/U *The Survival Guide for Kids with Learning Differences,* by Gary L. Fisher and Rhoda Woods Cummings (Free Spirit, 1990)
A handbook for kids with learning disabilities that discusses different types of disorders, programs at school, coping with negative feelings, and making friends. Includes a parent-and-teacher section.

U *Everything You Need to Know about Eating Disorders: Anorexia and Bulimia,* by Rachel Kubersky (Rosen, 1996)
Contains case studies to illustrate the role of food in our lives. A sensible approach to staying healthy is stressed.

U *Fighting Back: What Some People Are Doing about AIDS,* by Susan Kuklin (Putnam, 1992)
Real-life stories of people working together to fight AIDS, done with nice text and photographs.

U *Know about AIDS,* by Margaret O. Hyde (Walker, 1994)
Reports the origins and effects of AIDS, who may get it, how it is spread, and how to control its spread.

U *Nothing to Be Ashamed of: Growing up with Mental Illness in Your Family,* by Sherry H. Dinner, Ph.D. (Lothrop, Lee & Shepard, 1989)
Describes symptoms and treatments of major mental illnesses and techniques for lessening the effects on those around the victims.

U *100 Questions and Answers about AIDS,* by Michael Thomas Ford (William Morrow, 1993)
Frequent AIDS questions are answered; includes four interviews with young HIV-positive people, a resource list, a glossary, and a listing of state hotlines.

U   *Ryan White: My Own Story,* by Ryan White and AnnMarie Cunningham (Signet, 1992)
An autobiography, accompanied by photographs, about Ryan White's struggle with AIDS and educating the public.

U   *Stephen Hawking: Quest for a Theory of the Universe,* by Kitty Ferguson (Bantam Books, 1992)
A well-written biography about Stephen Hawking, the man and scientist, and his determination to lead a full life despite having Lou Gehrig's disease.

■ Reading Selections

Books marked with an asterisk (*) before and after the title are related to activities in the activity sections of this chapter.

Arnie and the New Kid, by Nancy Carlson (Puffin Books, 1992)
> A cat and dog take on human characteristics to provide insight into what life in a wheelchair is like.

Be Good to Edie Lee, by Virginia Fleming (Philomel, 1993)
> Touching story of a Down's syndrome child, considered a pest by others his age, who shares special discoveries with a girl next door.

Because She's My Friend, by Harriet Sirof (Atheneum, 2000)
> Two girls meet in a hospital; one is a volunteer and the other has lost the use of her leg. Antagonistic at first, they become friends and help each other face their problems. (Chapter Book)

Becky, by Karen Hirsch (Carolrhoda Books, 1981)
> A deaf child helps a family understand the problems facing the deaf.

A Button in Her Ear, by Ada B. Litchfield (Whitman, 1987)
> A humorous story of a little girl as she recalls how her hearing deficiency was detected and fixed with the help of a hearing aid.

A Cane in Her Hand, by Ada B. Litchfield (Whitman, 1987)
> Simple illustrations help describe how a young girl is able to cope with her failing vision.

Child of the Silent Night, by Edith Fisher Hunter (Houghton Mifflin, 1963)
> This story tells of the life of Laura Bridgman, the first deaf-blind child to be able to communicate with the outside world. Laura lived almost 50 years before Helen Keller. (Chapter Book)

The Cow Buzzed, by Andrea Zimmerman (Harper Trophy, 1995)
> The farm animals pass around their voices along with their coughs, sneezes, and sniffles.

The Crazy Horse Electric Game, by Chris Crutcher (Greenwillow, 1987)
> A high school star athlete is left with an awkward walk and slow speech after a water-skiing accident. His idea of coping involves running away. (Chapter Book)

Deenie, by Judy Blume (Laurel Leaf, 1991)
> When a girl learns that she must wear a back brace until she is 17, she becomes aware of prejudices about physical disabilities. (Chapter Book)

The Gift of the Girl Who Couldn't Hear, by Susan Richards Shreve (Beech Tree Books, 1993)
> Two friends, one of whom is deaf, help each other out in the tryouts for a play. (Chapter Book)

The Handmade Alphabet, by Laura Rankin (Puffin Books, 1996)
>Presents many different hands forming the symbols that represent the alphabet used in American Sign Language.

Harry and Willy and Carrothead, by Judith Caseley (Greenwillow, 1991)
>Harry, who wears a prosthetic hand, can easily join his friends in activities. However, he won't join in teasing a classmate because he knows how it feels to be "different."

Josh, a Boy with Dyslexia, by Caroline Janover (Waterfront Books, 1988)
>A boy tries to live with his disability, dyslexia, and to gain the respect and friendship of those around him. Information on the disorder and organizations that help are included.

Lucy Forever and Miss Rosetree, Shrinks, by Susan Richards Shreve (Henry Holt, 1996)
>Two sixth-graders encounter a mute child and determine to help her speak. (Chapter Book)

Mama Zooms, by Jane Cowen-Fletcher (Scholastic, 1993)
>A little boy plays imaginative games while sitting on his mom's lap as she "zooms" around in her wheelchair.

My Brother, Matthew, by Mary Thompson (Woodbine House, 1992)
>A boy explains his relationship with his new little brother, who has special needs.

My Buddy, by Audrey Osofsky (Henry Holt, 1992)
>A child with muscular dystrophy, confined to a wheelchair, explains how his dog is his arms and legs.

My Grammy, by Marsha Kibbey (Carolrhoda Books, 1988)
>Amy learns to treat her Grammy, who is suffering from Alzheimer's disease, with patience when they share a bedroom.

My Sister, Then and Now, by Virginia L. Kroll (Carolrhoda Books, 1992)
>A 10-year-old describes her 20-year-old sister's schizophrenia, its effect on the family, and the emotions involved.

Nick Joins In, by Joe Lasker (Whitman, 1980)
>Nick, a little boy confined to a wheelchair, is scared and nervous on the day he starts going to school.

Picking up the Pieces, by Patricia Calvert (Aladdin, 1999)
>A 14-year-old girl dreads her summer at a family cottage due to her newly acquired wheelchair. A neighbor helps her to look ahead to the future. (Chapter Book)

Princess Pooh, by Kathleen M. Muldoon (Concept Books, 1989)
>Patty Jean is jealous of her sister, who is confined to a wheelchair. When Patty Jean tries out her sister's chair, she finds that it is not fun at all.

Rabbie Starkey, by Lois Lowry (Yearling Books, 1988)
>Rabbie and her mother must move in with Rabbie's best friend's family after her mother becomes mentally incapacitated. (Chapter Book)

The Rough Face Girl, by Rafe Martin (G. P. Putnam's Sons, 1992)
>An Algonquin Indian version of the Cinderella story in which the young girl has noticeable facial scars to deal with.

The Secret Garden, by Frances Hodgson Burnett (Godine, 1987)
>Ten-year-old Mary comes to live in a lonely house on the Yorkshire moors and discovers an invalid cousin and the mysteries of a locked garden. (Chapter Book)

See You Tomorrow, Charles, by Miriam Cohen (Bantam Books, 1997)
> A class of first-graders learns that the blind boy in their class is just the same as they are.

The Summer of the Swans, by Betsy Byars (Viking, 1996)
> When her mentally retarded brother gets lost, a young girl gains insight into herself and her family. (Chapter Book)

A Summer to Die, by Lois Lowry (Laurel Leaf), 1984
> Meg, who has always envied her sister's beauty and popularity, finds it very hard to deal with Molly's illness and subsequent death. (Chapter Book)

Thrump-o-Moto, by James Clavell (Delacorte Press, 1986)
> A wizard takes Patricia and her crutches from Australia to Japan, where she hopes to find a cure for her physical handicap. (Chapter Book)

Where's Chimpy?, by Berniece Rabe (Whitman, 1988)
> A little girl with Down's syndrome reviews her day's activities as she and her father search for her pet monkey.

Witch's Fire, by Beverly Butler (Cobblehill Books, 1993)
> A girl faces a wheelchair, a new mother and sister, and living in a house that was once the home of a reputed witch. (Chapter Book)

Who Cares about Disabled People?, by Pam Adams (Child's Play, 1996)
> Stressing that we all belong together, the brief text explains different handicaps in a simplistic style, with illustrations.

The following books are out of print, but may be available at the local library.

Alex is My Friend, by Marisabina Russo (Greenwillow Books, 1992)
> Brightly colored illustrations help describe the friendship between two boys, one of whom has physical problems, but a great sense of humor.

Always Gramma, by Vaunda Nelson (G. P. Putnam's Sons, 1988)
> A little girl tells what it is like as her grandmother loses the ability to care for herself.

The Balancing Girl, by Berniece Rabe (E. P. Dutton, 1981)
> Margaret, who is very good at balancing things while in her wheelchair or on crutches, comes up with her best-ever balancing act to use at the school carnival.

Grandma's Soup, by Nancy Karkowsky (Kar-Ben Copies, 1993)
> A young girl must face the problems of her grandma's Alzheimer's disease.

Halsey's Pride, by Lynn Hall (Scribner, 1990)
> A 13-year-old girl with epilepsy moves with her father to a small, rural town and becomes afraid that she won't fit in. (Chapter Book)

Harry's Dog, by Barbara Ann Porte (Greenwillow Books, 1984)
> Harry wants to keep his new dog, even though his father is allergic to it.

Itchy, Itchy Chicken Pox, by Grace Maccarone (Scholastic, 1992)
> A humorous look at having the chicken pox.

Itchy Richard, by Jamie Gilson (Houghton Mifflin, 1991)
> Richard knows that someone in his classroom has head lice and is afraid that it is someone who sits at his table.

Jodie's Journey, by Colin Thiele (HarperCollins, 1990)
>Eleven-year-old Jodie, skilled in horse jumping, finds that she has rheumatoid arthritis, a painful disease without a cure. (Chapter Book)

Move Over, Wheelchairs Coming Through!, by Ron Roy (Houghton Mifflin, 1985)
>Presents the profiles of seven children who are confined to wheelchairs as they go through their active daily lives.

The Seeing Stick, by Jane Yolen (Thomas Y. Crowell, 1977)
>An old man and his "seeing stick" find a way to show the blind princess how to see the world around her.

When Daddy Had the Chicken Pox, by Harriet Ziefert (HarperCollins, 1991)
>A family is upset when Daddy gets the chicken pox.

Yes, I Can!, by Doris Sanford (Multnomah Press, 1992)
>Tells, from first-person point of view, the trials and tribulations of a physically impaired girl.

■ Science Activities

Speechless

- Have the students try to communicate an idea without talking or writing. How difficult was it? How did it make you feel? Were you frustrated? Have them write a short summary of what it was like to be without speech for communicating.

- Have several students wear earplugs for an hour. Ask them to share with the class: Was everyday life more difficult when you weren't able to hear as you are used to? How did it make you feel?

- Have the students make a list of changes they would make in their surroundings or actions if someone who was hearing impaired was staying with them for several days.

Who Said What?

Turn on a radio and tune it in-between stations so that you can hear a station but there is a great deal of static along with it. Have the students try to decipher what is being said on that station. Have them write down a summary of what they heard. Compare the students' stories. You will probably discover that each of you arrived at a different idea or caught different details. It's easy to misinterpret a topic or become mis-informed when you do not hear all of what is being said. This often happens with the hearing impaired. Ask the students: How did you feel when you couldn't understand all that was being said? Did you find yourself filling in the gaps?

Accomplishments of the Hearing Impaired

Discuss how being deaf would change your life. Have the students research a famous deaf person (Helen Keller, Beethoven, actress Marlee Maitlin, baseball player William (Dummy) Joy, Laurent Clerc, Thomas Hopkins Gallaudet, Julliette Gordon Law) and write a paper about the accomplishments of that person's life. How did being deaf make this person's accomplishments harder to achieve? Was there any way in which deafness actually helped this person?

Assistive Hearing Devices

There are many everyday devices or events that require hearing to be effective, such as an alarm clock, a fire alarm, calling out signals at a football game, using a telephone, or even hearing it ring. As a class, research special assistive devices and services (such as message relay services) available to the hearing impaired population. Have the students write letters to their congressional representative persuading him or her to contribute funds for purchasing such equipment for the hearing impaired children in their community.

Helping the Hearing Impaired

A difficult situation for a hearing impaired person who relies on lip-reading is to be part of a conversation involving several people talking. It's hard to keep up with who is talking. Often, by the time the hearing impaired person figures out who is talking, he or she has missed the beginning of what was being said. Have the students write up a guide of suggestions or ideas to keep in mind when a hearing impaired person is in your group. (Suggestions: Only one person talk at a time, point to yourself when you're going to begin talking, be sure the hearing impaired person is looking at you before you begin speaking.)

Hearing Dogs

You have probably heard of seeing-eye dogs for the blind, but have you heard of hearing dogs for the hearing impaired? These dogs are specially trained to assist an independent hearing impaired person or couple living alone. They alert their owners to auditory cues such as a baby crying, someone knocking at the door, or a smoke alarm going off. Have the students find out more about a hearing dog's training and write a news article about how these dogs serve humanity.

Low and Loud

Take the front cover off the speaker of a stereo, television, or radio. Turn on some loud music and watch the "cone" (the woofer) vibrate back and forth. What type of sounds caused more vibration, the high-pitched ones or the lower-pitched ones? (Low.) The hearing impaired population can often hear low-pitched sounds within speech (vowels, b, d, g, m, n) better than high-pitched sounds (s, t, p, k).

A World without Sight

What would it be like to live in the world without being able to see? Blindfold a student and instruct him or her to perform a relatively simple, everyday task (brushing teeth, pouring a glass of water, combing hair). Continue this simulation so that the student is left in the dark for about half an hour. Have the student write a summary of what the experience was like and how he or she felt in the dark.

Physical Disabilities

Sometimes an accident, a disease, or genetic makeup can leave a person unable to walk. More and more facilities are being adapted to make them accessible to the physically impaired. Have the students visit a local shopping mall or other public building and look for adaptations for the physically impaired. They should list the adaptations they find. Discuss what difficulties a disabled person might encounter while attempting to shop or do business in the place they visited. If appropriate, have students write a letter to the owner or manager offering suggestions for improvements.

Role Playing

Try some of the exercises listed below to give your students a feel for what it is like to live with a disability. Give the students the following instructions.

- Simulate being blind by either closing your eyes (no peeking!) or being blindfolded. Take a ball of modeling clay and try to mold a specific object out of it. Determine exactly what you are going to mold in advance. How did your sculpture turn out?
- While still blindfolded, try to pick out a cassette tape, place it in a recorder, and play it. How did you do? How can someone who is disabled compensate by using other senses and strengths?
- Tape the four fingers of your writing hand together. Try to paint a picture or color a drawing. How difficult was it?
- Place a nonsymmetrical object on a table. With your back to the object, look into a mirror to see the object. While you are looking into the mirror, attempt to draw a picture of the object you are viewing. Was it difficult to turn the object around in your mind? What would it be like to have dyslexia?

Vitamin and Mineral Deficiencies

Our bodies require a variety of vitamins and minerals to aid in normal bodily functions. Have the students identify the diseases associated with deficiencies in the following vitamins and minerals:

calcium (rickets and osteomalacia)

iron (anemia)

vitamin C (scurvy)

thiamin (beriberi)

vitamin A (night blindness and bone, teeth, and nervous system problems)

niacin (pellagra)

vitamin D (rickets)

iodine (goiter, cretinism)

floride (tooth decay and osteoporosis)

riboflavin (ariboflavinosis)

Have the students pretend that they are doctors and have patients with these diseases. What foods would they prescribe to remedy each illness?

Immune System

Your body has a complex immune system to fight germs and foreign invaders. Discuss what each of the following organs or tissues do to help protect our bodies:

tonsils lymph nodes
spleen blood antigens
eyelashes tears
thymus stomach juices

Immunizations

- Our bodies can build antibodies for certain diseases. Discuss how vaccinations encourage our bodies to create antibodies. Have the students look through their medical records to find out which diseases they have been immunized against. How many times were they vaccinated? How old were they when they were vaccinated against each disease? Have the students compare their findings with fellow classmates.

Teachers: This could be a good time to get a list of suggested vaccinations from your health department so that the students can compare their records with the recommended list. Students could bring any discrepancies to their parents' attention.

Challenge question: Why aren't we vaccinated against all diseases?

Parasites

Just as germs can invade our bodies and cause us to become ill, we can also react to parasite invasions. Have the students discuss the following parasites: lice, scabies, fleas, tapeworms, pinworms, threadworms, roundworms, and ticks. What can they do to prevent or reduce their chances of being exposed to these parasites? What should they do if they are exposed?

Bacteria

Many bacteria and viruses exist that invade our bodies. Often, the bacterium or virus will congregate in a particular organ or area of the body. Have the students identify the area of the body affected by each of the following:

pneumonia (lungs)

cystitis (bladder)

meningitis (brain)

staphylococcus (skin)

hepatitis A (liver)

streptococci (throat)

tuberculosis (lungs)

What other bacteria or viruses can the students name? Which area of the body do they affect?

Germs

- Discuss how germs are transmitted. Some germs are airborne, some are waterborne, some are present in food, and others can be transmitted only if you are in direct contact with an infected person's bodily fluids.
- Have the students make a list of good hygiene practices to be followed to reduce the chances of becoming ill. (Cover your mouth when you cough or sneeze, wash your hands before eating or preparing food, don't use eggs that come out of the carton already cracked, don't consume foods that have been left out in the heat too long, etc.)
- Discuss some diseases that are not contagious (cancer, muscular dystrophy, Alzheimer's disease). Are there any precautions you can take to reduce your chances of contracting these types of diseases?
- Depending on the age of your students, you may want to use this opportunity to discuss misconceptions about the transmission of the AIDS virus (e.g., shaking hands, hugs).

Hemophilia

Discuss what hemophilia is. (A blood disorder in which blood does not clot when the hemophiliac is bruised or badly cut.) Explain that hemophilia is often called the "Royal Disease." (Hemophilia was common in royal families because these families tended to marry close relatives to keep their wealth and power within the family.) Research British history to discover some famous members of royalty who were hemophiliacs. Ask the students: What does it mean when a disease is *genetic?* What does it mean to have a *recessive gene?* What are some other genetic diseases or traits?

The Plague

Ask the students to speculate as to what a "plague" is. Discuss the bubonic plague. What type of conditions must exist for it to spread? How did its presence affect the course of history? Are there any cases that have occurred in modern times? Have the students research the dramatic effect the bubonic plague had on the population. Have there been other devastating plagues in history?

Addictions

- While students are studying diseases and disorders of the body, it is a good idea to discuss different substances that the body can become addicted to. Discuss what it means to be physically addicted.

- Have the students list some of the substances they know to be addictive (be sure to include substances previously considered to be socially acceptable addictions, such as caffeine and nicotine). Research what treatments are available to help a person break an addiction to one or more of these substances. Why is it so difficult to break an addiction?

- Discuss the fact that alcoholism is an addiction but is also considered a disease. Have the students research the cause of alcohol addiction and identify organizations that help alcoholics and their families.

- Have the class discuss methods they think should be employed to reduce the availability of addictive substances in our society. You can have students send their suggestions to state and federal representatives.

■ Creative Writing Activities

Following are instructions to give students for various writing activities.

- Write a suspense story in which the detective solves a puzzling mystery through clues that involve sounds.

- A friend of yours is sick and must be confined to bed for the next month. You want to buy your friend something to help occupy his time while confined. What would you get? How would it occupy your friend's time? Make a list of possible gifts. Next to the name of the gift, write as many things as you can think of that your friend could do with the gift while in bed. Review your list and decide which would be the best gift to give.

- Write a story about someone who finds himself or herself in a humorous situation when he or she misunderstands something that is said to him. (*A Button in Her Ear* by Litchfield; *Mrs. Toggle and the Dinosaur* by Pulver)

- Pretend that you have a magical wheelchair that will take you anywhere you want to go. Where would you go? Write a story about your adventure. (*Mama Zooms* by Cowen-Fletcher)

- Pretend that you have a "seeing stick" that shows you the future when you rub it. Rub your magical stick and look at any day you wish. Write a newspaper for the day you "see." You can include a sports page, fashion updates, want ads, advertisements for new products, and so forth. (*The Seeing Stick* by Yolen)

- Sometimes we falsely think that because some people look different, they act or feel differently than we do. In reality, we are all unique, but we all have feelings. Write a descriptive paragraph about yourself, without giving your name, detailing ways in which you are unique. What hobbies do you have that your friends don't share? What special features do you have? Have someone in the class read the descriptions aloud and see if the other members can guess which student is being described in each.

- What would you choose to have for a pet? Would it be able to help you in any way? Write a letter to your parents requesting this pet and give examples of what this pet would be able to do for you and your family. (*My Buddy* by Osofsky)

- You are at home, and your mother has given you a map to the grocery store. However, she has forgotten to reverse the directions to account for your dyslexia. Everything on the map will appear backwards to you. You try to follow the map, but you end up in a totally different place. Describe where you ended up. What happened to you there?

- Imagine that, due to a small problem that you experience while walking, you must be confined to a wheelchair for one month. First, think about your current everyday activities. Then write down a list of changes that you will have to make in your daily routine because of your confinement. Which activities will have to be eliminated? Which activities will have to be altered, and how?

- You have a pet that has lived with your family for several years. You are very fond of your pet. One day, you find out that you are allergic to this special pet and must give it away. Write an advertisement that gives the reasons why one of your friends or neighbors would benefit from giving your pet a good home. (*Harry's Dog* by Porte) You can also use this scenario to have children write a letter to a friend or relative describing their feelings about having to get rid of their pet.

■ Art Activities

Following are instructions to give the students for various art activities.

- Create a greeting card or special message using sign language stamps. You can purchase a finger-spelling alphabet stamp set (see "Additional Resources" for availability from Evergreen) or make copies of the signals from an encyclopedia or library book (*The Handmade Alphabet* by Rankin). Decorate your card and practice the message yourself using your finger-spelling skills.

- Rent a television caption decoder (often available through your local Deaf and Hard of Hearing Institute) and watch your favorite shows captioned. (Some television sets have closed captioning built in.) Notice the words chosen for sounds that occur in the show that aren't spoken by the character; for example, "buzz" when a doorbell is rung or "ring" when a telephone rings.

- Have the students make their own television by washing and drying out a half-gallon milk carton. Fold down the top flaps and tape them in place. They can paint the outside of the carton or cover it with colored contact paper to make it look like a television. Students can put various dials or decorations on their television sets.

    Cut a square in the front of the television where the screen will be. Make slits in both sides of the television (close to the front edge) the same length as the television screen. Cut a long strip of white paper (tape pieces together if necessary to make the roll long enough) or use a roll of adding machine tape.

Have the students draw small pictures on the roll of paper and write the dialogue beneath the pictures to make their own television story. (You can also cut pictures out of magazines or catalogs instead of drawing them.) Thread the strips of paper into the slit on the left-hand side of the television and out through the slit on the right-hand side of the box. Pull the paper through to "show" the program.

• Have the students draw their own "germ." What does it look like? What type of disease does it cause? What are the symptoms of this disease? Draw a person who has the disease and show the physical symptoms.

• Have the students pretend that they have won a contest by designing an AIDS awareness poster. Part of the prize is the opportunity to have lunch with the president of the United States, who will present them with a merit medal. Have the students design the poster and then write about their lunch with the president.

• Have the students create a get well card for a special friend who has come down with chicken pox. Will the card be funny or sentimental? (*When Daddy Had Chicken Pox* by Ziefert)

• Have the students choose one of their favorite storybooks. They should practice reading them and then make an audiotape of the students reading the books. Donate the tape to the local association for the blind so that blind children can enjoy their favorite books, too.

• On a piece of white paper, have the students draw a picture of a typical downtown street scene. Include the street, sidewalks, buildings, buses, cars, and so forth. With a red pencil, mark the parts of the scene that could cause problems for someone who must use a wheelchair. On a separate piece of paper, have the students draw the street scene again, correcting the areas that were marked on their first drawing so that the obstacles are removed. (*Move Over, Wheelchairs Coming Through* by Roy; *Mama Zooms* by Cowen-Fletcher; *Nick Joins In* by Lasker)

• Read *The Cow Buzzed* by Zimmerman. Have the students draw their own illustrations for the book. Have them create their own version of this story and illustrate it (e.g., when the animals sneeze, a part of their anatomy—ear, nose, eye—flies off and onto another animal's body).

• On the front of a piece of paper, have the students draw a picture of a pleasant outdoor scene. On the back of the paper, have them draw the same scene as it might appear to someone who is confined to bed and can only watch through a window. Discuss what life might be like if they were afflicted with an ongoing illness.

• Give the students each two paper plates. On the bottom of a paper plate, have them draw a picture of a face of someone who is healthy and feeling good. On the bottom of a second plate, they should draw a face showing someone feeling ill. Staple the edges of the two plates together (pictures on the outside). Attach an ice cream stick to the bottom of the plates for a handle. Have children tell stories about people who suffer from an illness or disease. Switch the paper plates between pictures to depict what is happening in the story. (After the children make up their own stories, present one that revolves around someone with a disorder or disability who learns to deal with illness cheerfully.) (*The Balancing Girl* by Rabe; *Yes, I Can* by Sanford)

■ Experiment Books

How to Really Fool Yourself, by Vicki Cobb (John Wiley & Sons, 1999)
> Activities with explanations show how and why the senses can be fooled.

The Science Book of the Senses, by Neil Ardley (Gulliver, 1992)
> Science series with helpful photographs and good, simple instructions for experiments dealing with our senses.

■ *National Geographic* Articles

The Five Senses

November 1992—"The Sense of Sight," page 3

Diseases/Disabilities/Disorders

February 1992—"Alcohol, the Legal Drug," page 2; "Fetal Alcohol Syndrome," page 36
January 1991—"The Disease Detectives," page 114

■ Organizations

Hearing Impaired

Evergreen
P.O. Box 20003
Alexandria, VA 22332
finger-spelling alphabet stamp set

Gallaudet College Bookstore
Gallaudet College
Washington, D.C. 20002

National Association of the Deaf
814 Thayer Ave.
Silver Spring, MD 20910

National Information Center on Deafness
800 Florida Ave., NE
Washington, D.C. 20002
202-651-5051
materials on all aspects of hearing loss/deafness

Other

Alliance to End Childhood Lead Poisoning
227 Massachusetts Ave., NE, Suite 200
Washington, D.C. 20002
202-543-1147
low-cost publications on preventing and
dealing with lead poisoning

American Academy of Pediatrics
141 Northwest Blvd.
Elk Grove Village, IL 60007
708-228-5005
free pamphlets and information sheets
on health and safety issues

American Association on Mental
Retardation
1719 Kalorama Rd., NW
Washington, D.C. 20009
800-424-3688
publications about mental retardation

American Cancer Society
1599 Clifton Rd., NE
Atlanta, GA 30329
800-227-2345
information on the dangers of smoking
and cancer in general

American Health Foundation
320 E. 43rd St.
New York, NY 10017
410-859-1500
pamphlets on disease prevention, health
education programs

American Institute for Preventive
Medicine
24450 Evergreen Rd.
Southfield, MI 48075
800-345-2476
information on the dangers of smoking
and general health information

American Lung Association
1740 Broadway
New York, NY 10019
212-315-8700
information on the dangers of smoking

Asthma and Allergy Foundation Information
Clearinghouse
1125 15th St., NW, Suite 502
Washington, D.C. 20005
800-727-8462
information packets and medical information cards

Child Welfare League
440 First St., NW
Washington, D.C. 20001
202-638-2952
publications on child abuse and teen pregnancy

Children and Adults with Attention Deficit Disorders
499 NW 70th Ave., Suite 308
Plantation, FL 33317
305-587-3700
brochures with information specifically for teachers

Cystic Fibrosis Foundation
6931 Arlington Rd.
Bethesda, MD 20814
800-344-4823
information packets

Epilepsy Foundation of America
4351 Garden City Dr.
Landover, MD 20785
301-459-3700
publications, videos, and comic books

Juvenile Diabetes Foundation
432 Park Ave. South
New York, NY 10016
800-533-2873
pamphlets (one specifically for teachers)

National AIDS Hotline/Centers for Disease
Control and Prevention
800-342-2437
information on AIDS/HIV

National Center for Learning Disabilities
381 Park Ave., South
New York, NY 10016
212-545-7510
pamphlets and information sheets, plus
free referrals to local resources

National Center for Youth with Disabilities
P.O. Box 721 UMHC
420 Delaware St., SE
Minneapolis, MN 55455
800-333-6293
publications for educators, families,
and teens

National Easter Seal Society
230 West Monroe St.
Chicago, IL 60606
312-726-6200
brochures and information sheets for
people with disabilities and their families

National Federation of the Blind
800-227-8922
1800 Johnson St.
Baltimore, MD 21230
410-659-9314
materials on all aspects of blindness

National Institute of Mental Health
Office of Public Information, Room 7-99
5600 Fishers Ln.
Rockville, MD 20857
301-443-4536
pamphlets on mental health issues

National Institutes of Health
Building 10, Room 1C125
Bethesda, MD 20892
301-496-4000
publications on more than 60 diseases and
health issues

National Mental Health Association
1021 Prince St.
Alexandria, VA 22314
800-969-6642
information on mental illness and support for
people and their families

National STD Hotline/Centers for Disease
Control and Prevention
800-227-8922
information on sexually transmitted diseases

Drug and Alcohol Abuse

Alateen/Al-Anon Family Group
Headquarters
World Service Office
P.O. Box 862
Midtown Station
New York, NY 10018-0862
212-302-7240 (publications)
800-356-9996 (referrals)
information for children of alcoholics
and drug abusers and referrals for local
chapters and meeting locations

Alcohol Education for Youth
1500 Western Ave.
Albany, NY 12203

Alcoholics Anonymous
175 5th Ave.
New York, NY 10010

Alcoholism & Drug Dependency Council
1 Kings Hwy. North
Westport, CT 06880

American Council for Drug Education
204 Monroe St., Suite 110
Rockville, MD 20850
800-488-3784
low-cost teaching materials on drug abuse
prevention

Center for Substance Abuse Treatment Hotline
800-662-HELP
information about drug abuse and referrals to
local programs

Mothers Against Drunk Driving
5330 Primrose, Suite 146
Fair Oaks, CA 95628

National Center for Alcohol Education
1601 North Kent St.
Arlington, VA 22209

National Clearinghouse on Alcohol and
Drug Information
800-729-6686
pamphlets and information sheets on all
facets of drug and alcohol abuse

National Council on Alcoholism, Inc.
12 West 21st St.
New York, NY 10010

Eating Disorders

International Association of Eating
Disorders Professionals
123 NW 13th St. Suite 206
Boca Raton, FL 33432
407-338-6494
low-cost publications and audiotapes

National Association of Anorexia Nervosa
and Associated Disorders
P.O. Box 7
Highland Park, IL 60035
708-831-3438
publications about eating disorders

Nutrition

Center for Science in the Public Interest
1875 Connecticut Ave., NW
Washington, D.C. 20009
202-332-9110
low-cost booklets, posters, software,
and books

National Center for Nutrition and Dietetics
216 W. Jackson Blvd., Suite 800
Chicago, IL 60606
800-366-1655
24-hour hotline on nutrition, pamphlets on
nutrition and diet

International Food Information Council
1100 Connecticut Ave., Suite 430
Washington, D.C. 20036
booklets and brochures on food and
nutrition

National Heart Savers
9140 West Dodge Rd.
Omaha, NE 68114
402-398-1993
publications on nutrition and diet

■ Web Sites

The following Web sites reference additional Web sites related to the human body. These Web sites were created especially for children. All sites were accessed in February 2001 and were active at that time.

Diseases: http://yahooligans.com/science_and_oddities/Health_and_safety/diseases_and_conditions/
Drugs and alcohol: http://yahooligans.com/science_and_oddities/Health_and_safety/drugs_and_alcohol
Fitness: http://yahooligans.com/science_and_oddities/Health_and_safety/fitness
Nutrition: http://yahooligans.com/science_and_oddities/Health_and_safety/nutrition
Teeth: http://yahooligans.com/science_and_oddities/Health_and_safety/teeth

The following Web sites discuss specific topics related to the human body:

Allergies: http://kidshealth.org/kid/health_problems/allergy/allergies.html
Asthma: http://galen.med.virginia.edu/~smb4v/tutorials/asthma/
Bacteria and viruses: http://falcon.cc.ukans.edu/~jbrown/bugs.html

Cerebral palsy information: http://galen.med.virginia.edu/~smb4v/tutorials/cp

Children's Safety Network: http://www.edc.org/HHD/CSN

Diseases: http://kidshealth.org

First aid information: http://www.prairienet.org/~autumn/firstaid/

Kid's Section on Health: http://kidshealth.org/kid

Skin: http://www.medic.mie-u.ac.jp/derma/anatom.html

See Your Organs At Work: http://www.vis.colostate.edu/cgi-bin/gva/gvaview/

PLANTS

- Key Concepts

- Comprehensive Teaching Resources

- Chapter 1: Simple Plants, Fungi, and Bacteria

- Chapter 2: Plant Life

- Chapter 3: Trees

- Additional Resources

Key Concepts

■ Primary Concepts

Students will be able to:
1. Identify parts of a seed (Chapter 2).

2. Observe that different plants grow from different seeds (Chapter 2).

   Classify seeds according to color, shape, and size.

   Match each seed to the fruit or vegetable that it comes from.

3. Identify conditions necessary for seeds to grow (Chapter 2).

4. Sequence the stages of plant growth from seed to plant (Chapter 2).

5. Understand that each seed plant produces its own kind of seed (Chapter 2).

6. Understand how non-flowering plants produce seeds (Chapters 2, 3).

7. Observe different ways to grow a new plant (Chapters 1, 2, 3): from bulbs, seeds, or cuttings. Understand that most plants grow from seeds.

8. Label the root, stem, and leaves of a plant (Chapters 1, 2, 3).

9. Compare parts and structures of various plants (including flowering plants) and describe the function of each (Chapters 1, 2, 3).

10. Identify that most plants need air, water, soil, and sunlight to grow (Chapters 1, 2, 3).

11. Understand that plants supply food for people and animals (Chapters 1, 2, 3).

12. Observe and explain how the changing seasons affect plants (Chapters 1, 2, 3).

13. Describe the importance of plants in our environment (Chapters 1, 2, 3).

■ Intermediate Concepts

Students will be able to:
1. Distinguish between two groups of seed plants and cite examples of each (Chapter 2).

2. Differentiate between monocot and dicot plants (Chapter 2).

3. Identify and classify three kinds of leaves (Chapter 3).

4. Distinguish between seed plants that produce flowers and ones that produce cones and explain the difference between them (Chapters 2, 3).

5. Identify and explain the reproductive parts of a flowering plant (Chapters 2, 3).

6. Describe the growth patterns of flowering plants (Chapters 2, 3). Seven factors are necessary for plant growth:

> oxygen
>
> water
>
> soil
>
> light
>
> food
>
> carbon dioxide
>
> temperature

7. Describe the process by which green plants make their own food (Chapters 1, 2, 3). They need:

> sunlight
>
> air
>
> water
>
> soil

8. Explain food and non-food uses of plants (Chapters 1, 2, 3).

9. Identify common plants that can be harmful and others that can be useful (Chapters 1, 2, 3).

10. Identify ways in which plants can be classified (Chapters 1, 2, 3).

11. Explain the usefulness of this classification system (Chapters 1, 2, 3).

12. Distinguish between non-seed plants and seed plants and cite examples of each (Chapters 1, 2, 3).

13. Describe plant adaptations that allow them to obtain the water and sunlight they need (Chapters 1, 2, 3).

14. Describe the interaction of plants with other living organisms (Chapters 1, 2, 3).

15. Explain the process of photosynthesis and compare it to the process of respiration (Chapters 1, 2, 3).

16. Explain how plants grow in length and in thickness (Chapters 1, 2, 3).

17. Describe various structural adaptations of different plants (Chapters 1, 2, 3).

18. Demonstrate and discuss advantages and disadvantages of various stimuli to which plants respond (Chapters 1, 2, 3):

> tropism
>
> phototropism

■ Upper Concepts

Students will be able to:

1. Differentiate between types of protists and describe characteristics of each (Chapter 1).

2. Identify common fungi and describe their characteristics (Chapter 1).

3. List the major anatomy and physiology of each of the following plant groups:

Nonvascular	Vascular
algae	ferns
mosses	gymnosperms
liverworts	angiosperms

   Identify similar characteristics among groups.

   Understand an increase in complexity from one group to another.

4. Classify plants into a group by characteristics (Chapters 1, 2).

5. Use a taxonomic key to identify plants (Chapters 1, 2).

6. Identify parts of a plant cell (Chapters 1, 2, 3).

Comprehensive Teaching Resources

Listed in the table is a book that covers a wide range of topics in the area of plants. This book could serve as your main teaching guide while studying this unit. It is provided with a short summary, and the chapters it covers are noted.

BOOK AND SUMMARY	AUTHOR	CHAPTERS		
		1	2	3
The New Book of Popular Science—Vol. IV (Grolier, 1998) In textbook style, covers all areas of plant life: types of plants, vital processes, photosynthesis, parts of the plant, and adaptation.	Deluxe Library Edition	X	X	X

In addition to the comprehensive resource listed above, each chapter in this section lists reference books that focus on the specific area of plant life being addressed. These books can be used to complement and expand upon the basic information provided in the comprehensive resource book in the table. The reference books in each chapter have been classified by age level to allow you to select the ones that best fit the needs and interests of your student(s).

Chapter 1
Simple Plants, Fungi, and Bacteria

■ Teaching Resources

Books containing experiment(s) relating to the subject matter are marked with a plus sign (+) before and after the title.

P/I *Carnivorous Mushrooms, Lassoing Their Prey?*, by Victor Gentle (Gareth Stevens, 1996)
Introduces varieties of fungi that eat eelworms and describes how they trap their prey.

I *Mosses and Liverworts*, by Theresa Greenaway (Steck-Vaughn, 1992)
Focuses on varieties and life cycles of mosses and liverworts in different climates and habitats.

U *Dangerous Plants and Mushrooms*, by Michael Peissel and Missy Allen (Chelsea House, 1993)
Describes 24 dangerous mushrooms and other plants.

■ Reading Selections

Books marked with an asterisk (*) before and after the title are related to activities in the activity sections of this chapter.

Anansi and the Moss-Covered Rock, by Eric Kimmel (Holiday House, 1990)
> Anansi, the spider, uses a strange moss-covered rock in the forest to trick all the other animals, until Little Bush Deer decides to teach Anansi a lesson.

The Mitten, by Alvin Tresselt (Lothrop, Lee, & Shepherd, 1964)
> The animals of the forest try to find warmth by squeezing into a lost mitten.

Moss Pillows, a Voyage to the Bunny Planet, by Rosemary Wells (Dial Books for Young Readers, 1992)
> Robert has a disastrous visit with his relatives. But he is cheered up when he makes a trip to the Bunny Planet. (Other "Voyages to the Bunny Planet" books are available.)

Mushroom in the Rain, by Mirra Ginsburg (Aladdin, 1977)
> As different animals need protection from the rain, the mushroom expands to provide shelter.

Where the Red Fern Grows, by Wilson Rawls (Random House, 2000)
> A young boy achieves his dream when he becomes the owner of two redbone hounds and teaches them to be champion hunters. (Chapter Book)

The Wonderful Flight to the Mushroom Planet, by Eleanor Cameron (Little, Brown, 1988)
> Two boys build a spaceship in answer to an advertisement, and when fuel is supplied by a mystery man, they are on their way to the Mushroom Planet. (Chapter Book)

The Zabajaba Jungle, by William Steig (Sunburst, 1991)
> Leonard slashes his way through the jungle where no human being has ever gone. On his way, he is befriended by many plants, including a fern.

■ Science Activities

Growing Molds

Molds can be grown on many different foods that you eat. Place several scraps of different foods in plastic bags in the corner of the refrigerator. Watch for mold growth. When several types of mold are present, share them with the students. Have them look at the mold with a magnifying glass or microscope, keeping the specimens in the bags. Students should write down their impressions of what the mold looks like and how it grows. Good specimens to use are bread, green peppers, grapes, cauliflower, orange rind, and cold cuts.

Conditions that Promote Mold Growth

Give the students eight samples of bread and have them follow these instructions:

- Moisten two of the samples. Place one in cellophane and expose the other to the air.
- Using two more samples, expose one to light and keep the other in a dark place.
- With samples five and six, keep one sample very dry and moisten the other.
- Take the last two samples and place one in a warm, dark place while placing the other in a cold, dark place such as a refrigerator.
- Examine the samples daily with a magnifying glass. Record any changes and observations. What conditions promote mold growth? Where and how should bread be stored to prevent mold growth?

Types of Mushrooms

Look in the gourmet section of your grocery store or visit an oriental food market to find different types of edible mushrooms such as enoki, straw, button, black, cloud ear, or wood ear. You can also look up additional information in an encyclopedia. Have the students examine the mushrooms and answer the following questions:

- Is each type sold fresh or dried? Why?
- What characteristics do they have in common?
- How do they differ?

Look for a recipe in an oriental cookbook that uses an unusual kind of mushroom and prepare it as a class. How did the mushrooms taste?

It's Alive!

As a class, put clean tap water in a jar and let it sit for 24 hours without a lid to allow the chlorine to evaporate. In another jar, collect (about 16 ounces) of green pond water. (Wash your hands afterwards. Pond water can make you ill!) Add some of the clean water to the jar of pond water until the jar is full. Completely cover the jar with aluminum foil. Cut out a small hole in the foil on one side of the jar. Put the jar on a windowsill with the hole facing the window. After an hour or two, carefully lift the aluminum foil cover off the jar. What has happened? Why? (The green water has gathered around the hole in the foil. The algae, which makes the water green, needs sunlight to grow.)

Bread and Yeast

Yeast belongs to the fungi phylum. Demonstrate how yeast affects the making of bread by making two batches of bread dough, one with yeast added and one without. The yeast forms carbon dioxide, which forms small bubbles in the bread and makes the dough rise. Ask the students which ingredient the yeast is digesting to produce carbon dioxide (sugar). You may want to use some of this homemade bread to grow molds (see "Growing Molds" in this activity section). Many bakeries add preservatives to retard spoilage, which makes it take longer for mold to grow on the bread.

Yeast and Bread

Most Americans associate yeast with bread making. Ask the students: Do all countries make their bread with yeast? What countries do not? What about cornbread? Why did the slaves eat so much cornbread as opposed to white bread? Try some different kinds of breads, such as pita, or make some yeastless breads of your own.

Bacteria

Have the students research some of the uses of bacteria. Make a chart and list on one side situations in which bacteria are useful (e.g., making cheese, breaking down compost). List on the other side of the chart instances when bacteria are harmful (e.g., spoiling foods, causing diseases).

■ Creative Writing Activities

Following are instructions to give the students for various writing activities.

- Write a story in which you use a mushroom as a piece of furniture in your "special" playhouse. What piece of furniture would the mushroom serve as? How is the rest of your playhouse furnished?

- Compare and contrast *Mushroom in the Rain* (by Ginsburg) with *The Mitten* (by Tresselt). Write your own story in which animals are outside and want to escape the weather. Where do they go?

- Your grandmother has given you a magical mushroom that can change you into anything you wish for one day. What would you wish to be? How would you spend your magical day? You can vary this exercise by having the mushroom take you anywhere you want to go.

- Write a story about someone who is making bread and adds too much yeast. What happens if the bread won't stop rising?

- Pretend you are a fern growing in the jungle. What is your day like? What activities do you observe around you? (*The Zabajaba Jungle* by Steig)

- You are a farmer whose crop has been destroyed by fungi. Write a letter to your closest friend describing what you will do to recover from this catastrophe.

- Penicillin is a mold that was found to kill certain bacteria. When penicillin was tested on animals, they died. You now are very sick, and the doctor believes penicillin may kill the bacterium that is making you sick. If it cures you, it may cure hundreds of other people. Write entries in a diary describing the process you went through in deciding whether to take the penicillin. What did you decide? Why?

- You are diving deep in the ocean and discover an object covered with slimy algae. What have you found? Write a story about your discovery.

■ Art Activities

Following are instructions to give the students for various art activities.

- Make your own artificial fern. Cut leaves out of green construction paper and tape them to twigs you find in your yard. You can stick the twigs into a piece of Styrofoam to make your own plants. In the jungle, natives often use ferns and leaves as the roofs to their huts. Use the ferns you have made out of construction paper, along with Popsicle sticks, twigs, or tooth-picks, to make a small jungle hut.

- Draw your own jungle scene. What plants would you include in your jungle? What colors would you use?

- Draw a family of mushrooms. Think about what human characteristics you would give your mushroom people. Draw the family taking part in a favorite activity.

- Make mushroom spore prints. Carefully break off the stalk of a mushroom. Put the mushroom on a sheet of white paper with the gills face down. Cover the mushroom and paper with a bowl. Leave it for a few hours. Lift the bowl off and carefully pick the mushroom off the paper. The patterns that you see are the spore prints.

- Watch the portion of *Fantasia* by Disney that shows the mushrooms coming to life and danc-ing around. Choose a song and dance "like mushrooms."

- Dry small ferns or press them in a book. Glue them onto a piece of paper to make stationery or make a picture. The ferns could surround a poem to make a special gift.

- Make a forest scene out of modeling clay. Where would you place different kinds of mush-rooms and fungi?

- Draw an underwater scene of fish feeding on algae. Check one of the "Teaching Resources" books or an encyclopedia to get an accurate idea of how the algae should look.

Chapter 2
Plant Life

▪ Teaching Resources

Books containing experiment(s) relating to the subject matter are marked with a plus sign (+) before and after the title.

P   *Blue Potatoes, Orange Tomatoes,* by Rosalind Creasy (Sierra Club, 1994)
Gives instructions on how to plant and grow a variety of colorful vegetables, including yellow watermelons, red corn, and multicolored radishes.

P   *How a Seed Grows,* by Helene J. Jordan (HarperCollins, 1992)
A straightforward book about seeds.

P   *Linnea's Windowsill Garden,* by Christina Bjork (Farrar, Straus & Giroux, 1988)
An illustrated introduction to plants and how they grow. Includes information on creating a home garden.

P   *+The Popcorn Book,+* by Tomie de Paola (Holiday House, 1989)
Presents a variety of facts about popcorn and includes two recipes.

P   *+Potatoes,+* by Ann Burckhardt (Bridgestone Books, 1996)
Simple text introduces potatoes, and instructions are given for making a potato stamper.

P   *+From Seed to Plant,+* by Gail Gibbons (Holiday House, 1993)
Explores the intricate relationship between seeds and the plants they produce, including parts of the flower, pollination, and seed scattering.

P   *Sunflowers,* by Mary Ann McDonald (Child's World, 1997)
Discusses the physical characteristics, uses, and origins of the sunflower.

P   *The Tiny Seed,* by Eric Carle (Little, Simon, 1998)
A simple description of a flowering plant's life cycle through the seasons.

I   *Cactus,* by Carol Lerner (Morrow Junior Books, 1992)
Discusses the physical characteristics, growth patterns, habitats, and varieties of cacti.

I   *Desert Giant: The World of the Saguaro Cactus,* by Barbara Bash (Little, Brown, 1990)
Documents the life cycle and ecosystem of the giant saguaro cactus and the desert animals it helps to support.

I   *Rice,* by Jillian Powell (Raintree Steck-Vaughn, 1997)
Provides information on the cultivation, consumption, nutritional value, and varieties of rice, plus several recipes.

U *From Flower to Fruit,* by Anne Ophelia Dowden (Ticknor & Fields, 1994)
Text and botanical illustrations explain how flowers mature into seed-bearing fruits.

■ Reading Selections

Books marked with an asterisk (*) before and after the title are related to activities in the activity sections of this chapter.

The Celery Stalks at Midnight, by James Howe (Avon, 1989)
> Chester, the cat, is convinced that Bunnicula is a vampire when a harvest of white vegetables appears. (Chapter Book)

Dancers in the Garden, by Joanne Ryder (Sierra Club, 1992)
> Follows the activities of a hummingbird and his mate in a garden on a sunny day.

Flowers for the Snowman, by Gerda Marie Scheidl (North South Books, 1998)
> A snowman, tired of seeing only white snow, sets out on a journey to find colorful flowers.

The Great Pumpkin Switch, by Megan McDonald (Orchard, 1995)
> An old man tells his grandchildren how he and a friend accidentally smashed the pumpkin his sister was growing and how they found a replacement for it.

Growing Vegetable Soup, by Lois Ehlert (Harcourt Brace Jovanovich, 1987)
> A father and child grow vegetables and then make them into a soup.

The Legend of the Bluebonnet, by Tomie de Paola (Paper Star, 1996)
> The legend of how a little Indian girl's sacrifice brought the bluebonnet flower to Texas.

The Legend of the Indian Paintbrush, by Tomie de Paola (Econo-Clad, 1999)
> A legend explaining the beautiful colors of the Indian Paintbrush.

The Lotus Seed, by Sherry Garland (Voyager Picture Books, 1997)
> A young Vietnamese girl saves a lotus seed and carries it with her everywhere to remember a brave emperor and the homeland that she has to flee. (Chapter Book)

The Plant That Ate Dirty Socks, by Nancy McArthur (Camelot, 1995)
> A hilarious series book about Michael and his brother, Norman, and their adventures with their mysterious plants that eat socks for survival. (Chapter Book)

Planting a Rainbow, by Lois Ehlert (Harcourt Brace Jovanovich, 1988)
> A mother and child plant a rainbow of flowers in the family garden.

Rose in My Garden, by Arnold Lobel (Mulberry Books, 1993)
> A variety of flowers grow near the hollyhocks that give shade to the bee that sleeps on the only rose in a garden.

The Secret Garden, by Frances Hodgson Burnett (Godine, 1987)
> Ten-year-old Mary comes to live in a lonely house on the Yorkshire moors and discovers an invalid cousin and the mysteries of a locked garden. (Chapter Book)

Something Is Growing, by Walter L. Krudop (Simon & Schuster, 1995)
> When Peter plants a seed near a city street, things very quickly get out of control.

Sunflower, by Mielo Ford (Greenwillow, 1995)
> A young girl plants a sunflower seed, waters it, and watches it grow.

The following books are out of print, but may be available at the local library.

Amanda and the Magic Garden, by John Himmelman (Viking Penguin, 1987)
Amanda has great success growing vegetables from magic seeds until the animals who eat the vegetables grow, too.

Apples and Pumpkins, by Anne Rockwell (Macmillan, 1989)
In preparation for Halloween night, a family visits Mr. Comstock's farm to pick apples and pumpkins.

Backyard Sunflower, by Elizabeth King (Dutton, 1993)
Text and photos follow the life cycle of a sunflower, from the time that Samantha plants a seed in her garden to the maturity of the sunflower and the harvest of its own seeds.

The Big Seed, by Ellen Howard (Simon & Schuster, 1993)
As her mystery seed develops throughout the summer, Bess discovers that growing makes things just the right size.

City Green, by Dianne DiSalvo-Ryan (Morrow Junior Books, 1994)
Marcy and Miss Rosa start a campaign to clean up an empty lot and turn it into a community garden.

Daisy's Garden, by Mordicai Gerstein (Hyperion Books, 1995)
A young girl and all the animals of the field come together to plant and harvest a garden.

Family Farm, by Thomas Locker (Dial Books, 1988)
A family saves their farm by growing pumpkins and flowers to supplement their income.

How My Garden Grew, by Anne and Harlow Rockwell (Macmillan, 1982)
With pride and pleasure, a young girl describes growing a garden all by herself.

Jack and the Bean Tree, by Gail Haley (Crown Publishing, 1986)
A boy climbs to the top of a giant beanstalk where he uses his quick wit to outsmart a giant and make his fortune.

Jack and the Beanstalk, by Eric Metaxas (Picture Book Studios, 1991)
The classic story of a boy who climbs a giant beanstalk and outwits a giant to make his fortune.

McCrephy's Field, by Christopher A. Myers and Lynne Born Myers (Houghton Mifflin, 1991)
Describes how, over the course of 50 years, the plants and animals change.

Pumpkin, Pumpkin, by Jeanne Titherington (Greenwillow Books, 1986)
After planting a pumpkin seed and watching it grow, Jamie carves the grown pumpkin and saves seeds to plant next spring.

This Year's Garden, by Cynthia Rylant (Bradbury Press, 1984)
The effects of the different seasons are evidenced in the plants of the garden.

Wild, Wild Sunflower Child Anna, by Nancy White Carlstrom (Macmillan, 1987)
Anna spends the day outside and enjoys the sun, sky, grass, flowers, berries, and bugs.

■ Science Activities

Nature Hike

Take a walk with the students and identify as many different types of plants as you can. Ask the students to speculate: Which plants live all year long? Which plants must be replanted each year? Which plants die each year, but come back again the next year? What is the difference between an annual and a perennial? Have the students look through a seed catalog or garden magazine to find five examples each of annuals and perennials.

Venn Diagram

Using a Venn Diagram, have the students compare a fruit such as an apple with a vegetable such as a potato.

- Draw a red circle and a blue circle next to each other on a sheet of paper, with a portion of the two circles overlapping in the center of the page (Venn Diagram).
- List the characteristics that the two chosen objects have in common in the overlapping section of the circles.
- List characteristics that are unique to the fruit inside the red circle and list characteristics that are unique to the vegetable inside the blue circle.
- Discuss how fruits and vegetables are similar and how they differ.

Leaf Structure

Using microscopes, have the students examine the underside of some leaves and locate stomata. Very carefully cut a very thin cross-section of the leaf and look for the palisade layer, the epidermis, and the spongy layer. Students can look for a vein and stomata in the spongy layer.

A Look at Radishes

Have the students place a few radish seeds between moist paper towels for two or three days. Remoisten the towels periodically. Students should observe the seeds and see white fuzz on them. Have them make a microscope slide of a small section of the radish root or look at it through a magnifying glass. Discuss if they can see the root hairs. What do the root hairs do?

Plant Book

Have the students make a plant book containing examples of the different plant structures they have studied. Staple several resealable bags together along the bottom so that the bag openings are accessible. Each student should choose a plant to study, and into each bag insert an example of the different plant parts: roots, stems, seedpods, leaves, and so forth. They should label the fronts of the bags so that the openings of the bags are on the right-hand side, to indicate which plant part each contains. Students can then make a cover and back for the book (fold a piece of construction paper in half) and decorate it with a picture of the plant. Staple the cover over the bags on the left-hand side on top of the existing staples.

Color a Flower

Have the students cut 2 inches off the bottom of a flower stem (a white carnation works best). Put several drops of any color food coloring into the water in a vase or glass. Let the flower stand in the water for several hours. The flower's petals will begin to turn the color of the water. Discuss why.

Parts of the Flower

Study different types of flowers that grow in your yard or nearby. See if you can identify the parts of the flower (petal, pistil, stamen, etc.). (*Family Farm* by Locker; *Planting a Rainbow* by Ehlert)

Thirsty Plants

"Watch" plants drink water. Split a celery stalk lengthwise three-quarters of the way up the stem. Place one side of the stalk in a glass filled with red-tinted water. Put the other half of the stem in blue-tinted water. Have the students check on the plant periodically and note any observations.

Advanced Application: Students, or the teacher, can use a razor blade (adult supervision needed with children!) to slice a very thin cross-section of the celery stalk. Place it on a microscope slide. Add a drop of clear water to the slide and mount a cover slip on top. View the slide under a microscope. What part(s) are now red?

Lima Beans

Have the students take two or three lima beans and place them between two wet paper towels. Keep the towels moist for one week. At the end of the week, split the lima beans open. Locate the three parts of the seed (embryo, seed coat, and food source).

Dueling Plants

Give each student a small plant (or divide the students into several groups if you are working with a large number). Each group is to decide how to care for the plant: where it should be placed, when to water it, whether to talk to it, and so forth. The student or group should keep a journal recording what procedures were used and what results were observed. At the end of four to six weeks, compare plants and journals.

Apples, Apples, Apples

- Gather several different types of apples. Discuss why the apples have seeds and where the seeds are located.
- Have the students predict how many seeds each apple will have inside. Then cut open the apples and see if they are right.
- Have the students compare the different types of apples. How does the number of seeds compare among the varieties of apples? How do the size, shape, color, and taste differ among varieties?
- Upper-level students can make a chart with a picture of each apple at the top of a column and list a comparison of the apples' characteristics (weight, shape, color, taste, etc.) below it. Discuss: How are the apples similar? Different? How do they differ from a pear? What defines an apple?
- Ask the students: Which varieties are better for different uses? Which apple is most often used in applesauce? Apple juice? Baking pies?

Grow Your Own Plants

- Plant seeds in separate pots using different types of soil or materials e.g., shredded newspaper, moistened oasis, sand). How do the growth rates differ?

- Vary the experiment by planting seeds in the same type of soil but water one plant with regular water and the other plant with another liquid (coffee, tea, soda, milk, etc.). Does this make a difference in the growth rate?
- You can also vary the amount of sunlight that you give each plant. What differences in growth rate do you detect?

Temperature and Plant Growth

Give the students the following instructions to determine if temperature affects plant growth.

- Place moist paper towels in two jars. Place four or five beans between the paper towels and the bottoms of the jars.
- Cover the jars and keep one in the refrigerator and put the other in a warm place.
- Observe the seeds every day. Do they sprout at the same rate? Will the seeds in the refrigerator ever sprout? Why or why not? What do seeds need to germinate?

Survival Test

Have the students pretend that they must be totally self-sufficient and grow plants that will provide them with all the things they need to survive. They must plan for providing their own food, clothing, shelter, and so forth. Have them list what they would plant in their gardens and give uses for each type of plant.

Uses for Plants

Have the students divide a piece of paper into four sections and label each section with one of the four uses we make of plants (food, clothing, shelter, and by-products). Look through magazines to find pictures that are examples of these uses. Cut the pictures out and attach them to the appropriate section of the paper. Upper-level students can list the different examples in each section and then choose one by-product to research and report on.

Plants and Their Roots

To demonstrate that water diffuses into a plant through its roots, have the class perform the following steps:

- Obtain two similar plants.
- Place 1/2 cup of water in a spray bottle.
- Pour 1/2 cup of water into the soil of one plant. Mist the other plant with the water in the spray bottle two or three times each day.
- When the water in the spray bottle is gone, refill it. Pour another 1/2 cup of water in the soil of the first plant and continue misting the second plant as before.
- Compare the two plants. Which is doing better? Why?

Geotropism

- Have the students get two plastic cups filled with soil and two bean seeds.
- Plant one seed in each cup. Plant one seed properly and plant the other seed upside-down.
- Check the plants after they have begun to sprout. Discuss what they observe about the two seeds.

Phototropism

As a class, take any small plant and experiment with it in the sunlight. Set the plant in a spot where it is partially in the sun and partially in the shade. Make sure that the plant is set in exactly the same position each day (the same side of the plant should be in the sun). What do you notice about the growth of the plant? Turn the plant around so that the opposite side is toward the sun for the next several days. What happens to the plant now?

More Phototropism

Give the students the following instructions.
- Fill a small flowerpot or plastic cup with soil and plant several sweet corn seeds about 1/2 inch deep.
- Place the pot in a warm, dark place; keeping the soil damp but not soaked.
- After the shoots are about 1 inch long (after approximately three to five days), cut out some tiny pieces of aluminum foil and twist them into tiny cones. Put the cones over the tips of half of the shoots. Place the pot on a windowsill and leave it in the sun for another couple of hours.
- Ask the students: What has happened? Are all of the shoots growing in the same direction? Why or why not?

Find the Food in Plants

The following activity should be performed as a teacher demonstration.
- Heat some rubbing alcohol in a jar over boiling water.
- Break several green leaves off of a plant that has been in the sun for several hours (such as a geranium) and add them to the boiling alcohol. Boil the leaves until the chlorophyll has been removed (no green should remain in the leaves).
- Remove the leaves from the alcohol and rinse them in hot water.
- Spread one of the leaves out on a dish. Cover the leaf with iodine and let it sit for several minutes.
- When you return to the leaf, it will have turned dark. (Remember, iodine turns dark in the presence of starch. The dark color demonstrates the presence of starch in the leaf.)

No Light – No Lunch

- To determine how light affects food production, have the class cover a few leaves on a growing plant with foil on both sides. Let the foil remain on the leaves for one or two days and repeat the experiment, using some foil-covered leaves and some uncovered leaves. What happens?

Monocots versus Dicots

- Secure the stems of a monocot plant such as corn, sugar cane, a lily, or bamboo. Cut across the stem with a very sharp knife or razor blade. Notice that the tubes, or fibrovascular bundles, are scattered throughout.

- Cut across the stem of a dicot plant such as a geranium, a tomato, or a small tree. Observe that, just under the outside layer, there is a bright green layer called the cambium layer. Observe that the tubes, or fibrovascular bundles, are arranged in a ring around the central, or woody, part of the stem.

- Discuss in what other ways monocots and dicots differ. (Dissect the seeds of each and observe the leaves of each.)

What Happens to Seedlings without Sunlight?

- Have the students cover two paper plates with damp (but not soaking) cloths and scatter some mustard seeds over the cloths.
- Place one paper plate in the sunlight and the other paper plate in a dark place (like a cupboard or a closet).
- Check the plates each day to be sure the cloths are still damp. Be careful not to let light into the dark area for longer than a few seconds. Have the students record their observations.
- Seedlings in the sunlight should be green and straight. Those in the dark will be yellow and weak looking. Seeds have enough food and water in them to start growing, but they need sunlight to make more food. Plants lose their green color without sunlight and will soon die.

Math Facts

Practice math facts by using dried seeds (lima beans or corn). Color or paint one side of each seed. Choose the group of seeds to equal a sum that needs review. Put the group into an empty film canister. Have a student shake the canister and pour out the seeds. Some seeds will drop colored side up, and others will drop colored side down. Write a number sentence that describes the combination. (For example: If you put five seeds into the canister, and two come out colored side up, and three come out colored side down, your number sentence would look like this: $2 + 3 = 5$ and $3 + 2 = 5$.

Which Way is Up?

- Soak several kidney beans or pea seeds for a few hours.
- Have the students pour about 1/2 inch of water into a jar and place a few pieces of damp paper towel around the sides of the jar. Arrange the seeds between the side of the jar and the paper towel.
- Place the jar in a warm place. Be sure to always keep approximately 1/2 inch of water in it.
- In a few days, a root will start to grow out of the seed. Have the students observe which direction the root is growing in.
- The shoot will appear later. Have the students observe in which direction the shoot is growing.
- Turn the jar onto its side. The shoots and roots are now pointing sideways. Leave the jar this way overnight. Discuss what you see in the morning.

Seeds and Germination

As a class, complete the following instructions:

- Get four jars with tight-fitting lids and number each one (1 through 4). Lay the jars on their sides. Place two paper tissues in each jar. Using a spoon, sprinkle some seeds into jar 1 and screw on the lid.
- Pour a little water into the other three jars to dampen but not soak the tissues.
- Sprinkle some seeds on the damp tissues in each jar. Tightly screw on the lids for jars 2 and 3.
- Put a piece of moist steel wool (without soap) into jar 4, sprinkle it with some seeds, and screw on the lid.
- Place jars 1, 3, and 4 in a dark cupboard. Put jar 2 in the refrigerator.

- Have the students record their observations of the seeds every couple of days. Discuss which seeds are germinating. Which aren't? Why?

- After a week, compare the students' notes to the following conclusions:

  The conditions for germination were right in jar 3. The seedlings here should be tall and thin. The seeds had water, oxygen, and warmth.

  Jar 1 had oxygen and warmth, but no water.

  Jar 2 had oxygen and water, but no warmth.

  Jar 4 had water and warmth, but no oxygen. (The steel wool used up the oxygen as it rusted. Take out the steel wool and the seeds will grow.)

- **Note:** The seeds didn't need sunlight to germinate. All seeds begin growing in the dark. Seeds have their own food supply to start with, but need sunlight to grow bigger.

■ Creative Writing Activities

Following are instructions to give the students for various writing activities.

- Write your own version of *Jack and the Bean Tree* by Haley, with you playing the part of Jack. Would you use a beanstalk? Where would your magic plant take you? What kind of adventure would you have?

- Have vegetable soup for lunch. Write a letter to a grandparent, cousin, or friend telling about your lunch and how the vegetable soup looked, smelled, and tasted (*Growing Vegetable Soup* by Ehlert). Older students could choose one of the vegetables found in the soup and do a research paper on it.

- Look at different types of flowers and see if you can locate the parts of a flower (pistil, stamen, etc.). Pick one of the flowers, do some research on it, and write a short paper about it. You can also draw a diagram of the flower and its parts to go along with your research paper.

- Write a story about a wonderful summer day you spent outside enjoying nature. (*Wild, Wild Sunflower Child Anna* by Carlstrom)

- Write a letter to a friend in which you describe how you grew your own garden. What vegetables or flowers did you grow? How did the garden look after everything came up? How did you feel?

- Pretend you sent flowers to a friend for a special occasion. What would the occasion be? What type(s) of flower(s) would you send? Why? Write a story that includes your friend's reaction to your gift.

- You are part of a pioneer family in early America. You must grow all the food for your family to survive. What crops would you grow? Write a journal detailing the decision-making, planting, and harvesting procedures you followed. The journal can be a weekly or monthly account of your progress.

- Research some legends about plants. Some give reasons for the names of the plants, while other tales explain how a certain plant shaped history. Examples of legends that have developed are the thistle (the national flower of Scotland), the French legend of the lily of the valley, and the Greek myth of clytie. (*The Legend of the Bluebonnet* by de Paola)

- Make a menu for a vegetarian, but instead of having sections such as "Appetizers" and "Entrees," use "Leaves," "Stems," "Roots," and "Seeds." What foods are you serving?

- Make up plant riddles and play "What Am I?" On one side of 3-by-5-inch cards, write clues that describe a plant. On the other side of each card, write the name of the plant being described. Read your clues to family members or friends and see if they can guess what plant is being described.

- You have just returned from a vacation to the deep Amazon jungle and have unknowingly brought back seeds from an exotic, rare plant home with you. You discover these seeds and plant them. What kind of plant grows from the seeds? Describe what it looks like and how you care for it. What uses does your plant have?

■ Art Activities

Following are instructions to give the students for various art activities.

- Draw a garden or a backyard as it would appear in the springtime. Color your picture using every color of the rainbow. (*Planting a Rainbow* by Ehlert)

- Using orange construction paper, draw and cut out a pumpkin. Cut out two eyes, a nose, and a mouth from black paper. Paste or tape this "face" onto your pumpkin. You can also make several different "faces" and interchange them to make many funny faces. (*Pumpkin, Pumpkin* by Titherington)

- Make a mosaic of a flower. Tear different-colored sheets of construction paper into small pieces. Glue the small colored pieces onto a sheet of paper, arranging them to resemble a flower or flower garden.

- Arrange several flowers (real, silk, or plastic) in a vase. If desired, other items can be placed on a table around the vase. Draw, sketch, or paint the arrangement to make a still-life picture. Older students may do several paintings of the still life, each from a different angle.

- Using smooth but not shiny paper, draw a flower shape with four petals. The shape should have a square in the middle with a petal coming off each side of the square. Color the petals of your flower. Cut out the flower and fold the petals toward the center of the square on the lines that make the sides of the square. Float the flower in some water. As the water rises up through the holes in the fibers of the paper, the petals will open up like a real flower.

- Draw a winter scene. Add flowers, leaves, and other foliage to give it spring-like color. (*Flowers for the Snowman* by Scheidl)

- Draw a line down the middle of a piece of paper on both sides. In each of the four blocks, draw a garden scene, changing it to show how it would look during each of the four seasons. (*This Year's Garden* by Rylant)

- Read *Amanda and the Magic Garden* by Himmelman. Draw a picture of an animal in the story before and after eating some magic seeds.

- Make a picture using a variety of dried beans or seeds. Glue the beans or seeds on a piece of paper in any design you want. You can also use the beans or seeds to decorate a paper plate. Use the paper plate as a picture or poke holes in the sides of the plate, run string or ribbon through the holes, and make a hat.

- Make a painting using pieces of fruits or vegetables you have at home. Cut an apple, orange, lemon, potato, or cucumber in half. Using your fingers or a small paintbrush, spread a thin layer of finger paint over the inside of the fruit or vegetable. Press the painted side of the fruit or vegetable down onto a piece of paper. The design of the fruit or vegetable will appear on the paper.

- Several books give directions for drying and pressing leaves and flowers. These dried plants can be used in several art projects, such as:

Making wildflower candles—Get a candle (or make it yourself) and decide where you want to place your dried flowers on the candle. Then brush melted paraffin over your dried arrangement to seal it to the candle in the spot you have chosen.

Decorating stationery, note cards, and bookmarks—Affix your dried flowers and leaves to the paper with glue in pretty designs.

- Make designs with flowers:

  Make a flower bookmark by cutting a rectangle out of cardboard, construction paper, or any heavy-duty paper. Cut the rectangle the width of a ruler and any length you desire. Create the flower(s) on your bookmark with paint, sequins, buttons, beads, and so forth.

  Make a fan using a cutout shape of your favorite flower made from cardboard, construction paper, or any heavy-duty paper. Decorate the flower and attach it to the top of an unsharpened pencil with tape.

  Do a sponge painting by cutting a small sponge into the flower shape you desire. Dip the sponge into a container of tempera paint and dab it onto a piece of paper to make your design. Dab it on a piece of scrap paper first to remove excess paint. Add leaves and stems to your flowers. Glue real leaves and stems to the "paint" flowers or dip the leaves and stems into the paint, place them on your picture, and carefully lift them after letting them set for about one minute.

- Make your own bouquet of sunflowers. You will need: a small piece of cardboard, brown poster board, crepe paper in brown and green, glue, yellow and green construction paper, several dowel rods, and tape.

  Using the brown poster board, cut out two 4-inch diameter circles for each sunflower you want to make. Cut small squares (1 inch) out of the brown crepe paper, scrunch them up, and glue them to one side of one of the brown circles. This makes the center of your flower.

  On the cardboard, draw a pattern for the petal of the flower. It should be about 3 inches tall and 1 1/2 inches wide. Trace and cut the petals out of the yellow paper. You will need about 12 per flower. Pleat the petals by making a slight crease in the center of the petal from the lower edge to about halfway up the petal. This gives your flower a more lifelike look. Glue the petals to the back edge of the brown circle that you covered with crepe paper. Make sure you overlap the petals.

- Make a leaf pattern from the cardboard. Cut the leaves out of the green construction paper. Twist the bottom of the leaves to make a small stem. Place the leaves along the dowel rod and attach them with tape. Wrap the green crepe paper around the entire dowel rod to cover it. Tape the flower to the top front of the dowel rod. Glue the plain brown circle to the back of the flower to cover where it is attached to the rod. Make as many sunflowers as you want and arrange them in a vase.

- Make potato prints. (**Adult supervision is required.**)

  Lay out several layers of paper towels on your work surface for protection (you can also use newspapers). Pour some thick tempera paint into a shallow bowl (use several bowls if you are making prints in several different colors).

  Place a large sheet of shelf paper (shiny side down) on the paper towel. You will make your potato prints on the dull side of the paper.

  Cut a potato in half, then use a pencil to scratch a design into the middle of the cut side of the potato.

Scoop out the parts of the potato around your design with a spoon. Only the raised parts of the potato will print.

Dip the raised design into the paint and carefully press the design onto the shelf paper. You will be able to press the design two or three times on the paper before you need more paint.

Potato printing can also be done on cloth using textile paints that don't wash out. Be careful! Mistakes don't wash out either. If you print on a shirt put several layers of paper inside the shirt so that your print won't bleed through to the back.

Chapter 3
Trees

■ Teaching Resources

Books containing experiment(s) relating to the subject matter are marked with a plus sign (+) before and after the title.

P   *Ancient Ones: The World of the Old-Growth Douglas Fir,* by Barbara Bash (Sierra Club for Children, 1994)
A description of the life cycle of the Douglas fir.

P   *Apple Tree,* by Gail Saunders-Smith (Pebble Books, 1998)
Describes an apple tree as it goes through the seasons.

P   *Crinkleroot's Guide to Knowing the Trees,* by Jim Arnosky (Bradbury Press, 1992)
An illustrated introduction to trees and woodlands, with information on how to identify trees by the bark and the leaves, the many ways that animals use trees, and how to read the individual history that shapes every tree.

P   *The Gift of the Tree,* by Alvin Tresselt (Lothrop, Lee & Shepard, 1992)
Traces the life cycle of an oak tree and describes the animals that depend on it for shelter and food.

P   *It Could Still Be a Tree,* by Allan Fowler (Children's Press, 1991)
Identifies characteristics of trees and gives examples.

P   *Red Leaf, Yellow Leaf,* by Lois Ehlert (Harcourt Brace, 1991)
A child describes the growth of a maple tree from seed to sapling.

P   *+The Seasons of Arnold's Apple Tree,+* by Gail Gibbons (Harcourt Brace, 1988)
As the seasons pass, Arnold enjoys a variety of activities as a result of his apple tree. Includes a recipe for apple pie and a description of how an apple cider press works.

I   *An Apple Tree Through the Year,* by Claudia Schnieper (Carolrhoda Books, 1988)
Follows an apple tree through the four seasons, detailing the yearly growth cycle and examining the ecosystem of the entire apple orchard.

I   *+How the Forest Grew,+* by William Jaspersohn (Greenwillow, 1992)
Describes, in storybook form, the gradual transformation of a cleared farm field into a dense forest.

■ Reading Selections

Books marked with an asterisk (*) before and after the title are related to activities in the activity sections of this chapter.

Birches, by Robert Frost (Henry Holt, 1990)
> A poem that gives the author's impressions of what a birch tree says to him.

Chicka Chicka Boom Boom, by Bill Martin, Jr. and John Archambault (Simon & Schuster, 1989)
> An alphabet rhyme/chant that relates what happens when the whole alphabet tries to climb a coconut tree.

The Giving Tree, by Shel Silverstein (HarperCollins Juvenile, 1999)
> An apple tree nurtures a little boy while he is young, and the tree is happy. As the boy grows older, he wants more and more from the tree.

The Great Kapok Tree, by Lynne Cherry (Voyager Picture Books, 2000)
> The many different animals that live in a great Kapok tree in the Brazilian rain forest try to convince a man with an axe of the importance of not cutting down their home.

James and the Giant Peach, by Roald Dahl (Alfred A. Knopf, 1996)
> When given magic crystals, James's clumsiness causes a peach tree to grow wild. (Chapter Book)

"Leaves" poem in *A Child's Garden of Verses,* by Robert Louis Stevenson (Smithmark, 1997)
> A collection of Stevenson's poems, softly illustrated.

Night Tree, by Eve Bunting (Voyager Picture Books, 1994)
> A family makes its annual pilgrimage to decorate an evergreen tree with food for the forest animals at Christmas time.

Once There Was a Tree, by Natalia Romanove and Gennady Spirin (E. P. Dutton, 1992)
> Many creatures, including humans, are attracted to a tree stump. When the stump is gone, a new tree attracts the same creatures.

The Singing Tree, by Kate Seredy (Puffin Books, 1990)
> A prince takes a magic tree to a beautiful, but spoiled, princess and brings an evil curse on them both. (Chapter Book)

The Sword in the Tree, by Clyde Robert Bulla (Harper Trophy, 2000)
> Recreates the time of King Arthur and a brave young knight's adventures. (Chapter Book)

A Tree Is Nice, by Janice May Udry (Harper Trophy, 1987)
> A child gives many wonderful and funny reasons why a tree is nice to have.

Tree of Life, the World of the African Baobab, by Barbara Bash (Sierra Club Books, 1989)
> A folk tale describing the baobab tree and how the people and animals use the tree.

Uncle Foster's Hat Tree, by Doug Cushman (Puffin Books, 1996)
> Merle hears four entertaining stories about the hats on his uncle's hat tree and then gets to try on the hats.

The following books are out of print, but may be available at the local library.

I Wish I had a Big, Big Tree, by Satoru Sato (Lothrop, Lee & Shepard, 1986)
>A boy dreams of building a treehouse to visit the squirrels and birds, but needs a big, big tree.

I'm Going to Pet a Worm Today: and other Poems, by Constance Levy (M. K. McElderry Books, 1991)
>Contains 39 poems, mostly about nature, covering subjects from leaves on trees to petting worms.

In My Treehouse, by Alice Schertle (Lothrop, Lee & Shepard, 1983)
>A child shares the real and imaginary adventures of a treehouse.

The Legend of Johnny Appleseed, by Reeve Lindbergh (Little, Brown, 1990)
>The life of John Chapman (Appleseed) is told through rhyming text.

My Father Doesn't Know About the Woods and Me, by Dennis Haseley (Macmillan, 1988)
>On a walk with his father, a child relates to the animals in the woods and enjoys the freedom of nature.

Rhinos Don't Climb, by Ruth Rosner (Harper & Row, 1984)
>Two young rhinos who love to climb build a mountain and inadvertently teach the adults the joys of climbing.

The Talking Tree, by John Himmelman (Viking Penguin, 1986)
>A tree appears to talk, but in reality it is only Skylar who is stuck in a hollow tree trunk.

Trees, by Harry Behn (Henry Holt, 1992)
>A simple poem describing the benefits of trees.

■ Science Activities

Upper-Level Challenge

Ask the students what would happen if a band of bark is completely removed from around a tree. Have them support why they believe the tree will die. (*Hint:* A tree is a dicot.)

Answer: The weakest layer in a tree is the cambium layer, which lies under the bark. When bark is peeled away, it breaks away from the stem at this cambium layer. The phloem layer (which transports food) lies between the bark and the cambium layer and is removed with the bark. Without the phloem layer, the tree has no method of transporting food, and the tree would then die.

Book of Leaves

- Have the students collect leaves from different types of trees in their neighborhood or at the nearest park. Compare the leaves to pictures in the encyclopedia or in a tree guide. Determine which tree each leaf came from. Study the shape and design of each leaf.

Create a class book by giving each student a leaf and follow these steps:

- Place each leaf on a separate sheet of paper. The size should be determined by the size you want your book to be. Spread glue over the entire sheet of paper.
- Place a piece of plastic wrap over the leaf and glued paper to mount the leaf for the book. Trim away excess plastic.

- Put holes in the sides of the leaf papers and the written text and bind them together in a book. You can use a binder from the store or have children make a front and back cover for the book out of decorated cardboard and tie everything together with string or ribbon.
- Have older students research and write a short story about each type of tree. Have younger students draw a picture of the tree or write a simple explanation of the tree, depending on their abilities.

No Trees?

What would the world be like with no trees? Discuss this idea with your students. Have them guess how the world would be different if all the trees were destroyed. Have younger students record their findings in picture form. Have older students write a summary based on their findings.

Bark Rubbings

Have the students firmly hold a piece of paper against the bark of a tree. Rub a crayon over the paper and bark to make the pattern of the bark appear. Have them identify each type of tree. These rubbings can be labeled and made into a booklet.

Stages of a Pine Cone

This activity will continue throughout the changing seasons. Have the students observe changes in pine cones on some nearby trees:

- Small male cones are grouped at the ends of twigs and produce yellow pollen. During the hot months, you can see clouds of pollen if you shake a branch.
- Female cones are produced upright and singly at the ends of the twigs. At first they are pink but then become green and turn downward.
- Pollen grains fall between the scales of the young female cones and carry the cells into the ovules.
- Cones open their scales to let the seeds blow away in dry weather. Some types of cones fall apart to release their seeds. When it rains, the scales close again.

Chewing Gum

Have the students research how chewing gum is made. Who discovered it, and who determined that it would make a good snack food? Where does the sapodilla tree grow?

Coniferous Versus Deciduous

Have the students compare coniferous and deciduous trees. What are the characteristics of each? Have them collect twigs, leaves, bark, and so forth for both types of trees and make a poster comparing the two.

Landscaping

Visit a nursery, or look at a catalog of plants and trees, and select trees that would be nice to plant in your schoolyard. How much would it cost to buy these trees? Where would you plant them? Have the students design blueprints and calculate the costs to implement their plan.

Trees and Shade

People sometimes say, "It's 100 degrees in the shade." Discuss whether there is a difference in temperature in the shade as compared to being out in the direct sunlight. As a class, place one thermometer in the shade and another one in direct sunlight. Have the students read the two thermometers several times during the day and record the readings. How do the temperatures compare?

Of All the Gall!

As a class, examine the twigs of an oak tree during the heat of the summer. You may see many tiny, brown, spongy balls called oak apples, or galls. These galls are not a fruit but are made when insect larvae feed on the tree. If you open a gall, you can see the larvae inside. If you find a gall with no holes in it, the larvae are still inside. Place the gall in a glass jar and put a piece of cloth over the top of the jar. Wait and watch the gall insects as they come out.

■ Creative Writing Activities

Following are instructions to give the students for various writing activities.

- What is a "hat" tree? Show the children several hats. Write a story about a person who might wear one of the hats. (*Uncle Foster's Hat Tree* by Cushman)
- Write a description of a place you find comforting or special. (*My Father Doesn't Know About the Woods and Me* by Haseley)
- Pretend you are spending the afternoon in a tree house. Write a story about your adventures. (*In My Treehouse* by Schertle)
- Write and illustrate your own storybook in which you have a conversation with a very old (or a brand new) tree. What would you ask the tree? (*The Talking Tree* by Himmelman)
- Write a story about a tree house you would build. What would it contain? Who would visit you there? (*I Wish I Had a Big, Big Tree* by Sato)
- Pretend you are a reporter and are going to interview Johnny Appleseed. Write a news article about the interview in which you chronicle the events of Johnny Appleseed's life (*The Legend of Johnny Appleseed* by Lindbergh) Older students could research the life of John Chapman and write a report on him.
- Write a story about an unusual animal action, like an elephant climbing a tree. How and why does it get up in the tree? How will it get down? (*Rhinos Don't Climb* by Rosner)
- Write a letter to a pretend neighbor to convince him or her not to cut down a large oak tree that is the home for a family of robins and a rambunctious squirrel.
- Write an essay about the excitement and delight felt by a child as he or she helps Daddy put up a swing in the old oak tree in the backyard.
- What is your favorite tree in your yard or in your neighborhood? What do you see in this tree that makes it special to you? Which season of the year is your favorite as far as the tree is concerned?
- When the American settlers crossed the United States heading west, they chopped down trees to make houses and to clear land for farming. Native Americans, on the other hand, had lived for many years on the same land and had done so without destroying the trees. Write an editorial on the two different sides of this issue. Should the trees have been cut down by the settlers? Why or why not?
- What is a family tree? Create a family tree of your relatives.

- You are a bird looking around for the perfect tree to make your nest in. Write a list of the attributes that a "perfect" tree must have if you are to build your nest there. Then go looking for such a tree around your neighborhood. Can you find one that matches all of your requirements? If not, what did you have to settle for? Write a letter home describing the location and the tree that you chose to build your nest in. Include how the tree worked out for you and whether you would return to the same location next year.

■ Art Activities

Following are instructions to give the students for various art activities.

- Draw a picture of a tree near your house and the animals who live in it. (*The Great Kapok Tree* by Cherry)

- Read *The Legend of Johnny Appleseed* by Lindbergh or tell the story to your students, if you are familiar with it. Draw a picture of how you think Johnny Appleseed looked.

- Make your own tree out of cardboard and green construction paper. Draw and cut the trunk out of a piece of cardboard. Color it brown, black, or whatever color you choose. Draw and cut leaves out of the green construction paper. Have the students make different kinds of leaves (simple, compound, toothed, smooth) and group them together on the tree according to their common characteristics. Paste or glue the leaves in place. You can have the students add a bird's nest, birdhouse, or animals. This would be especially meaningful if the next science subject to be studied is birds.

- Have the students draw evergreen trees on large pieces of paper. Have the students decorate their trees for some special occasion (Christmas, Valentine's Day, Fourth of July, a birthday, etc.), using colored paper, stickers, and pictures from magazines. Remember, evergreen trees are with us all year long; that is, they do not shed their needles like leaves of deciduous trees.

- Choose a leaf from your backyard or a park or woods near you. With a small brush, spread finger paint on one side of the leaf. Gently press the painted side of the leaf onto a piece of white paper. After several seconds, carefully pull the leaf off the paper to reveal your "leaf painting." You can use several different sizes and shapes of leaves and many combinations of colors to make a fall scene.

- Using bark rubbings (see last item under "Science Activities") as a background, arrange several leaves from the tree on the paper. Trace around each leaf with a contrasting color.

- Draw the trunk of a tree with branches on it. Reproduce this trunk on several sheets of paper. Have students decorate four different trunks to illustrate how the tree would look in each of the four seasons. (Students could use paints, crayons, tissue paper, berries, or popcorn to achieve the desired effect.)

- Fun things to do with pine cones:

    Paint pine cones and design animals using pipe cleaners and pieces of felt for their eyes, ears, tongues, and so forth.

    Put some peanut butter on a pine cone and sprinkle birdseed over it. Then hang the pine cone bird feeder on a nearby tree and watch the birds flock to it.

    Make a mobile. Decorate pine cones with glitter, paint, or sequins. Tie a string around the pine cones and then tie each one to a branch or stick. Hang the pine cones from varying lengths of string. Be sure to balance out the weight of your pine cone mobile so that it will hang level.

- Have fun with nuts and twigs:

    Make an owl by gluing two small pine cone "feet" to the bottom of a large nut. Glue two acorn caps onto the top of the nut to make eyes. (You could glue tiny seeds or beads inside the caps.) Glue a small piece of bark between and below the eyes to make the owl's beak. Glue your owl onto a twig or broken branch for a perch.

    Make a climbing cat by gluing two different-shaped nuts together, one on top of the other, to make the body and head. Attach thin twigs for legs and the tail or use a pipe cleaner for the tail. Glue on corn kernel eyes and small pine cones for ears. To make your cat a climber, you can find a twig of a tree that has several branches and a few little leaves on it. Attach your cat to this small "tree."

    Make a person flying a kite by gluing together two different-shaped nuts, one on top of the other, for the person's body and head. Attach twigs for the arms and legs. Attach one end of a piece of thin wire to one of the arms and the other to the end of a diamond-shaped piece of cornhusk (the kite). Add tissue paper, a small piece of cloth, or a thin strip of cornhusk to the bottom of the kite for a tail.

    There are many different people, animals, and objects that you can make by using nuts and twigs. See if you can think up some of your own. Try to identify the type of tree used in your objects.

- Make a tree out of a lunch bag using the following instructions:

    Stuff the bottom of a lunch bag with crumpled paper to make the trunk.

    Cut the upper third of the bag into 1/2-inch strips for branches.

    Twist the trunk several times just below the 1/2-inch strips.

    Cut leaves out of green construction paper and glue them in place on the branches.

    Twist the branches and position them to finish your tree.

Additional Resources

■ Experiment Books

The Everyday Science Sourcebook, by Lawrence Lowery (Dale Seymour, 1997)
   Contains sections on just about every science-type subject one could imagine. Has an excellent section of experiments on plants.

The Kid's Nature Book, by Susan Milord (Gareth Stevens, 1997)
   Contains a nature activity for each day of the year. Activities are grouped in weekly themes that match the time of the year.

More Mudpies to Magnets, by Elizabeth A. Sherwood, Robert A. Williams, and Robert E. Rockwell (Gryphon House, 1991)
   A collection of experiments for young children on the subjects of plants, animals, and space.

Nature Crafts for Kids, by Gwen Diehn and Terry Krautwurst (Sterling, 1997)
   More than 50 outdoor projects, for every season of the year, will show you how to learn by doing. Discover facts about how nature works. Provides clear, step-by-step instructions.

Science in Your Backyard, by William R. Wellnitz, Ph.D. (TAB Books, 1992)
   Includes experiments involving plants, animals, and earth sciences that can be done close to home and that encourage the development of observation and measurement skills.

■ Organizations

American Paper Institute, Inc.
260 Madison Ave.
New York, NY 10016

Industrial Forestry Association
225 S. W. Broadway, Room 400
Portland, OR 97205

Nova Scotia Department of Lands
and Forests
Forest Resources Education
Box 68
Truro, Nova Scotia B2N 5B8

Sierra Club
530 Bush St.
San Francisco, CA 94108

Trees for Tomorrow
Environmental Center
P.O. Box 609
Eagle River, WI 54521

■ Further Reading

Listed below is an assortment of books pertaining to the world of plants. Students who express a desire to delve deeper into this subject may want to use these additional resources to research their favorite topics.

The Audubon Society Field Guide to North American Mushrooms, by Gary Lincoff (New York: Alfred A. Knopf, 1981)

The Audubon Society Field Guide to North American Trees, by Little Elbert (New York: Alfred A. Knopf, 1980)

The Audubon Society Field Guide to North American Wildflowers, by William A. Niering (New York: Alfred A. Knopf, 1979)

Carnivorous Plants of the United States and Canada, by Donald E. Schnell (Winston-Salem, NC: John F. Blair, 1976)

Edible Wild Plants, by Lee Allen Peterson (Boston: Houghton Mifflin, 1977)

Edible Wild Plants and Useful Herbs, by Margaret McKenny (Boston: Houghton Mifflin, 1968)

Fall Wildflowers of the Blue Ridge and Great Smokey Mountains, by Oscar W. Gupton and Fred C. Swope (Charlottesville, VA: University Press of Virginia, 1987)

Forests: A Naturalist's Guide to Trees and Forest Ecology, by Laurence C. Walker (New York: John Wiley & Sons, 1990)

A Guide to Field Identification: Trees of North America, by C. Frank Brockman (Racine, WI: Western, 1986)

How Did We Find Out about Photosynthesis?, by Isaac Asimov (New York: Walker, 1989)

How to Know the Wild Flowers, by Mrs. William Starr Dana (Boston: Houghton Mifflin, 1989)

Leaves: The Formation, Characteristics, and Uses of Hundreds of Leaves Found in All Parts of the World, by Ghillean Tolmie Prance (New York: Crown, 1985)

Mushrooms in Color, by Orson K. Miller, Jr. and Hope H. Miller (New York: E. P. Dutton, 1980)

Peterson Field Guides: Mushrooms, by Kent H. McKnight and Vera B. McKnight (Boston: Houghton Mifflin, 1987)

Peterson Field Guides: Wildflowers of Northeastern and Northcentral North America, by Roger Tory Peterson and John Tomikel (Elgin, PA: Allegheny Press, 1986)

Plants Do Amazing Things, by Hedda Nussbaum (New York: Random House, 1977)

Pods: Wildflowers and Weeds in Their Final Beauty, by Jane Embertson (New York: Charles Scribner's Sons, 1979)

Poisonous Plants of Eastern North America, by Randy G. Westbrooks and James W. Preacher (Columbia, SC: University of South Carolina Press, 1986)

The Secret Life of Flowers, by Bob Gibbons (New York: Sterling, 1984)

Simon & Schuster's Guide to Trees, by Paola Lanzara and Mariella Pizzetti (New York: Simon & Schuster, 1977)

The Trees of North Amerca, by Alan Mitchell (New York: Facts on File, 1987)

A Weed Is a Flower: The Life of George Washington Carver, by Aliki (Englewood Cliffs, NJ: Prentice Hall, 1965)

Wildflowers Across America, by Lady Bird Johnson and Carlton B. Lees (New York: Abbeville Press, 1988)

■ Web Sites

The following Web sites discuss specific topics about plants. All sites were accessed in February 2001 and were active at that time.

Australian plants: http://www.anbg.gov.au

Carnivorous plants: http://www.labs.agilent.com/bot/cp-home

Gardening—Kid Style: http://aggie-horticulture.tamu.edu/kinder/

Gardens: http://www.yahooligans.com/science_and_oddities/Living_things/botany/gardens

Hawaiian plants: http://www.hawaii_nation.org/canoe

Hydroponics: http://www.viasub.net

New York Botanical Gardens: http://pathfinder.com/vg/Gardens/NYBG

Photosynthesis: http://www.yahooligans.com/science_and_oddities/Living_things/botany/photosynThesis

Plants and Our Environment: http://tqjunior.thinkquest.org/3715

Time Life's Library of Plants: http://pathfinder.com/vg/TimeLife/

Visit an Arboretum: http://ag.arizona.edu/BTA/btsa.html

About the Authors

Amy J. Bain is a teacher in the Miami Elementary School system, Milford, Ohio, and is president of Solomon Publishing. **Janet Richer** has worked extensively writing and presenting training workshops and videos for homeschooling families throughout the Midwest. **Janet Weckman** is a teacher at Blanche Moore Elementary School, Corpus Christi, Texas, with more than 20 years of teaching experience, including working with hearing-impaired students.

from *Teacher Ideas Press*

CELEBRATING THE EARTH: Stories, Experiences, Activities
Norma J. Livo

Invite young readers to observe, explore, and appreciate the natural world through engaging activities. Livo shows you how to use folk stories, personal narrative, and a variety of learning projects to teach students about amphibians, reptiles, mammals, constellations, plants, and other natural phenomena. Designed to build a Naturalist Intelligence in young learners, these stories and activities are packed with scientific information. **All Levels.**
xvii, 174p. 8½x11 paper ISBN 1-56308-776-6

FAMOUS PROBLEMS AND THEIR MATHEMATICIANS
Art Johnson

Why did ordering an omelet cost one mathematician his life? The answer to this and other questions are found in this exciting new resource that shows your students how 60 mathematicians discovered mathematical solutions through everyday situations. These lessons are easily incorporated into the curriculum as an introduction to a math concept, a homework piece, or an extra challenge. Teacher notes and suggestions for the classroom are followed by extension problems and additional background material. **Grades 5–12.**
xvi, 179p. 8½x11 paper ISBN 1-56308-446-5

SCIENCE AND MATH BOOKMARK BOOK: 300 Fascinating, Fact-Filled Bookmarks
Kendall Haven and Roni Berg

Use these 300 reproducible bookmarks of fascinating facts, concepts, trivia, inventions, and discoveries to spark student learning. They cover all major disciplines of math and physical, earth, and life sciences—ready to copy, cut out, and give to your students. **Grades 4 and up.**
xii, 115p. 8½x11 paper ISBN 1-56308-675-1

WRITE RIGHT! Creative Writing Using Storytelling Techniques
Kendall Haven

Haven's breakthrough approach to creative writing uses storytelling techniques to enhance the creative writing process. This practical guide offers you directions for 38 writing exercises that will show students how to create powerful and dynamic fiction. All the steps are included, from finding inspiration and creating believable characters to the final edit. Activities are coded by levels, but most can be adapted to various grades. **All Levels.**
240p. 8½x11 paper ISBN 1-56308-677-8

VISUAL MESSAGES: Integrating Imagery into Instruction
2d Edition
David M. Considine and Gail E. Haley

The authors provide effective media literacy strategies, activities, and resources that help students learn the critical-viewing skills necessary in our media-dominated world. Various media and types of programs are addressed, including motion pictures, television news, and advertising. Activities are coded by grade level and curriculum area. **Grades K–12.**
xxiii,371p. 8½x11 paper ISBN 1-56308-575-5

For a free catalog or to place an order, please contact:
Teacher Ideas Press
Dept. B051 • P.O. Box 6633 • Englewood, CO • 80155-6633
800-237-6124 • www.lu.com/tip • Fax: 303-220-8843